Frank Schalow
**Departures**

# Quellen und Studien zur Philosophie

Herausgegeben von
Jens Halfwassen, Dominik Perler, Michael Quante

## Band 112

Frank Schalow

# Departures

At the Crossroads between Heidegger and Kant

DE GRUYTER

ISBN 978-3-11-048164-8
e-ISBN 978-3-11-029138-4
ISSN 0344-8142

**Library of Congress Cataloging-in-Publication Data**
A CIP catalog record for this book has been applied for at the Library of Congress.

**Bibliographic information published by the Deutsche Nationalbibliothek**
The Deutsche Nationalbibliothek lists this publication in the Deutsche Nationalbibliografie;
detailed bibliographic data are available in the Internet at http://dnb.dnb.de.

© 2013 Walter de Gruyter GmbH, Berlin/Boston
Typesetting: jürgen ullrich typosatz, Nördlingen
Printing: Hubert & Co. GmbH & Co. KG, Göttingen
♾ Printed on acid-free paper
Printed in Germany

www.degruyter.com

# Acknowledgments

This book pursues the open-ended task of unfolding a dialogue between two legendary thinkers, Martin Heidegger and Immanuel Kant. In the course of formulating this project and bringing it to fruition, I have received many helpful suggestions. First and foremost, I would like to thank Professor Parvis Emad: his comments were not only insightful on various fronts, but also allowed me to identify the precise strategy by which Heidegger initiates his *Auseinandersetzung* with Kant and opens the dialogical space for their conversation.

I would also like to express my gratitude to Chris W. Surprenant for helping me to negotiate some of the more difficult passages in *Kants Gesammelte Schriften* (*Akademie Ausgabe*). Thanks also goes to Ivo De Gennaro, George Kovacs, and Michael E. Zimmerman for their continuing support. In addition, I wish to acknowledge the conscientious guidance which Dr. Gertrud Grünkorn of de Gruyter Verlag has provided in overseeing the publication of this book.

Finally, I would like to thank Lisa Dunn, Kenneth Kahn, and Brittany Tucker for their encouragement over the years, as well as Lyn and Debra Rollins for providing me a safe haven during hurricane season.

# Table of Contents

# Abbreviations

| Sigle | Author | Titel | Title |
|-------|--------|-------|-------|
| AA | Immanuel Kant | *Kants Gesammelte Schriften, Akademie Ausgabe* | |
| GA | Martin Heidegger | *Gesamtausgabe* | |
| Gr | Immanuel Kant | *Grundlegung zur Metaphysik der Sitten* | *Grounding for the Metaphysics of Morals* |
| KpV | Immanuel Kant | *Kritik der praktischen Vernunft* | *Critique of Practical Reason* |
| KrV | Immanuel Kant | *Kritik der reinen Vernunft* | *Critique of Pure Reason* |
| KU | Immanuel Kant | *Kritik der Urteilskraft* | *Critique of Judgment* |
| MdS | Immanuel Kant | *Metaphysik der Sitten* | |
| Pr | Immanuel Kant | *Prolegomena zu einer jeden künftigen Metaphysik* | *Prolegomena to Any Future Metaphysics* |
| RGV | Immanuel Kant | *Religion innerhalb der Grenzen der blossen Vernunft* | |

# Introduction

Of Martin Heidegger's myriad philosophical contributions, his interest in the inherent creativity of language can be matched only by the depth by which he probed the history of philosophy. If by name only, the linguistic philosophy of the 20<sup>th</sup> century can also be seen as emphasizing the importance of language. Heidegger's seminal insight, however, is that language cannot be reduced to the (grammar of) the spoken word, since what remains unspoken, or unsaid, remains equally as important. He arrives at this insight by recognizing that the philosophical tradition provides a repository for these unspoken gestures. To bring what remains unsaid itself to speech, Heidegger proposes an ingenious strategy of "destructive-retrieval." By engaging his predecessors in a critical exchange or *Auseinandersetzung*, he gives voice to what otherwise remains muted − and thereby forgotten − in the most perennial of all philosophical concerns, the question of being. Through a dialogue with the greatest thinkers of the tradition, Heidegger shifts the philosophical landscape in such a way that whatever insights we attain are projected against a prior historical backdrop. Conversely, by participating in and extending the debates between the greatest thinkers, we evolve new distinctions in our own language and thereby reformulate the perennial questions of philosophy.

Of all the thinkers who epitomized this historical approach, Heidegger did so, first and foremost, by engaging the most influential philosopher of modernity, Immanuel Kant. As Heidegger remarks in reflecting upon the significance of his epoch study, *Kant and the Problem of Metaphysics* (1929): "an attempt to question what has not been said, instead of writing in a fixed way about what Kant said. What has been said is insufficient, *what has not been said is filled with riches*."[1] More than eighty years later, we are drawn back into that debate, not simply as a monument to intellectual history, but because of what continues to circulate at the periphery of that discussion in accord with the challenges of our contemporary situation. The historical unfolding of the Heidegger-Kant debate breathes new life into our situation, by spawning those issues that speak to the problematic character of our existence: questions concerning our place on the earth, the quality of the habitat in which we live, our affinity with nature and responsibility toward our animal counterparts, along with our obligation to future generations. While these concerns may appear last on the agenda of what the dialogue

---

1 Heidegger, *Kant und das Problem der Metaphysik*, p. 249; *Kant and the Problem of Metaphysics*, p. 175 (emphasis my own). Hereafter, references to Heidegger's *Gesamtausgabe* ("Complete Edition") will be abbreviated as GA; where available, the corresponding English translation will also be given (GA, p.; tr.).

between Heidegger and Kant explores, my study aims to make them a priority by pushing the language in which that debate is couched to its limits. What has changed not only since the appearance of the Kant-book, but more recently during the last decade, is the continuing publication of Heidegger's Complete Edition (*Gesamtausgabe*). Through the appearance of such pivotal texts as *Contributions to Philosophy (From Enowning)* and *Mindfulness*, we can appreciate the full magnitude of Heidegger's "being-historical thinking," the strategy for his appropriation of the philosophical tradition.[2] As a result, we have a greater opportunity to explore the frontiers of Heidegger's exchange with Kant, in order to "mine" its enormous "riches."

To be sure, Heidegger and Kant are among the most difficult philosophers who employ the most technical jargon of almost anyone in the history of philosophy. The tendency is to add further complication to this mixture by characterizing it as a battle over the preeminence of one thinker's position over another's, for example, ontology versus epistemology. What sets these thinkers apart, however, is not an explicit doctrine either may advance, but rather the *innovation each pioneers* about how to practice philosophy, in short, *the implementation of distinctive methodologies and the freedom that they embody*. Throughout this study, I will accent this innovativeness in order that, by allowing less obvious dimensions of the relationship between Kant and Heidegger to emerge, the contemporary relevance of their thinking can be expanded on multiple fronts. In this way, we reach an equilibrium in which the difficulty of their philosophies is not over exaggerated, but, at the same time, the seminal insights of each thinker — concerning time and finitude, self and society, being and truth — *can be retrieved within the wider scope of their implications for today.*[3]

In the course of our discussion, we will seek *new entry point* to the dialogue between Kant and Heidegger, which follows the swing of the pendulum whereby a concern seemingly irrelevant to the thought of the former can emerge as the key to the thinking of the latter, specifically, language itself. Because the interest in Heidegger and Kant has remained more doctrinal than methodological, much of the scholarship has overlooked the crucial disparity whose explication reanimates the exchange between the two as well as expands its purview. To pose a simple question: why should philosopher like Kant, for whom (the phenomenon) of language seemed to be almost inconsequential, become the crucial counter point

---

**2** GA 65, pp. 405–417; tr. 285–293. GA 66, pp. 333–342; tr. 297–305. See Emad, *On the Way to Heidegger's Contributions to Philosophy*, pp. 7–11. Also see Schalow, "Heidegger and the Hidden Task of Kant's Schematism", pp. 425–436.

**3** For Heidegger's discussion of how "today" offers "hints" of what is worthy of questioning, see GA 66, pp. 46–47; tr. 38–39.

for a thinker like Heidegger to develop a novel way to address, understand, and, ultimately, express the most perennial of all philosophical concepts, namely, "being" as such? By making this concern for language paramount, I will identify the *point of crossing* where the *differences*,[4] as well as the similarities, between these great thinkers shape a new landscape of philosophical inquiry. At this crossing (*Übergang*) it becomes possible to "translate" the key motifs of transcendental philosophy into terms that pertain to the question of being. Here we will consider the transformation of the philosophical tradition into a task parallel to that of translation, i. e., as understood in the "broadest" sense, not merely as a process of transposing meanings from one language into another, but also as an *imaginative venture that spawns new idioms of thought at the threshold where the word emerges from silence.*[5] Within this newly forged landscape of imagination, I will be able to highlight the issues which are normally relegated to the *periphery* of the exchange between Heidegger and Kant, including *spatiality and embodiment,*[6] *nature and art, religion and politics.*

In Chapter One, I provide an overview of the historical circumstances that prompt, and the nexus of issues which shape, Heidegger's appropriation of Kant's transcendental philosophy. In Chapter Two, I will locate the exact point of "crossing," which allow Heidegger to develop his own ontological concerns for temporality, truth and being on the adjacent front of Kant's epistemic focus on the human finitude, predication, and knowledge. We will see how Heidegger develops a "translation key" by which to render the apparently disparate concepts of Kant's philosophy in terms that serve the more "original" task of re-formulating the question of being. As we unlock this key, we will discover that Heidegger's search for a new linchpin to connect the parts of Kant's Critical philosophy, most notably, the creative power of the imagination has, as its unstated converse, rediscovering language as the pre-articulated wellspring of meaning. In this way, we distinguish between language as emerging directly as a phenomenon, as *logos,* and indirectly through the figure of an emissary, intermediary, or a "go-between" (the example of "Hermes.")

---

4 See Schalow, *The Renewal of the Heidegger-Kant Dialogue,* pp. 7–21. This book arrives at the importance of the problem of language, rather than *beginning* from it, as the counter point that gives momentum to Heidegger's exchange or *Auseinandersetzung* with Kant. Only by emphasizing this divergence can we outline the panorama of issues which punctuate that exchange. For the first major treatment of this topic, see Sherover, *Heidegger, Kant, and Time,* pp. 8–12.
5 See Emad, *Translation and Interpretation: Learning from Beitrage,* pp. 61–70. Also see Emad, *On the Way to Heidegger's Contributions to Philosophy,* pp. 21–26. Of special note is his key distinction between "interlingual" and "intralingual" translation.
6 See Schalow, *The Incarnality of Being,* pp. 1–12.

In Chapter Three, I situate Heidegger's exchange with Kant within the wider context of his appropriation of the tradition, including its relevance for understanding the so-called "turning" (*Kehre*) toward a new philosophical beginning. In the fourth chapter, I address the "practical" implications of Heidegger's retrieval of Kant, the importance of recovering space, in conjunction with time, as establishing the place (*Ort*) for being's manifestations as well as our inhabitation of the earth. I argue that experiencing being is indispensable to understanding it, and that our engagement in the domain of *praxis* — along with our correlative exercise of freedom — enables Heidegger to translate Kant's notion of autonomy into the more concrete terms of moral responsibility. In the fifth chapter, I outline the transition from the experience of being, to its expression in language, while showing how the exchange between thinkers serves as a linguistic vehicle to evoke the most basic idioms of thought. In the process, we will enter into a controversial debate concerning Heidegger's stance toward the politics, and raise a question as to whether it is possible to transform that realm by undergoing another form of translation: that is, "translating" social policies (designed to regulate human conduct) into terrestrial (ecological) ones (aimed to facilitate our manner of "dwelling" on the earth).

In Chapter Six, I show how the task of retrieving the nascent concern for language throughout the whole of Kant's philosophy, and particularly its potential for "figurative" expression, extends Heidegger's own hermeneutic mission to rediscover language as a wellspring of the most primordial idioms and gestures. By harboring an "unstated" clue, the *Critique of Judgment* opens a new path for Heidegger's philosophy: specifically, that "thought" need no longer assume a subordinate position to language, because, quite the reverse, *the words themselves are vital to the creative thrust and task of thinking*. In this way, I emphasize the "other side" of Heidegger's exchange with Kant, in which the voice (*Stimme*) of the latter reverberates in the former's search for a new philosophical beginning under the heading of "being-historical thinking." In Chapter Seven, I explore an area of Kant's thinking that Heidegger largely circumvented, the concern for art and nature in the third *Critique*, even though Heidegger's discussion of these topics forms the cornerstone for radicalizing his own philosophy. We will discover that the numeric characterization of "three" signifies a path of inter-mediation leading back and forth between Heidegger and Kant, marking a "crossroads" bridging their philosophies. For Kant, the crossing is configured through the power of imagination, for Heidegger, through the figure of Hermes and its ontological enactment in translating the grounding words of philosophy. By following this ellipsis which returns us to the ultimate presupposition of Kant's philosophy, we arrive at the "crossroads" where it becomes possible to forge a "departure" for philosophy and thereby address the most pressing issues of today.

# Chapter One
# Why Did Heidegger "Turn" to Kant?

Whenever we consider the greatest philosophers, Immanuel Kant (1724–1804) and Martin Heidegger (1889–1976) are among the first names that come to mind. And yet, despite the fact that they share a common heritage, and the former profoundly influenced the latter, there are noticeable differences as well. Among twentieth-century thinkers, Martin Heidegger stands out as the philosopher par excellence for whom the question of the meaning of being constitutes the primary philosophical problematic. If only because we assume what being "means" in an everyday context, however, *turning what is obvious into what is most question-worthy* poses the utmost challenge. A century and a half earlier, Immanuel Kant faced his own challenge when he made the concern for circumscribing the limits of human knowledge predetermine the scope of all philosophical questions. Given the "epistemic" slant of his *Critique of Pure Reason*, and, by implication, its indifference to the "ontological" concern for being, Kant's philosophical approach stands in stark contrast to Heidegger's.

Indeed, on the surface the gulf between these two thinkers appears almost insurmountable, with only the intervening passage of years allowing for an exchange between them. As Heidegger suggests, in quoting an all-too prophetic remark of Kant's: "In the last years of his life, in the course of a conversation, Kant once said: 'I came with my writings a hundred years too early. A hundred years from now they will understand me better and will study and accept my books anew.'"[7] And are we, likewise, in any better position to understand Heidegger's thought, including the intricacies of his appropriation of transcendental philosophy? So why did Heidegger "turn" to Kant's transcendental study of the nature and limits of human knowledge, in an effort to discover the outline for the development of his own fundamental ontology?

In this chapter, I will try to answer this pivotal question, which remains in the background of most attempts to unravel the parallels between Heidegger's and Kant's thinking. Despite Kant's neglect for the question of being, he leaves the trace of an access to it through his emphasis on time. But is that emphasis only what directs Heidegger to Kant's thinking? Or instead is it the case that time is so endemic to the organization of human understanding, as to exhibit a universality on par with the most universal of all concepts, namely, being? What Heidegger saw in Kant, then, was a unique approach to time, whose explicit formulation

---

7  GA 25, p. 1; tr. 1. Also see GA 41, p. 41.

would yield clues to the possibility of understanding being and expressing its meaning in conceptual terms. That is, Kant's treatment of time included a methodological component, allowing it to serve as an "intermediary" whereby terms infused with temporal connotations, e. g., presence and permanence, would "signify" being. By examining the methodological precepts of this form of intermediation, which Kant called "schematism," Heidegger believed he could reenact the process of projecting being upon time, thereby articulating its meaning in words. Time in the strictly Kantian sense would then yield a vocabulary to articulate being, not arbitrarily, but in accord with a universality of expression which would culminatge in a "science of being" or ontology.[8]

By providing the key to articulate being and universalize the language thereof, temporality serves as an intermediary in the classical, hermeneutic sense of a "go-between," which translates what is otherwise indeterminate and occult into intelligible and communicable terms. In its most basic form, hermeneutics is a strategy to bring forth what is hidden to our understanding, in order that what is implicit can be made explicit and its meaning can be expressed. Though this strategy can be applied in different areas, Heidegger maintained that the primary mission of hermeneutics was to address the enigma surrounding "being," in order that its "meaning" could be conveyed in philosophical terms with a concreteness that remain anchored in, rather than detached from, the inquirer's lived-experience. On the one hand, Heidegger uncovered in Kant's attempt to transplant philosophy on the soil of human finitude a nascent form of hermeneutics. Ironically, Heidegger's depiction of Kant as a proto-hermeneuticist remains underappreciated in most studies of the relation between these two thinkers. On the other hand, through his appropriation of Kant, Heidegger took one of the greatest steps to radicalize his hermeneutic task. That is, he sought to liberate it from its confinement to cultural (e. g., Wilhelm Dilthey) and religious (e. g., Rudolf Bultmann) inquiries, and wed it to the distinctly philosophical pursuit of developing a science of being.

Heidegger, like Kant, used the term "science" in a way directly correlated with philosophical inquiry, rather than with the form of empirical investigation we tend to construe as "scientific" today. Indeed, Heidegger characterized "science" in the phenomenological sense of conforming our analyzes to the self-showing of the phenomenon, in this case, to being, while inviting the inquirer's participation in the singularity of its manifestation. Through his destructive-retrieval of Kant, Heidegger found testimony to how the dynamic of being's manifestation could include the potential for its own transcription into words, the

---

**8** GA 24, p. 22; tr. 17.

unfolding of the "meaning" of being as such. And this testimonial in turn bears further witness to the radicalization of the phenomenology through hermeneutics, the rebirth of hermeneutics in harmony with, rather than in opposition to, ontology as the *science* of being.

I will begin by outlining the key steps which comprise Heidegger's destructive-retrieval of Kant's transcendental philosophy, and locate it more broadly within his understanding of the Western tradition. Then I will consider the parallels between the Kantian account of synthetic a priori knowledge and the hermeneutic exercise of interpretation, as a way of laying out the temporal determinations of being. Finally, I will address the objections that Heidegger's so-called "transcendental turn" constitutes a perversion of hermeneutics.

## 1 Attunement and Meaning: Saying the "Unsaid"

From the early days as a novice philosopher after World-War I, Heidegger undertook one primary mission: to breathe new life into the most perennial, if not also the most overlooked of all philosophical questions, the question of being (*die Seinsfrage*). As he states in one of his most famous works, *Contributions to Philosophy* (1938): "The question of the 'meaning of being' is the question of all questions."[9] In retrospect, Heidegger's way of reformulating this question continues to be influential today, if only because he *forged his own novel methodology* by appropriating the insights of an extraordinary litany of predecessors: from Aristotle to Hegel, from Duns Scotus to Schelling, from Plato to Nietzsche, from Kant to Kierkegaard — only to name a few of the West's greatest thinkers. Along with an uncanny ability to address his contemporaries, and yet develop an alternative path of thinking (*Denkweg*) to them — from Husserl to Scheler, Jaspers to Bultmann, Lask to Cassirer — Heidegger chiseled out a completely new philosophical landscape within which to recast an age-old problem. Undoubtably, Heidegger's contributions are both diverse and significant, including his unparalleled foresight in anticipating the dangerous implications of modern technology. Yet perhaps it is as a virtuoso for reinterpreting the greatest philosophical texts, from Aristotle's *Ethics* to Kant's *Critique of Pure Reason*, that Heidegger's creative spirit shines most brightly.

With perhaps greater flare than even Hegel, Heidegger stands out as the historian of philosophy par excellence. Yet "historian" in this sense does not simply involve passively studying the works of past thinkers, but rather entails

---

**9** GA 65, p. 11; tr. 8.

creatively wrestling with their writings, in order to "mine" the hidden gems of insight buried deeply within them. Because more than any other thinker Heidegger sows the seeds of his philosophy within the soil of the Western tradition, his *legacy* hinges on his success at reclaiming, appropriating, and transmitting the insights of his predecessors. Indeed, given that Heidegger advances his philosophical project by retrieving these insights, as well as dismantling the obstacles obscuring them, the *future impact of his thinking depends upon rediscovering its historical roots.* Accordingly, it is by addressing one thinker in particular with whom he shares a common ancestry, and who also stands out among the handful of the greatest philosophers, namely, Immanuel Kant, that Heidegger offers one of the most compelling and controversial examples of his "destructive-retrieval" of the Western tradition. How can we cast new light on a quest that returns Heidegger to one of the most profound of all catalysts in the development of his thinking?

While much has been written concerning Heidegger's relation to Kant, perhaps there is still more to be told. In attempting to trace the stages of Heidegger's destructive-retrieval of Kant, the tendency is to proceed in an exegetical manner either by providing a detailed analysis of pivotal texts, e. g., *Kant and the Problem of Metaphysics* (1929) or the immediately proceeding lecture-course, *The Phenomenological Interpretation of Kant's Critique of Pure Reason*, or to proceed thematically by examining distinctive topics, e. g., the phenomenon of transcendence. From Sherover to Dahlstrom to Weatherston, these approaches have served us well.[10] But what is the variable which now renders them more problematic, if not the continual renaissance in the interpretation of Heidegger's thought? The publication of Heidegger's *Beiträge zur Philosophie (Vom Ereignis)* [1989], along with its translation as *Contributions to Philosophy (From Enowning)* [1999], as well as, even more recently, *Besinnung* (1997) and its translation as *Mindfulness* (2006), has sparked this resurgence of interest in his philosophy by bringing the task of "being-historical thinking" to the forefront. Given this new fulcrum for addressing Heidegger's thought, it is incumbent to supplement my earlier work, *The Renewal of the Heidegger-Kant Dialogue* (1992), and make explicit the "being-historical perspective," which establishes the *distance* as well as the proximity between

---

**10** Sherover, *Heidegger, Kant and Time*, pp. 9–15. Because of its clarity, this work sets the standard for interpreting the Kant-book. We might say that the sequel to this work is a collection of essays, which reveal a "pragmatic" bent to Sherover's approach. See Sherover, *From Kant and Royce to Heidegger: Essays in Modern Philosophy*, pp. ix-xvi. Dahlstrom, "Heidegger's Kant-Courses at Marburg", pp. 293–308. See Dahlstrom, "Heidegger's Kantian Turn: Notes on His Commentary to the *Kritik der reinen Vernunft*", pp. 329–361. Weatherston, *Heidegger's Interpretation of Kant: Categories, Imagination, and Temporality*, pp. 8–15.

these two thinkers. As Parvis Emad suggests, such a perspective carves an original pathway for thought, which becomes "mindful of be-ing's historically self-transforming showing,"[11] and thus alert to the inception (*Anfang*) of all thinking throughout the history of philosophy.

Of course, analyzing a spectrum of Heidegger's texts and developing the correlative topics is as laudable as it is unavoidable. In this study, I venture a different approach, which begins by seeking an ambiance or atmosphere, the grounding-attunement (*Grundstimmung*), for unfolding Heidegger's *Auseinandersetzung* with Kant. Even when I originally referred to the "Heidegger-Kant dialogue," this attunement is presupposed as *opening the dialogical space for the exchange between these two thinkers.*[12] While perhaps appearing capricious, my approach nevertheless squares with the novelty of Heidegger's radical interpretation of Kant's transcendental philosophy. For of the variety of dramatic claims which Heidegger advances throughout his interpretation, two standout as setting the guidelines thereof: 1) that Kant's thought has profound ontological implications for re-asking the question of being and 2) that despite the title of Kant's *magnum opus*, the *Critique of Pure Reason*, the basic thrust of transcendental philosophy is to restore the affective dimension of our experience, which is the hallmark of our human constitution as finite. As a constant thread running throughout his various studies of Kant, Heidegger argues that the power of imagination (*Einbildungskraft*) usurps reason as the organizational stem whereby human beings can project a horizon of meaning (transcendence) within which to encounter things/objects. The imagination, by defining the finite origin of time, provides a more primordial point of departure than does reason from which to develop the most basic philosophical questions, including *die Seinsfrage*. Given this radical subversion of reason, a clue arises as to the atmosphere surrounding Heidegger's interpretation when, in the "Preface to the Second Edition" (1950) of the Kant-book, he alludes to its necessary "violence" (*Gewalt*) in dislocating the center of transcendental philosophy.[13] As Hans-Georg Gadamer, one of Heidegger's most prominent students, summarizes his initial turn to Kant: "Precisely the two-sided nature of the two sources of knowledge, precisely the restriction of reason to that which could be given in intuition seemed to offer Heidegger a foundation for an alliance with Kant. Of course, his attempt to cast Kant in light of a 'finite metaphysics' was a highly violent deed …"[14]

---

**11** For a further discussion of this "being-historical perspective," see Emad, *On the Way to Heidegger's Contributions to Philosophy*, p. 158.

**12** See Schalow, *Renewal of the Heidegger-Kant Dialogue*, p. 128.

**13** Heidegger, *Kant and the Problem of Metaphysics*. "Preface to the Second Edition"; tr. xx.

**14** Gadamer, *Heidegger's Ways*, pp. 161–162.

According to Heidegger, the grounding-attunement which best characterizes this violence is distress (*Not*). For him, distress is a response we experience from standing on the cusp of a historical decision, that is, by anticipating how possibilities dormant in the past come to fruition through their arrival in the future. Distress alerts us to the uniqueness of our historical situation, the pervasiveness of history in everything we do as well as in the quest to develop philosophical insight into the meaning of being. As Heidegger states in *Contributions to Philosophy*:

> All necessity is rooted in distress. As the first and utmost mindfulness of the truth of be-ing of the be-ing of truth, the necessity of philosophy lies in the first and utmost distress ...
> The necessity of philosophy consists in the fact that as mindfulness it does not have to eliminate that distress but rather must persevere in it and ground it, i. e., make it the ground of man's history.[15]

Friedrich Nietzsche was one of the first philosophers to consider the possibility of a transition, a "going under," and crossing (*Übergang*) in history. In his famous work, *Thus Spoke Zarathustra*, the dwarf taunts Zarathustra as he ascends toward the overman, exclaiming: "You philosopher's stone. You throw yourself so high. But what goes up must come down."[16] We might paraphrase that statement by saying that no ascent to philosophical heights is possible without a parallel descent into the depths of history – every "crossing" entail a parallel moment of "going-under." Indeed, this paradox proves to be especially compelling in the case of the most fundamental philosophical pursuit of all, the inquiry into the meaning of being or what traditionally has been called "ontology." Due to its obviousness if not ubiquity, the meaning of being is inherently elusive, receding in the background of what appears in its wake or beings (*Seiende*) themselves. Correlatively, philosophical understanding is equally elusive; and, contrary to a logic of linear progress, philosophy predicates its advance on recovering its origins. Two implications immediately follow from this observation.

First, despite constituting the primary and most time-honored of all philosophical topics, the question of being, and its ultimate meaning, lies in its forgottenness (*Vergessenheit*). Second, because of its dormancy throughout two millennia of the philosophical tradition, the question of being is inherently historical. Due to this fact, Heidegger can only re-ask the question of being by engaging his predecessors in conversation. Such a conversation implies speaking, but, when considered in light of the preceding, speech assumes the characteristics most

---

15 GA 65, pp. 45–46; tr. 32.
16 Nietzsche, *Thus Spoke Zarathustra*, p. 268.

endemic to what it expresses or being, that is, giving way to and preserving what is unspoken. Curiously, then, an *Auseinandersetzung* with previous philosophers proves fruitful by considering precisely how being withdraws from their thinking; and, then, conversely, the nooks and crannies, the breaks and ruptures, in their thought where being can re-emerge into questioning, that is, a new formulation of the question (*Fragestellung*) can once again occur. In this spirit, we refer to a "destructive-retrieval" of a previous thinker's thought, in order to distinguish the dual character by which the acknowledgment of the omission of neglect yields a clue to what is most question-worthy, and hence the dynamic of *Auseinandersetzung* transforms forgottenness into recollection. In his dialogue with Kant, Heidegger first alludes to his attempt to elicit what remains *"unsaid"* in transcendental philosophy concerning the question of being, its affiliation with temporality, and the primacy of imagination as the vehicle of time-formation. Correlatively, *Kant and the Problem of Metaphysics* sets the precedent for all of Heidegger's subsequent exchanges with previous thinkers, including Nietzsche.[17]

Heidegger's destructive-retrieval of the tradition becomes possible only given the contingency of his own historical situation, his thrownness into it. Only by measuring his own thought against his predecessors — comparing and contrasting — can he underscore its originality. By the same token, Heidegger's attempt to re-ask the question of being does not emerge *sui generis*, but instead is prefigured in the investigations of previous philosophers. Specifically, Kant's transcendental philosophy prefigures Heidegger's task by shifting the focus of inquiry to the inquirer's capacity to address his/her own finitude. Kant's way of shifting the fulcrum of philosophy back to this preliminary stage of investigation into human finitude parallels Heidegger's own attempt to inaugurate his formulation of the question of being in and through the "existential analytic" or provisional analysis of human existence. In his 1928 lectures on German Idealism, Heidegger describes "the finitude of Dasein as the basic happening of metaphysics" (*Endlichkeit des Daseins als Grundgeschehen der Metaphysik*).[18] The self-implicatory pattern of the investigation, that allows the inquirer's preunderstanding to suggest guidelines for what the inquiry addresses, yields the movement for re-asking the question of being. By showing how Kant employs a philosophical strategy parallel to his own, Heidegger undertakes a destructive-retrieval of his thought which in effect re-enacts or "repeats" the selection of his own point of departure of hermeneutic-phenomenological investigation.

---

17 See Schalow, "The *Gesamtausgabe* Nietzsche: An Exercise in Translation and Thought" pp. 139–152.
18 GA 28, p. 47.

For Heidegger, repetition or retrieval (*Wiederholung*) is an essential dimension of the hermeneutics which Heidegger employs, if not its heart. Retrieval is a strategy for clarifying the presuppositions from which an inquiry begins, and to when we return, in light of the understanding which has been achieved in the course of the investigation. By clarifying these presuppositions, we 1) make explicit what lends intelligibility to understanding, yielding its measure of determination and allowing what is understood to be articulated; 2) justify the point of departure, thereby opening up a more radical avenue of investigation from which new possibilities of understanding, concerning the meaning of being, can arise; 3) show how philosophical knowing exhibits the contours of human understanding as such, doubling back upon its own beginnings and unfolding in a circular pattern. According to this dynamic, what we understand undergoes change, revision, and clarification in light of the path it follows. For what allows understanding to proceed remains concealed from the start, only to be revealed subsequently, thereby expanding the horizon of understanding itself. When we read a great work of literature for the second time, for example, we gain a greater appreciation of it precisely by recognizing the limits of our first reading and thereby freeing new possibilities of understanding. The fact that all human understanding develops in this way, and exhibits this circular dynamic of unfolding its own possibilities, indicates its inherent dependence upon boundaries, that is, its essential *finitude*; 4) as repetitive in its development, understanding displays the "self-disclosive" character of original truth. Accordingly, Heidegger claims that philosophical understanding is a "radicalization" of the pre-understanding of being, which is implicated in the course of human existence and enacted through each individual. Given the concrete thrust of his hermeneutics, Heidegger thereby insures that philosophy is not an esoteric study, but instead springs from our "temporal sojourn in the world."[19]

What distinguishes Heidegger's hermeneutic phenomenology is the inclusion of this pre-philosophical, pre-theoretical orientation, insuring that the conceptualizing of being speaks to and from the lived-experience of the inquirer, rather than becoming lost in esoteric speculation. In this spirit, Heidegger first develops an interest in the emergence of "meaning" *per se*, as the primary philosophical orientation, from out of which he first ventures to address being in its manifold dimensions of meaning, as Franz Brentano had done before.[20] In his 1918 lectures comprising *Towards the Definition of Philosophy*, Heidegger makes a pivotal re-

---

19 GA 2, p. 263. For an English translation, not based on the *Gesamtausgabe* volume, see *Being and Time*, p. 243.

20 Gadamer, *Heidegger's Ways*, p. 83. See Friedrich-Wilhelm von Herrmann, *Subjekt und Dasein*, p. 17.

mark that prefigures his subsequent hermeneutic strategy for re-asking the question of the *meaning* of being: "The immanent historicity of life as such constitutes hermeneutical intuition. Once these insights are obtained, it emerges that the meaningfulness of language does *not* have to be theoretical."[21] Language itself, including that pertaining to being, acquires its scope of relevance prior to, and from a broader horizon than, the merely theoretical attitude. Only give this pre-theoretical orientation, from the roots of hermeneutics spring, can philosophy address the "meaning" of being through a language that preserves our experience of it (being) and seeks in that pre-understanding the guidelines of developing the concepts for its articulation. Experience and concept form a reciprocal partnership, and it is this methodological insight of his early hermeneutics that Heidegger initiates in his interpretation of Kant in the late 1920s. And, conversely, in order to explore the dynamic integration of that partnership, Heidegger turns to Kant's schematism as the key strategy for deriving from time an original lexicon of being.

Interestingly enough, Heidegger develops his interest in "meaning" by rebutting the Neo-Kantian stalwarts of his day, including his thesis advisor, Heinrich Rickert. What is important in this early development is that it gives a stamp of inevitability to Heidegger's subsequent attempt — etched a decade later — to reinterpret anew Kant's transcendental philosophy. Indeed, Heidegger's appropriation of transcendental philosophy appears almost inevitable, insofar as it is only by counterposing his own interpretation of Kant from the Southwest German school of Neo-Kantian in the work of Lask, Windelband, and Rickert,[22] as well as Cohen,[23] and later Cassirer, that Heidegger can accentuate the originality of his own "hermeneutic breakthrough." Even though the influence of Neo-Kantianism — and particularly that of the Marburg school — diminishes throughout the course of Heidegger's career, he continues to separate his own interpretation of transcendental philosophy from that movement, as witnessed even as late as his lecture course from the Winter Semester 1935/36, *Die Frage nach dem Ding.*[24]

To bring this discussion to a head, we must recall what was stated at the outset concerning the role of hermeneutics as an intermediary. Hermeneutics is the method that allows the example of my own existence to speak 1) to the structures constitutive thereof, of care (*Sorge*) as the being of Da-sein and then, subsequently 2) to the possibility of understanding being. As a form of retrieval,

---

21  GA 56/57, p. 219; tr. 187.
22  See Risser, *Hermeneutics and the Voice of the Other*, p. 27. For a further discussion of the Neo-Kantians, see Orth, "Martin Heidegger und der NeuKantianismus", pp. 421–429.
23  GA 56/57, p. 168; tr. 142. See Gadamer, *Philosophical Apprenticeships*, pp. 8–11.
24  GA 41, p. 59; tr. 59–60.

hermeneutics proceeds to another level to match what understanding discloses concerning being, with the language capable of expressing it. Being, however, is a concept which has a significant ancestry, the most perennial of all concepts. As a result, we must trace the origination of the vocabulary to articulate being back to its birth within the philosophical tradition. In this case, the destructive-retrieval of Kant's thought serves to exemplify the hermeneutic maneuvers Heidegger which undertakes in *Being and Time*, in order that his inquiry can be traced back to its historical roots and thereby shown to have an antecedent within the tradition. Then, a crossing of the language(s) can occur, in which the more "conventional" way of employing Kantian terms can be reinformed with Heidegger's language. Given this crossing, the latter can become a conduit for re-expressing the former, of saying what is "unsaid"; and, conversely, the success by which Heidegger reformulates Kant's task in terms parallel to his own can serve as a litmus test to the originality of his own project of re-asking the question of being. Under this umbrella of retrieval, the reciprocal implication which occurs in the dialogue between Heidegger and Kant thereby embodies another instance of the hermeneutical circle. However, it is now the entire background of the philosophical tradition, and the inherently historical character of the question of being, which determines the scope of this circularity.

There is a misperception that by the "unsaid" in Kant Heidegger has in view something mysterious to which only he has access, lending a kind of arbitrariness to his vision. Compounding the problem is a belief that Heidegger is providing the interpretation of all interpretations of Kant's transcendental philosophy. But perhaps what is controversial is not whether Heidegger merely distorts transcendental philosophy or arrogantly provides a definitive interpretation thereof. On the contrary, what is often lost in the "violence" of Heidegger's reading is how his reciprocal rejoinder (*Erwiderung*) with his predecessor transposes his own language into a historical context where words can reverberate with the power of tradition, and acquires the nuances to articulate the most primeval concept of all, namely, being. To put matters in the clearest way, the reciprocal implication between Heidegger's and Kant's thought evokes the key distinctions to formulate the concept of being and thereby signify its meaning. By restoring what is "unsaid" in Kant, Heidegger's destructive-retrieval of transcendental philosophy becomes an exercise whose mission is "to preserve the force (*Kraft*) of the *most elemental words (elementarsten Worte)* by which Dasein expresses itself."[25]

By allowing the words to speak with the reverberations of tradition, Heidegger reciprocal-rejoinder with Kant restores a depth to the basic philosophical

---

**25** GA 2, p. 291; tr. 262.

concepts in accord with their ancestry. In *Contributions to Philosophy*, Heidegger characterizes this historical occurrence as an "echoing," in which words resound across the chasms that separate distinct historical epochs and allow for meanings to recede, be rediscovered, and transmitted again. This echoing implies a prior acclimation, tonality, and attunement, which harbors a reciprocal invitation for each of us to heed the word and allow for the play of its various inflections of meaning.

> The *guiding-attunement* of echo: shock and deep awe, but always rising out of the grounding-attunement of *reservedness* (*Verhaltenheit*).
> The utmost distress: the *distress of lack of distress*. First of all to let this reverberate, whereby much must necessarily remain incomprehensible and unquestionable; and nevertheless a faint hint becomes possible.[26]

With this observation, we return to our starting point where the grounding-attunement of distress strips away the familiar cloth of our proximity to tradition, so that in the intervening distance being-historical thinking can be enacted in order to rekindle interest in perennial philosophical questions. Such thinking allows the "distress to become more distressing, and the questioning more hearable."[27] In accord with this attunement, a destructive-retrieval of the tradition, of Kant's thought in particular, becomes possible. As Heidegger states in *Contributions*, "*retrieval* here means to let the *same*, the uniqueness of be-ing [*Seyn*], become a distress *again* — and that means *thus from a more originary truth*."[28] In the end, novelty is a function of reclaiming the origins by deferring to the future as the gathering-point for their appropriation. In the hiatus of this deferral the echo resounds, signifying the dynamic of giving and reserving, of offering and refusing.[29]

## 2 "Philosophy on this Earth" — The Lasting Importance of the First Critique

Much has been said about Heidegger's abrupt decision to reexamine Kant's *Critique of Pure Reason* in order to establish a ground plan for the development of his own project of "being and time." Indeed, Heidegger recounts the suddenness, during the winter break of 1925, that he decided to change the topic of his next

---

26 GA 65, p. 107; tr. 75.
27 GA 66, p. 361; tr. 250.
28 GA 65, p. 73; tr. 51.
29 GA 65, p. 108; tr. 75.

course — *Logik: Die Frage nach der Wahrheit* — to a study of Kant's first *Critique*.[30] Heidegger concludes his 1928 lecture course, *The Phenomenological Interpretation of Kant's Critique of Pure Reason*, with this memorable statement:

> When some years ago I studied the *Critique of Pure Reason* anew and read it, as it were, against the background of Husserl's phenomenology, it opened my eyes; and Kant became for me a crucial confirmation of the accuracy of the path which I took in my search ... Kant has *the* immense significance in education for scientific, philosophical work; and one can trust him fully. In Kant as in no other thinker one has the immediate certainty that he does not cheat. And the most monstrous danger consists in cheating, because all efforts do not have the massive character of a natural scientific experiment or that of an historical source. But where the greatest danger of cheating is, there is also the ultimate possibility for the genuineness of thinking and questioning. The meaning of doing philosophy consists in awakening the need for this genuineness and keeping it awake.[31]

As we will discover at the close of this chapter, it is debated how pivotal to the development of Heidegger's thinking his turn to Kant is. But one thing is certain: Heidegger never lost his reverence for Kant's thought, even if he became increasingly aware of the latter's "entanglement" in metaphysics.[32] In what followed the Kant-book as his second major study of the *Critique of Pure Reason, Die Frage nach dem Ding*, Heidegger remarks: "Kant's *Critique of Pure Reason* is among those philosophical works, as long as there is philosophy on this earth at all, that daily becomes inexhaustible anew. It is one of those works that have already pronounced judgments over every future attempt to 'overcome' them by only passing them by."[33]

In *Die Frage nach dem Ding*, Heidegger offers one of his most lucid summaries of Kant's critical enterprise:

> Critique thus becomes the surveying which sets the boundaries for the entire domain of pure reason. This surveying does not take place, as Kant expressly and ever again enjoins, by referring to "facts" ("*Faktis*"), but it occurs from principles; not by determining qualities met somewhere, but by determining the whole enactment of pure reason out of its own principles. Critique is a setting of boundaries, a surveying projecting of pure reason.[34]

For Kant, the "critique of pure reason" reason's self-examination of its own capabilities, the circumscription of its powers, in order to determine in advance

---

30 GA 21, pp. 407–411.
31 GA 25, p. 431; tr. 293.
32 Gadamer, *Heidegger's Ways*, p. 162.
33 GA 41, p. 60; tr. 61. For an early essay dealing with Heidegger's 1935/36 lectures, see Edward G. Ballard, "Heidegger on Bringing Kant to Stand", pp. 91–103.
34 GA 41, p. 123; tr. 121 (translation modified).

what the most basic metaphysical questions are and how they might be legitimately answered. When cast in phenomenological terms, reason's exercise of self-criticism amounts to "laying the foundation of metaphysics" on the soil of human finitude, of appealing to a preliminary analysis of human existence (as finitude) to establish he ground plan of ontology. Heidegger found in Kant's Critical enterprise, in his portrait of the problem of human finitude, the prefigurement of his own fundamental ontology. In adopting the phenomenological method, Heidegger followed in his mentor's, Edmund Husserl's, footsteps. Yet, curiously enough, when the need arises to establish the key for formulating the question of being, Heidegger finds a closer allegiance in Kant than in Husserl.

As the name suggests, the destructive-retrieval of Kant proceeds on two fronts: integrating those dimensions of transcendental philosophy that contribute to re-asking the question of being, and discarding those aspects which would otherwise obstruct that task. Obviously, most attention drifts to the first front, because that is where the true payoff of Heidegger's endeavors lie. But the importance of the issues played out on the second front cannot be underestimated, if only because the reciprocal rejoinder between these two thinkers occurs when we negotiate the chasm separating them. Though terminological differences are a factor, Heidegger can unfold the ontological implications of Kant's thought only by divorcing it from a derivative preconception of being qua "nature" defined as the totality of physical objects. By the same token, Heidegger rescues Kant's interest in the problematic of time, as it serves to couch the concern for being in the most universal terms, by denouncing the modern prejudice of limiting being to a circumscribed region of beings. The tension that governs Heidegger's destructive-retrieval of Kant, then, can be summarized this way: Kant's predilection to restrict human knowledge to the sphere of nature must be sacrificed in order to allow a preconception of being to guide us which is sufficiently universal as to suggest its own linkage to a parallel problematic of time. At the close of *Phenomenological Interpretation*, Heidegger emphasizes the importance of the hermeneutic fore-concept linking being to time:

> If we radicalize the Kantian problem of ontological knowledge in the sense that we do not limit this problem of the ontological foundation of the positive sciences and if we do not take this problem as a problem of judgment but as the radical and fundamental question concerning the possibility of understanding being in general, then we shall arrive at the philosophically fundamental problematic of *Being and Time*. Time will then no longer be understood in terms of the ordinary concept of time, but in terms of temporality as the original unity of the ecstatic constitution of Dasein. Being will then no longer be understood in terms of nature's being extant, but rather in that universal sense which encompasses in itself all possibilities of regional variation. *Universality of being and radicality of time are the*

*two titles which together denote the tasks which a further thinking of the possibility of metaphysics calls for.*[35]

Though going unnoticed to a large extent, this hermeneutic guideline yields the direction which Heidegger takes in initiating his dialogue with Kant. The hermeneutic foreconcept has the effect of circumscribing the scope of the inquiry, of distinguishing the relevant from the irrelevant, of sorting out the chaff from the straw. When we think of hermeneutics, we also think of understanding (*Verstehen*), a term in English whose corollary in a Kantian context (*Verstand*) has epistemic connotations pertaining to the possibility of knowledge. The issue at stake, however, is more than just terminology. Through a critique of pure reason, Kant seeks to uncover the preconditions of knowledge, which coincide with the application of pure concepts or categories originating from understanding. As a term taken from Dilthey, understanding (*Verstehen*) pertains to a general capability that the individual possesses to project possibilities and see him/herself disclosed thereby. Understanding in this regard pertains more broadly to the determination of meaning, and, by forming the backdrop for any theoretical pursuits involved in knowledge, also includes the cognitive awareness implied in practical dealings, e. g., driving a car. When Heidegger addresses "understanding" in the Kantian mode, he formalizes the notion in accord with this broadest sense. In taking up the problem of knowledge, Heidegger then imports the dynamic proper to understanding (*Verstehen*) to distinguish the capability proper to knowledge, that is, as projecting-open in advance a horizon within which something can emerge as an object to be known. Heidegger's way of transposing Kant's problematic of knowledge into an ontological concern about the dynamic presupposed in the capacity to know, the horizonal preview of the possibility, constitutes a crucial step in his appropriation of transcendental philosophy.

When first examining Heidegger's interpretation of Kant, there is a tendency to polarize these two thinkers in terms of a false dichotomy between ontology and epistemology, particularly by making the concern for knowledge irrelevant to the former. In *Kant and the Problem of Metaphysics*, for example, Heidegger does not merely circumvent the problem of knowledge. Instead, he attempts to show how the concern for knowledge harbors a prior question about the constitution or being of the knower, the "subjectivity of the subject," apart from its reduction to the Carestian *cogito*. If we base the possibility of knowledge on Descartes's premise that the knower is an isolated ego separated from the natural realm of inanimate objects, then, as Heidegger argues in *Being and Time*, knowing is a

---

35 GA 25, pp. 426–427; tr. 289.

"founded" or derivative mode of being-in-the-world. If, on the other hand, we relocate the knower within its proper place in the world, in the "there" of Da-sein, a completely different picture emerges. The knower is not simply divorced from what it knows, but is already pre-oriented towards it; and, reciprocally, the object to be known must already be capable of appearing within a pre-given horizon of manifestation. According to Heidegger, Kant's "transcendental" concern for the possibility of knowledge involves shifting the focus to the knower's participation in forming this horizon. The horizon constitutes a field of inter-mediation, as it were, which enables the knower to "surpass toward" and encounter what becomes manifest within this field, or the object as such. In the *Critique of Pure Reason*, Kant defines "transcendental knowledge" as concerning not so much the objects themselves as the preconditions of knowledge. With an eye to rendering that Kant means by his term "transcendental," Heidegger reserves the term "transcendence" to capture the dynamic (i. e., temporal) movement of surpassing toward and passing over to the object, that is, as circumscribing the entire arc of the horizon itself. As Heidegger remarks in his 1930/31 lectures on Hegel: "Certainly this transcendence undergoes a peculiar contraction and formalization through its orientation toward the relational character of knowledge (thinking, understanding, *logos*), which is already to be found in Kant."[36]

Heidegger's way of defining the transcendental in terms of transcendence may on the surface seems somewhat strange. For Kant distinguishes between the sense of "transcendental," as emphasizing a critical focus on the finite conditions of knowledge, and a contrary sense of "transcendent," a referring to the spurious attempt by human reason to cognize super sensuous objects, i. e., God, freedom, and immortality, which lie beyond the possibility of experience. Correlatively, for his part, Heidegger distinguishes between finite transcendence, which has as its target "world" as the pre-theoretical horizon of manifestation, and a religious form of transcendence, which seeks the Divine as its point of culmination. Heidegger finds the latter variation of transcendence expressed best in his contemporary, Max Scheler's, phenomenology. For the religious person transcendence assumes a higher spiritual plane beyond "this" world of ordinary existence. Heidegger maintains, on the other hand, that the world is as much a place of "exteriority" in the sense that it is what allows everything else to become manifest, and it is only by already residing therein, or being-in-the-world, that we can understand any other possibility of transcendence. For Heidegger, then, *finite* transcendence constitutes the self's path of "entry" into the world. In turn, the world emerges when Dasein projects its open, and the self, qua transcendence,

---

**36** GA 32, p. 195; tr. 135.

exists "in" the world in the dual sense as both its point of origination (the "there") and as an occupant alongside everything else (e. g., beings) that becomes manifest.

The fact that Heidegger equates the "transcendental" with transcendence, which takes world as its cornerstone, has an important repercussion for his radical reinterpretation of Kant. For world now forms the axis to mediate the relation between knower and known, in a way that undercuts the Cartesian subject-object dichotomy. In turn, the axis of this mediation turns on a more primeval distinction, which the act of transcendence brings to the forefront, the pre-understanding of being which governs our interaction with beings. The pre-understanding gives the form of organization to whatever we can understand, pre-determining the scope of relevance of whatever can appear as intelligible to us. The allusion "to us" proves crucial. For as finite, we require an horizon to open up what we can understand, and this reference back and forth between the horizon and what appears within it allows increasingly differentiation to be etched in whatever we understand. Put more simply, lacking totality, understanding develops through various stages that interweave more intricate strands of nuance and differentiation. By revolving in a circular arc, understanding testifies to its finitude.

In undercutting the subject-object dichotomy, Heidegger recasts the problem of knowledge in terms of a dynamic that joins knower and known in their reciprocal relationship with each. Heidegger's own concept of transcendence as being-in-the-world permits radicalizing the problem of knowledge in this way. But how can we illustrate corollary development in the lexicon of Kant's own terminology which, despite its orientation to finitude, is for the most part "pre-hermeneutical." Yet Kant envisioned a similar transposition in the relation between knower and known when he proclaimed, in his celebrated Copernican revolution in philosophy, that the problem of (synthetic a priori) knowledge could be solved only by adopting the hypothesis that the "object conform to (the conditions of) our knowledge, rather than the other way around."[37] Kant developed this hypothesis through an analogy with Copernicus's insight that the movement of the celestial bodies could best be explained by making the sun the center of the solar system and have the earth revolve around it. Kant's analogy, however, has always been somewhat puzzling. Given his emphasis on shifting the focus of knowledge away from the object, it would appear that the knower re-emerges

---

37 Immanuel Kant, *Kritik der reinen Vernunft*, B xvii. Hereafter, all references to this text will be included within the text, in reference to the "A" (1781) or "B" (1787) editions, followed by the page number. All other notes to Kant's works will cite *Kants Gesammelte Schriften* (*Akademie Ausgabe*), Hereafter "AA" (Academy Edition), followed by the English translation (where available).

as the center of knowledge. Yet, if we assume that the earth and knower are analogical pairs, as would be natural to do, the analogy does not seem to hold. For in Copernicus's model the earth is actually de-centered in favor of the sun, rather than transposed into the center. However cryptically, Kant says instead that just as it is in relation to the coordinates of the earth's orbit that everything becomes visible in the sky, so the appearance of order in the realm of objects occurs in relation to the preconditions of the trajectory of knowing. Thus, to extend the analogy, even while knowledge appears to be fixed like the earth, the knower is actually part of a dynamic, unfolding, revolving process, i.e., of surpassing toward the horizon within which objects can *appear* (as the earth rotates around the sun). As Sherover explains the Copernican analogy: "Just because *we are traveling around the sun*, judgment of the accuracy of any description of the sun depends upon our own changing position in regard to it. This means we experience a radically changing perspective in a continually dynamic field of vision."[38] That Kant did not do the best job in clarifying this analogy, as Paton argues, goes without saying.[39] Yet it is equally interesting to note that in connection with his "Copernican turn" Kant employed the term "horizon," to accent the limited character of human knowledge, as the following statement from his *Logic* illustrates: "By the absolute and universal horizon (*Horizont*) is to be understood the congruence of the limits of human cognition with the boundaries (*Grenzen*) of the complete human perfection as such, and here the question is: What can man, as man, know at all?"[40]

The Copernican revolution is one of the most brilliant of all philosophical hypotheses. And yet it is predicated on a concession: that the problem of how we can know an object in advance of any encounter with it — synthetic a priori knowledge — can be solved only by conceding that human finitude predetermines the conditions in conformity with which can object an be given to us and hence the object becomes knowable only in the restricted guise of its appearance. Any object, in order to be an object, must be able to present itself in accord with space and time as pure forms of intuition. Correlatively, the pure concepts of the understanding can apply to an object only in conjunction with these forms of intuition, and the former can apply only when they serve in this restricted employment as preconditions under which an object can be known. Only by implicating the circular dynamic of human understanding, can the Copernican revolution answer the challenge of solving the enigma of synthetic a priori knowl-

---

**38** See Sherover, *From Kant and Royce to Heidegger*, p. 29.
**39** Paton, *Kant's Metaphysics of Experience*, pp. 22–36.
**40** AA 9, p. 42; tr. 46 (translation modified).

edge. As Heidegger states: "Thus true to its inner core, thinking proceeds in a *roundabout way*; thinking moves through the determining representation; thinking is a *running through* — *is discursive*. The *finitude* of thinking gets manifested in the character of thinking as roundabout and discursive, i. e., in the fact that, as a function of understanding, judging is a representation of a representation, a mediated representing."[41]

This circular dynamic becomes evident in Kant's formulating of his "transcendental turn." Object can be objects only insofar as they preconform to the precise determination provided by the pure concepts of the understanding (e. g., substance, cause and effect, and existence); but, reciprocally, the pure concepts remain empty or void unless, in conjunction with the pure concepts of space and time, they can serve as predicates which stand for or signify the general characteristics of any possible object. On the one hand, objects must preconform to the pure concepts in order to be admitted into the circumference of knowledge; on the other hand, the pure concepts themselves cannot have any significance or import through their potential to refer to, and designate an object of experience itself. And this back and forth dynamic exemplifies the finitude in whose "*image*" we are to construct the "first principles" that govern the possibility of knowledge as such.

In the guise of the Copernican revolution, Kant's transcendental philosophy spins along the axis of human finitude. And this shift in the direction of human finitude, as providing the new fulcrum from which to solve the enigma of synthetic a priori knowledge, defines his so-called "transcendental turn" or shift in the direction of the subject/subjectivity. But because the term "subject" can be taken in two different ways, as a world-less "I" in Descartes' sense or as a subject whose capacity to know stems from a deeper root of being-in-the-world, the allusion to a "transcendental turn" is ambiguous. Heidegger tries to avoid this ambiguity because for him 1) the epistemic concern for synthetic a priori knowledge already implies the ontological problematic of world and 2) the constitution of the subject, in its finitude, comes radically into question in relation to *die Seinsfrage* rather than, as in Descartes's case, in exclusion thereof. As Heidegger makes this distinction in *Basic Problems*: "Philosophy must perhaps start from the 'subject' and return to the 'subject' in its ultimate questions and yet for all that it may not pose its questions in a one-sidedly subjectivistic manner."[42]

When Heidegger then emphasizes the transcendental subject, he distinguishes the dimensions of the knower which exemplify its finitude. And all of

---

41 GA 25, p. 172; tr. 188.
42 GA 24, p. 220; tr. 155.

those factors which distinguish human finitude, relative to the capacity to know one restriction stands out: that in order to be known an object must be given through our senses, and thereby conform to the preconditions of sensibility, space and time. Yet, as Heidegger argues, it is not simply the object's ability to affect our five senses which distinguishes human finitude, but the reverse: it is because we are finite, and must depend upon the object's presentation to us, that we require sense organs:

> If human intuition as finite is receptive and if the possibility of its receiving something "given" presupposes affection, then organs capable of beings affected — the organs of "sense" are necessary. Human intuition, therefore, is not "sensible" because its affection takes place through "sense" organs. Rather, the converse is true: it is because our Dasein is finite — existing in the midst of beings which already are and to which our Dasein is abandoned — that it must of necessity receive beings, that is, offer it the possibility of giving notice of itself.[43]

With this remark, Heidegger exemplifies his hermeneutic strategy that allows the pre-understanding of being to access the relevance of certain "facts" about human nature. The simple fact that we have sense organs points to a deeper root of *facticity* by which we find ourselves already delivered over to a situation and depends upon the manifestation of the beings surrounding us. When Heidegger addresses the phenomenon or appearance in the Kantian sense, he considers a further, ontological connotation that includes the dynamic of beings becoming manifest, as well as how we, in the facticity of being-there, participate in that manifestation. Thus, Heidegger construes "appearance" in the Kantian sense not simply as denoting a domain of physical objects equivalent with nature, but instead as a self-originating event that cannot be encapsulated by one region of beings or another. To employ terminology that reflects the influences of such contemporary phenomenologists as Husserl and Scheler, Heidegger distinguishes between appearance and what appears, the so-called "ontological" and the instance of its unfolding or the "ontic." Being (*Sein*), in contrast to beings (*Seiende*), implies an allocation of possibility, allowing its manifestation to yield novelty and otherness. While seeming indeterminate, being is prohibitively determinative by allowing the play of new possibilities of manifestation.

What, then, does Heidegger mean when he characterizes his 1928 lecture course as a "phenomenological interpretation" of Kant? More specifically, what constitutes the phenomenon to be addressed and why does it require interpretation? For Heidegger, "being" always constitutes the phenomenon of phenomenol-

---

43 GA 3, p. 28; tr. 18–19.

ogy, though in what fashion needs to be clarified. Given the hermeneutic profile of phenomenology, being shows itself first and foremost through its reciprocity with the inquirer, who, through his/her inquisitiveness, displays an understanding thereof (*Seinsverständnis*); and hence it is the inquirer's being that constitutes the phenomenon initially, albeit as harboring the possibility of understanding being. Through a phenomenological interpretation of the first *Critique*, Heidegger addresses the being of the knower, the subjectivity of the subject, indeed, as finitely constituted. And human finitude in turn emerges as a phenomenon, insofar as it points back to the temporal origination of the subject, and, accordingly, anchors the possibility of understanding being in temporality. By unraveling this nexus of considerations, the reciprocity between the inquirer's being and the understanding thereof, the interweaving of the problem of being with time, a "phenomenological interpretation" approaches transcendental philosophy insofar as it prefigures the development of fundamental ontology. The "phenomenon," then, is the question of being as it recoils from its own roots, indeed, the infrastructure for its reformulation as such.

An interpretation, however, necessarily accompanies phenomenology, insofar as we ascribe the richest texture to its phenomena. As Heidegger emphasizes in *Being and Time*, what characterizes the phenomena of phenomenology is, paradoxically, the tendency *not* to show itself. As a hermeneutic venture, an interpretation flags this tendency toward concealment, and, then, by allowing its own occurrence to serve as a *contrary indicator*, to elicit the counter possibility of unconcealment. In the initial phase of developing hermeneutics, Heidegger pioneered a strategy called "formal indication." Through this strategy, the individual's concrete experience points to more general structures, including those pertaining to the inquirer's being, which in turn become open to phenomenological investigation. But just as an individual whose personal mistakes can point in the opposite direction of a proper path to follow, so the exposure of "misunderstandings" can redirect us along the proper avenue of inquiry.[44] If phenomenology in the Husserlian sense emphasizes "evidentiary" self-showing, then a hermeneutic phenomenology allows "negative evidence," or the neglect and omission of the concern for being, to implicate an alternative constellation of factors. As the phenomenological inquiry broadens, it addresses various factical elements, including the self-inquisitiveness of the inquirer, its finitude, its proximity to time, the temporal organization of understanding (transcendence).

---

44 See Kalary, "Towards Sketching the 'Genesis' of *Being and Time*" pp. 199–200. The entire key to formal indication, as Kalary emphasizes, is not just to point us along the path for investigating being, but also to provide signposts to order that the inquirer does not "stray" from that path.

By "pointing away" from abstractions and misunderstandings, these "factical" elements shape the tapestry to reformulate the question of being (*Fragestellung*). A phenomenological interpretation of Kant, then, becomes a springboard for re-asking the question of being, for relocating its origin within the compass of the philosophical tradition. This radical retrieval of Kant's thought, however, includes its own important repercussion: that philosophizing necessarily turns in an historical orbit. As Heidegger states at the beginning of his 1928 lectures on Kant: "The intention of this course is to achieve a philosophical understanding of Kant's *Critique of Pure Reason*, and that means to learn how to do philosophy."[45] How can doing philosophy, as Heidegger's opening remark suggests, dovetail with the history of philosophy? The obvious answer is: because the question of being is inherently historical.

Through his reciprocal rejoinder with Kant, Heidegger "loosens up" or "unbuilds" the sedimented layers of the philosophical tradition which obstruct the questions of being. Rather than allowing the basic philosophical motifs and concepts to stagnate, this loosening-up process returns them to circulation in serving to animate discussion and opening new channels of philosophical debate (*Auseinandersetzung*). The debate, however, is not simply contentiousness for its own sake. Rather, it seeks to bring to the forefront that constellation of issues that may easily be overlooked, allowing for the recovery of what otherwise goes unnoticed as far as the concern for being goes. The opposition of the exchange, then, coincides with the tension of revealing-concealing within the phenomenon itself. Accordingly, it is by participating in the self-showing that the adversaries advance their points of contention, and each remains subordinate to and is "enowned" by the process of disclosure itself. The more extreme the opposition of the debate, the more differentiated does its language become; and this differentiation provides the sources of generating more nuanced forms of expression, which correspond to the self-showing of the phenomena and allow them to manifest themselves in commensurately distinct ways. This reciprocity between the *logos* and the phenomenon, between the letting be seen and what shows itself, lies at the heart of phenomenology. And yet it is by moving within the historical orbit of philosophical debate, as it were, that phenomenology comes into its own and assumes its mission as a science of being. As Heidegger states in a Supplement to his 1962 essay, "My Way to Phenomenology," echoing his earlier statement from *Being and Time* (1927): "'Higher than actuality stands *possibility*. We can understand phenomenology only by seizing upon it as a possibility.'"[46]

---

45 GA 25, p. 1; tr. 1.
46 Heidegger, "My Way to Phenomenology," p. 82.

What remains missing in Husserl's concept of phenomenology, and which Heidegger adds to his hermeneutics, is the unfolding of philosophy as a historical possibility. By incorporating the backdrop of the tradition, philosophy arrives at that most elemental differentiation that informs the development of all philosophical concepts, namely, the distinction between being and beings. Heidegger reserves the term "ontological difference" to describe this most primitive of all distinctions. It is in respect to the ontological difference that the evolution of all other distinctions must defer, in prompting the development of new idioms to express the meaning of being. The transition from a pre-understanding of being to the articulation thereof, from the experience of being to its conceptualization, presupposes the ontological difference. As Heidegger states in his 1928 lectures the foundations of logic:

> Being is different than beings, and only this difference is general, this possibility of distinction, insures an understanding of being. Put another way, in the understanding-of-being this distinction of being from being is carried out. It is this distinction that makes anything like an ontology possible in the first place. We thus term this distinction that first enables something like an understanding-of-being the *ontological difference.*[47]

The ontological difference's import is so great, according to Heidegger, that the degree to which the ontological difference has been acknowledged or neglected has shaped the entire course of the history of philosophy. Correlatively, as a historical possibility, the science of being has its birth in and through the explicit formulation of the ontological difference.

Within the published portion of *Being and Time*, Heidegger never employs the term "ontological difference," although he does allude to its significance. Is it more than coincidental that, when he coins this term, he does so through various discussions which are punctuated with detailed references to Kant's transcendental philosophy? These discussions, which lay out the set of presuppositions or hermeneutical situation surrounding his *magnum opus*, include the *Basic Problems of Phenomenology*, *The Metaphysical Foundations of Logic*, and *Vom Wesen des Grundes*. Relative to their importance in carrying out Heidegger's reciprocal rejoinder with Kant, these texts provide intricate synergies between fundamental ontology and transcendental philosophy. In completing the decade of the 1920s, the *Phenomenological Interpretation of Kant* and *Kant and the Problem of Metaphysics* bring these synergies to expression as the key for "translating" the question of being into historical terms. Interestingly enough, in his "Letter on 'Humanism,'" (1947), Heidegger cites the Kant-book as one of his first discussions of the

---

47 GA 26, p. 192; tr. 152 (translation modified).

ontological difference. "[Metaphysics] does not think being as such, does not think the difference between being and beings. (Cf. *Kant the Problem of Metaphysics* [1929])."[48] Heidegger, then, turns to Kant, in order to reclaim the historical roots of his own task, thereby radicalizing the question of being by transposing it into a historical arena. Phenomenology can be recovered *as* a possibility, since history can then be seen to yield the pre-understanding of being, as contrasted with beings (the ontological difference), from which Heidegger's own inquiry originates. By subordinating itself to this difference, philosophy arrives at the point of its own re-inception, its return to beginnings, albeit now played out on an historical stage. "The finitude of philosophy consists not in the fact that it comes up against limits and cannot proceed further. It rather consists in this: in the singleness and simplicity of its central problematic, philosophy conceals a richness that again and again demands a renewed awakening."[49]

The beginnings, then, are never simply stationary, since they are that toward which philosophy is always underway, and in whose historical orbit we are already thrown. If we assume that the problem of ontology betrays both a systematic avenue, by which we conceptualize/articulate our experience of being,[50] and a historical avenue, by which we situate that inquiry topic, then Heidegger discovers their intersection through his exchange with Kant. In an important passage from the conclusion to the Kant-book, Heidegger emphasizes how the ontological difference, even as it remains withdrawn through the history of philosophy, influences in its very forgottenness any subsequent attempt to formulate the question of being. "... the *difference* between being and beings *as such* remains concealed."[51] Through his destructive-retrieval of Kant, Heidegger arrives at this point where the ontological difference's abeyance can spearhead an inquiry into the possibility of any understanding of being whatsoever. The promise of reaching this zenith point, as it were, where thinking can revolve within this historically structured hermeneutical circle, as much as anything explains the importance of Heidegger's "turn" to Kant. In his 1930 lectures on Kant, Heidegger gives his own phenomenological spin to the Copernican revolution: "Even if we leave open the inner connection between being and the understanding of being, one thing is certain, namely that we have *access* to the problem of being only through the understanding of time."[52]

---

48 GA 9, p. 322; tr. 246. Heidegger cites page 225 of the Kant-book (GA 3 [tr. 157]).
49 GA 26, p. 198; tr. 156.
50 GA 26, p. 192; tr. 152.
51 GA 3, p. 235; tr. 165.
52 GA 31, p. 125; tr. 86–87 (emphasis my own). See de Boer, "The Temporality of Thinking: Heidegger's Method", p. 43.

We have now seen uncovered much of the motivation behind Heidegger's interest in appropriating transcendental philosophy, as least as a counterpoint to highlight his own projecting-open of "being and time." But to gain a full appreciation of this development, we must still discover not only to what extent Kant can be read as a "pre-Heideggerian," but, conversely, how Heidegger's own task assumes Kantian overtones in the sense of employing the grammar of Kant's "transcendental" terminology, what we might call a "language of possibility" (echoing the dynamic of the verbal form of expression).

## 3 Addressing the Critics

*Being and Time* is as complicated of philosophical text as we might find, at least as far as Heidegger's success goes in weaving together an eclectic number of historical sources, from Aristotle to Husserl, from Kant to Kierkegaard. Yet among these various influences, perhaps Kant's goes unnoticed as much as any, if only because so much of the narrative of *Being and Time* occurs on an existential plane which appears far-removed from Kant's preoccupation with the conditions of human knowledge. Yet, when viewed within the context of Heidegger's contemporaries a confrontation with Kant's thought become inevitable, if only because of the prevalence of Neo-Kantian within German intellectual circles. Not only was this Neo-Kantian movement, with its "epistemic focus," embodied in Heidegger's teacher, Heinrich Rickert.[53] But that movement was also championed by one of Germany's leading philosophers, Ernst Cassirer, although his interest shifted more explicitly into the direction of language, culture, and symbol.[54] In *Introduction to Philosophy* (1928/29), Heidegger emphasizes his attempt to anchor the activity of thinking through categories in our intuitive capacity to allow objects to present themselves, in opposition to the Neo-Kantian trend to privilege thought at the expense of intuition.[55] Reflecting later (1935/36) on his divergence from this Neo-Kantian school, Heidegger cites his resistance to reduce Kant's vision of human intuition and sensibility to the structures of thought as a major bone of contention with the Neo-Kantians.

> Generally, the Neo-Kantian interpretation of the *Critique of Pure Reason* leads to a depreciation of intuition as the basic component of human knowledge. The Marburg school's interpretation

---

53 See Bambach, *Heidegger, Dilthey, and the Crisis of Historicism*, p. 5.
54 See Schalow, "Thinking at Cross Purposes with Kant: Reason, Finitude and Truth in the Cassirer-Heidegger Debate", pp. 198–217.
55 GA 27, p. 259.

of Kant even went so far as to eliminate altogether from the *Critique of Pure Reason* intuition as a foreign body. The downgrading of intuition had the consequence that the question of the unity of both components, intuition and thinking — or, more exactly, the question of the ground of the possibility of their unification — took a wrong turn, if it was never seriously asked at all.[56]

Conversely, we can trace part of the evolution of Heidegger's *Kant and the Problem of Metaphysics* back to his attempt to differentiate his hermeneutic phenomenology (including its implications for re-interpreting Kant's transcendental philosophy) from Cassirer's appropriation of Kant in the form of a philosophy of culture.[57] This clash between Germany's leading philosopher, Ernst Cassirer, and the rising star, Heidegger, came to a head in a famous debate at Davos, Switzerland. Heidegger composed the Kant-book after his debate with Cassirer in March, 1929.[58] A close friend of Heidegger, Heinrich Petzet, recounts this seminal importance of this debate at Davos:

> Conversations during the winter were fed by reports brought back by participants in the "Davoser Hochschulkurse," in which Heidegger debated Ernst Cassirer. These reports reminded us of the period of the important *disputations* during the middle Ages, when the best minds of the time struggle with one another. It seemed that a rich tradition, which protected goods declared holy, was again under attack. One specific statement by Heidegger excited those whose minds had become sleepy on their convenient paths of thinking. Heidegger has said that the task of philosophy is "somehow to jolt human beings out of their laziness and in a certain sense back into the rigor of their destiny, using only the works of the mind." Who could not have paid attention to this? It was no wonder that this statement, which fifty years earlier could have come from Sils Maria, was ardently discussed in the lecture halls of the University of Freiburg and even became a topic for evening discussions in ski huts. This venture into a meditation on thinking was not about theoretical points of view, but rather about the very roots of one's own being.[59]

In his celebrated exchange with Heidegger at Davos, and in his review of the Kant-book which followed, Cassirer makes this point:

> Goethe once said to Schopenhauer that, when he read a page of Kant, he felt as if he were entering a bright room. From the very outset Heidegger's philosophy obeys, as it were, a different principle of style. For Kant, metaphysics is the doctrine of 'the first principles of human knowledge.' And the concept of principle is understood here in the straightforward and harmless sense that metaphysics is to exhibit and make the first principles of this

---

**56** GA 41, p. 148; tr. 145. See Dahlstrom, "Heidegger's Kant-Courses at Marburg", p. 294.
**57** See Schalow, "Thinking at Cross Purposes with Kant: Reason, Finitude and Truth in the Cassirer-Heidegger Debate", pp. 198–217.
**58** GA 3, Preface to the First and Fourth Edition(s); tr. xviii, xix.
**59** Petzet, *Encounters Dialogues with Martin Heidegger (1929–1976)*, p. 13.

knowledge intelligible. On the other hand, for Heidegger transcendence is the proper 'region of the question about the essence of the principle.' The principle arises out of finite freedom. As a principle of this kind, however, freedom is the chasm of existence. 'It is not as if individual free attitude were groundless. Rather, freedom in its essence as transcendence places existence as capability in possibilities that open up before its finite choice, that is, in its fate.' 'The opening of this ground in grounding transcendence is ... the primary movement that freedom accomplishes with us.' Such sentences, through which, according to Heidegger, the idea of logic cancels itself out 'in the whirlpool of a primordial questioning,' are explicable in terms of the world of Kierkegaard; but in Kant's intellectual world they have no place. For Kant it was not fear that revealed the nothing to him and which opened the area of metaphysics to him and drove him into it ... That was Kant's metaphysics [of critical rationality] — his way of dispelling the fear of nothingness ...[60]

Though we need to consider more closely how Heidegger modifies the Kantian notion of transcendence, Cassirer's allusion to how Heidegger links that notion with his concept of freedom. As we have already seen, Heidegger defines transcendence, as the self's projecting-open of possibilities, in terms of finitude. And, by implication, he anchors freedom in finitude as well. Because Heidegger construes freedom in this way, and Kant characterized freedom as a moral presupposition of a purely rational moral will, these two notions of freedom, as Cassirer argues, may not be easily reconciled. And yet one of the most poignant ironies of his destructive-retrieval of Kant is that Heidegger finds the former concept of freedom, for all its apparently a-temporal, infinite grounding, to be relevant to explaining the presupposition of the impetus to philosophize, the premise of our engagement in philosophy or the intrinsic possibility of that enterprise as such. In his "Introduction" to the *Phenomenological Interpretation*, Heidegger begins his exchange with Kant by making general observations about the constitution of Dasein. In the process, he emphasizes that Dasein is defined through its freedom. "The existence which always makes up our being — though not the only determinant — is a matter of our *freedom*; and only a being which can be resolved and has resolved itself in such and such a way can have a world. World and freedom as basic determinations of human existence are most closely related."[61] More than a year earlier in *The Basic Problems of Phenomenology*, Heidegger remarks that philosophy becomes possible only when we exercise our freedom.[62]

---

60 Ernst Cassirer, "Kant and the Problem of Metaphysics: Remarks on Martin Heidegger's Interpretation of Kant", p. 156. See the original publication of this review. "Kant und das Problem der Metaphysik: Bemerkungen zu Martin Heideggers Kant-Interpretation", pp. 1–26. See Lynch, "Ernst Cassirer and Martin Heidegger: The Davos Debate", p. 363. Also see Schrag, "Heidegger and Cassirer on Kant", p. 98.
61 GA 25, p. 20; tr. 15.
62 GA 24, p. 17; tr. 12.

Put simply, philosophy presupposes an open forum of exchange, of which Heidegger's dialogue with Kant bears witness. In addition, philosophy extends the frontiers of investigation in a manner which, unlike the regional sciences, refuses to compromise for the security of convenient answers. As we will discover, Heidegger adopts a polyvalent concept of freedom, which simultaneously incorporates different variables, a choosing that must be informed by openness, a willing that is still yielding in its responsiveness. Yet if we look at freedom insofar as it is indicated by the form of human ex-istence itself, then we experience freedom through the development of possibilities. This experiential ground of freedom includes both the "factical" dimension of already finding oneself delivered over to a pre-given set of circumstances, and the trajectory of transcendence from which issues a horizon of possibilities. When formalized in this way, freedom includes a characteristic which overlaps with Kant's sense of the transcendental, namely, referencing the organization of our knowledge with the possible, our potential or capability. That which "makes possible" or provides the conditions from something else arises, in Kant's terminology, is also that which, in Heidegger's lexicon of "formal indicators," is originative, freeing, and enabling.

For Heidegger, it is no accident that a concept of freedom lurks in the background of Kant's transcendental language of possibility. What for Kant may have been mere coincidence becomes for Heidegger a methodological necessity in the sense that he uncovers, rather than assumes, the intersection of freedom and transcendence. Through the phenomenon of transcendence, Heidegger pinpoints that primeval act that transmits the dynamic of the possible, to any mode of organization, e. g., understanding, investing in the possible its own power to configure and supply determination. While world, as the horizon of transcendence, yields this nexus of determination, freedom constitutes the agency of this act, harnessing its power in which the demarcation of the possible transforms indeterminacy into determinacy. In appealing to "demarcation" in this way, we make explicit the concern for finitude which both Heidegger and Kant share, and point to a common ancestry between the former's ontologically defined sense of transcendence and the latter's epistemically colored meaning of the transcendental as "transcendental knowledge." As Heidegger remarks in *The Basic Problems of Phenomenology*:

> We define the philosophical concept of transcendence following the pattern of the original meaning and not so much with regard to traditional philosophical usage, which besides is quite ambiguous and indefinite. It is from the ontological concept of transcendence properly understood that an understanding can first of all be gained of what Kant was seeking, at

bottom, when transcendence moved from him into the center of philosophical inquiry, so much so that he called his philosophy transcendental philosophy.[63]

Given this lineage with Kant, Heidegger can then employ the term "transcendental" in a sufficiently broad context to include another connotation from Medieval thought, that is, concerning determinations of being which are to be found "higher up" (than categories). When Heidegger reserves the term "transcendental truth/knowledge" to describe the disclosure of being (and not just beings), he brings to fruition his way of cross fertilizing the manifold senses of transcendence. In a passage from the close of the second chapter of the "Introduction" to *Being and Time*, Heidegger summarizes the goal of his project:

> Being, as the basic theme of philosophy, is no class or genus of entities; yet it pertains to every entity. Its 'universality' is to be sought higher up. Being and the structure of being lie beyond every entity and every possible character which an entity may possess. *Being is the transcendens pure and simple*. And the transcendence of Dasein's being is distinctive in that it implies the possibility and the necessity of the more radical *individuation*. Every disclosure of being as the *transcendens* is *transcendental* knowledge. Phenomenological truth (*the disclosedness of being*) is *veritas transcendentalis*.[64]

At a pivotal point in this *magnum opus*, Heidegger suggests why the Kantian problematic is so compelling: specifically, Kant's implicit reference to the transcendence points to the convergence between our experience of being and the universal dimension of our understanding of it. Insofar as transcendence has a temporal origin, temporality provides the linchpin to develop the universality of human understanding in concert with the dynamics of our experience of being. This temporal inter-mediation, as it were, prevents the sacrifice of either side of the equation, the universality of the concept of being and the dynamics of our concrete experience thereof. "Thus the way in which being and its modes and characteristics have their meaning determined primordially in terms of time, is what we shall call its 'temporal' determinateness. Thus the fundamental ontological task of interpreting being as such includes working out the *temporality of being*."[65] In this way, philosophy ascends to the level of "transcendental truth." For temporality is so pre-eminently universal in its composition as to provide the conceptual thread to interweave the manifoldness of our ways of experiencing being into a single unity.

---

63 GA 24, p. 423; tr. 298.
64 GA 2, p. 51; tr. 62.
65 GA 2, p. 26; tr. 40.

Can we locate a corollary formulation or slogan within the first *Critique* which prefigures Heidegger's hermeneutic strategy on the one hand and, on the other, simplifies it according to a vocabulary which becomes part of a philosophical folklore known to those who have only been marginally initiated into the writings of either Heidegger or Kant? In the opening to his section on "Transcendental Logic," Kant makes the celebrated remark: "Thoughts without content [intuitions] are empty; intuition [percepts] without concepts is blind."[66] Serving as this intermediary, temporality gathers up and discharges the possibilities of being's manifold ways of appearing. In the *Basic Problems*, Heidegger argues that, while throughout the philosophical tradition being exhibits various meanings, temporality provides the root from which diversity arises. Put in Kantian language, temporality is the "condition for the possibility" of any understanding of being as such.

How significant to the development of Heidegger's project of *Being and Time* is Heidegger's destructive-retrieval of Kant? Gadamer offers an illuminating perspective on this question:

> Then, during the period when he was on the way to an ontological deepening of his own approach to a philosophy of life and when he was immersed in these criticisms of modern philosophy and consciousness, Heidegger suddenly discovered Kant. And, indeed, it was precisely the Kant that the Neo-Kantianism and its phenomenological elaboration had concealed: the reference [*Angewiesenheit*] to that which is given. The human Dasein is neither a free self-projection nor a self-realization of an intellect, but rather is being toward death — and that means that it is essentially finite. It was precisely due to this finitude of Dasein that Heidegger was able to recognize a premonition of his own insights in Kant's doctrine of an interaction between the understanding and intuition and of the restriction of the use of the understanding to the realm of possible experience. Especially the transcendental imagination, this puzzling mid-ability of the human soul in which intuition, the understanding, receptivity, and spontaneity cooperate, allowed Heidegger to interpret Kant's own philosophy as a finite metaphysics. The being of an object is not defined through a reference to an infinite spirit (as in the classical metaphysics). Precisely the human understanding in its openness to accepting that which is given defines the object of experience.[67]

Though the importance that the Kantian influence has upon the development of Heidegger's thought can hardly be denied, among Heidegger scholars not everyone would agree. Most notably, Theodore Kisiel calls into question the "Kantian stage" in the "genesis" of *Being and Time*, characterizing it as an "aberration." According to Kisiel, there are two prior stages to the genesis of Heidegger's *magnum*

---

66 Kant, *Critique of Pure Reason*, A 52 / B 75.
67 Gadamer, *Heidegger's Ways*, p. 57.

*opus*, one devoted to a treatment of Aristotle, the other to Dilthey, that more faithfully incorporate the precepts of his "hermeneutics of facticity."[68] Conversely, by adopting Kant's transcendental methodology in the summer semester of 1926, Heidegger sacrifices the concreteness of that early hermeneutic perspective in favor of an esoteric rendition of phenomenology as a "science." To be sure, Heidegger adopts Kant's subtitle of the *Prolegomena* in order to characterize his own project as an endeavor that would be able to "come forth as science."[69] As our previous discussion establishes, however, hermeneutics does not clash with science, but instead seeks to transplant that latter on the historical soil of the philosophical tradition. The transformation of science through a critical exchange with his predecessors (e. g., Kant) separates Heidegger's phenomenology from Husserl's. For phenomenology becomes a hermeneutical exercise aimed at *relocating our place within history*, within the historical crucible of the forgottenness and recollection of being.

To contrast his methodology from that of Husserl, Heidegger introduces the threefold methodology of "reduction," "construction," and "destruction" in *The Basic Problems of Phenomenology*.[70] With a twist on Husserl's version of this procedure, Heidegger redefines the phenomenological reduction of his mentor as an undertaking that leads back to the factical roots of the inquirer's pre-understanding of being. Phenomenological construction formulates a concept of being, as defined through time, by which philosophy ascends from its pre-philosophical to the level of the science of ontology. But in order that this endeavor remains on the proper path, and avoids the misunderstandings which have plagued philosophers previously, Heidegger proposes a third moment of destruction: "a critical process in which the traditional concepts ... are deconstructed down to their sources from which they are drawn."[71] By virtue of joining these three moments of inquiry, philosophy becomes an historical enterprise and Heidegger, by necessity, becomes the "historian" of philosophy *par excellence*.

> These three basic components of phenomenological method ... receive grounding in their mutual pertinence. Construction in philosophy is necessarily destruction, that is to say, a

---

68 Kisiel, *The Genesis of Heidegger's Being and Time*, pp. 5–10, 415–420. See Schalow, "Questioning the Search for Genesis: A Look at Heidegger's Early Freiburg and Marburg Lectures", pp. 167–186.

69 GA 25, pp. 44–45; tr. 30–31. See GA 24, 468; tr. 328. For Heidegger's detailed exposition of Kant's *Prolegomena*, see GA 86, pp. 204–210. Also see AA 4, Pr, tr. 3.

70 GA 24, pp. 28–32; tr. 21–23. See de Boer, "The Temporality of Thinking: Heidegger's Method" pp. 42–45.

71 GA 24, p. 31; tr. 23

deconstructing of traditional concepts carried out in a historical recursion to the tradition. And this is not a negation of the tradition or a condemnation of it as worthless; quite the reverse, it signifies precisely a positive appropriation of the tradition. Because destruction belongs to construction, philosophical cognition is essentially at the same time, in a certain sense, historical cognition. "History of philosophy," as it is called, belongs to the concept of philosophy as science, to the concept of phenomenological investigation.[72]

By employing the tactic of destructive-retrieval, Heidegger allows Kant's own "critical" exercise to be deployed anew through the cutting edge of history. Through his dialogue with Kant, Heidegger does not pervert hermeneutics, as Kisiel contends, but instead radicalizes it by reclaiming history as the emissary to transmit the meaning of being. As George Kovacs argues, from the outset Heidegger construes phenomenology as a "primordial science." "Philosophy as primordial science is understood by Heidegger as a method, as primordial disclosure, as a way of knowing prior to and thus more radical than any theoretical construction or presupposition."[73] Far from an aberration, Heidegger's destructive-retrieval of Kant constitutes an indispensable step in the historical development of the question of being.

We have now documented the various factors which surround Heidegger's turn to Kant. We must still address a number of issues in order to appreciate the implications of this turn. Foremost among these is exploring the intricacies of the "crossing" between Heidegger and Kant, and specifically, how the issue language gradually emerges as the cornerstone of the reciprocal rejoinder between these great thinkers.

---

72 GA 24, p. 31; tr. 23.
73 George Kovacs, "Philosophy as Primordial Science", p. 97.

# Chapter Two
# The Crossing from Kant to Heidegger

The reference to a "crossroads," in the title of our study, implies a separation as well as a joining (*Fuge*). The more we come to appreciate the former, the more we must be careful to map out the juncture that joins Heidegger and Kant. Indeed, we must approach this joining from two different directions, in order to establish the common thread of a vocabulary which sustains a conversation between these two thinkers. The "signpost" which points in both directions is more than just a metaphor; for it already illustrates the traversal from one side to another, the "crossing" whose paths forge the most venturesome of all journeys through language itself. Indeed, that venture with language which marks every crossing is none one other than "translation" itself, that is, as an exercise which is simultaneously interwoven into the birth of the most primordial philosophical terms as well as their utterance by participants in a dialogue.

The fact that translation is involved in the most basic in spawning philosophical idioms does not discount its most familiar character as a practice in which we engage and participate in the disclosive power of language. We must rediscover the historical root of language in the Greek *logos* itself, however, in order to show how the two possibilities of its enactment pertain equally to Kant's as well as Heidegger's thinking. In this way, the "crossing" not only upholds the side of Heidegger's participation in this exchange, but also preserves the possibility of a counter reply from Kant's perspective. In this way, the conversation maintains its dynamism as open and ongoing, as well as occurring "alternatively" between these two thinkers. Heidegger offers this unique angle of approach, not in any explicit attempt to appropriate Kant's philosophy, but, instead, as an example to illustrate how translation already shapes the task of thinking. In his lecture course on Heraclitus's philosophy, Heidegger states that in order to understand Kant's *Critique of Pure Reason* it is first necessary to "translate" it.[74]

The translation, however, does not merely transpose into ontological terms the chief epistemic motifs of the *Critique*. Rather, according to his own lexicon, Heidegger uncovers new avenues for expressing Kant's thinking, which replaces his own claim as an authoritative commentator on the *Critique* with the precedent set by uncovering the power of the most basic philosophical idioms of all. It is by inviting the emergence of an "emissary" – the directive of hermeneutics as transmitting the claim and meaning of being – that Heidegger undertakes his

---

74 GA 55, p. 63. For further discussion, see Emad, *Translation and Interpretation*, pp. 59–69.

"translation." He thereby stands apart from his Neo-Kantian counterparts by initiating this radical shift in the strategy for *reading* Kant's *Critique of Pure Reason*, and thereby crossing over to a thinking capable of re-asking the question of being – the "onset" of being-historical thinking

Heidegger's divergence from the Neo-Kantians, however, is not merely an academic dispute, but corresponds to historical character of the crossing he undertakes: that is, in following one path of thinking (*Denkweg*) over another. While his split with the Neo-Kantian serves as a sign, Heidegger's strategy for reading Kant precipitates a decision (*Entscheidung*). The nature of this decision appears not only in hindsight as we access the ingenuity of his radical reinterpretation of by exploring his voluminous writings on the topic. On the contrary, we must also consider whether there are other ways to address Kant's Critical philosophy which, at least momentarily, withdraw into the background. But if the crossing is a movement that leads in one direction, possibly to the exclusion of another, can we characterize Heidegger's strategy as much by what it seems to foreclose as include? Indeed, we will discover that Heidegger implements his plan for a destructive-retrieval of transcendental philosophy through a kind of *shortcut*, an "*economizing*" of steps by which the language of his own hermeneutics provides the key to translate Kant's "critique of pure reason" into "the problem of metaphysics" (i. e., the quest to address being in its relation to time).

Let us begin by outlining the basic thrust of Heidegger's "decision" to engage Kant's Critical philosophy, and establish the distinctive strategy of "translating" the *Critique of Pure Reason*. In the process, I will outline the key motifs of Heidegger's interpretation that form the "jointure" between his own thinking and Kant's, including the synergy between imagination, temporality, and disclosedness. Then I will take a "detour" that Heidegger suggests, but does not himself explicitly follow, which supplies direct evidence "testimony" on Kant's behalf of the nascent concern for language in the first *Critique* — in the part devoted to the "Transcendental Dialectic" as well as the "Transcendental Analytic." Finally, having shown how Kant also harbors a reciprocal concern for language, I will detail specifically how he leaves behind clues that foreshadow Heidegger's own attempt to develop a "*logos*" of being, that is, to express its "meaning" in "temporal" idioms. In this way, we will discover how Heidegger's *Auseinandersetzung* with Kant proceeds by an "intralingual" translation of the grounding or "elemental" words of philosophy, that is, *a nomenclature of being in terms of time*.

# 1 The Translation "Key": Heidegger's Decision

At the conclusion of the *Phenomenological Interpretation of Kant's Critique of Pure Reason*, as we saw in the previous chapter, Heidegger recounts how his "eyes" were "opened" the importance of re-reading Kant's *magnum opus*.[75] In retrospect, Heidegger's "decision" takes a unique form that sets him apart from all his contemporaries, including his counterpart in the subsequent "Davos Disputation," Ernst Cassiser. For Heidegger's reinterpretation of transcendental philosophy requires a distinctive hermeneutic engagement with his predecessor, a unique venture of "translating" his most pivotal work. The hallmark of this hermeneutic engagement is that, despite appearances to the contrary (or even from the perspective of his critics), Heidegger relinquishes the claim of providing either an authoritative commentary or a definitive refutation of Kant's philosophy. Almost imperceptibly and without fanfare Heidegger puts aside these "external criteria" of evaluation. Instead, he allows the directions of his own hermeneutic inquiry, the dictates of the "thing itself," to elicit a common setting that allows a conversation between Kant and himself to unfold. Accordingly, his "decision" includes an innovative tactic, a (hermeneutic) strategy which Heidegger articulates later in the remark from the Heraclitus seminar quoted above. The translation involves rendering the key terms of Kant's transcendental philosophy in a new light, that is, which can be re-employed within the new context of Heidegger's inquiry into being and thereby extends our understanding of this new "problematic" (i. e., as reflected in title of his book, *Kant and the Problem of Metaphysics*). But as in the case of any translation, there are certain "directives," *keys* as it were, which allow us to zero in on the "crossover" in terminology. *Whenever we attempt to navigate the labyrinth of Heidegger's exchange this Kant, this provisional step is largely presupposed.*

Yet what are precisely these "keys," which in the language of vernacular we might characterize as "cracking the code" of translation? For Kant, the leitmotif marking the thrust of his entire enterprise is the "a priori," as in the "synthetic a priori," which takes center stage through his fore-most question: "how are synthetic a priori judgments possible?" The terms "a priori," as in "earlier," and "synthetic," as in "joining," have origins in Greek as well as in Latin — the latter which was "closest" to Kant in lineage, and thereby most prominent. Yet the "translation" that Heidegger proposes is not one which simply assumes as its entryway the pages of a dictionary and matching of reciprocal terms. Rather it is by bypassing this linear approach, and proceeding alternatively along a "circuitous path," that

---

75 GA 25, p. 431; tr. 292.

Heidegger will give the keys for translating this term ("synthetic a priori"), but also put forth the example of the "methodology" for doing so. The "earlier" of the "a priori" no longer points *only* to what "comes before," "precedes," and "makes possible" (the determination of) the object of knowledge (yet includes this designation). Instead, Heidegger "transfixes" the simple sequence of "first" and "last," of "earlier" and "later," by incorporating each into a circular motion from which *springs* the origin, development and unfolding of understanding (*Verstehen*) in its expanse of possibilities. The "earlier" is no longer a "fixed" designation, but instead gives way to inception, point of departure, being-underway, which is requisite for all understanding, that is, in simultaneously *beginning from and returning to its own presuppositions.* Losing its fixity as a designator of sequence, the "a priori" now literally *bends* in service of the circularity of understanding, of what Heidegger calls the "hermeneutical circle." By this initial translation, Heidegger sets the stage for recasting the compass of a circular orbit what the chief capacity of the "knower," which Kant had sought to redefine through the "synthetic a priori." For Heidegger, the hermeneutic directive of "understanding" takes lead in describing what Kant meant by knowledge, i. e., the level of "pre-understanding" which harbors the "pre-articulated whole" of "meaning" from out which anything can be understood, defined, and ultimately known. But that "pre-understanding" is simply an acronym for what Heidegger call the "pre-ontological understanding of being" which governs each and every attempt at relating to things, to beings, including the proposed knowledge thereof.

Yet, while the "keys" in question are beginning to emerge, the initial "translation" of the *Critique of Pure Reason* is still not complete. Given that we can distinguish for Heidegger and Kant two usages of the word, *Verstandnis* as "pre-theoretical" orientation to the possibilities within the concrete circumstances of (factical) life, and *Verstand* as a "theoretical" knowledge of physical objects or nature, we must still be able to make mark their overlap and "crossing." For by marking this crossing, and refraining from reducing one to the other, we maintain the tension that sustains a conversation between these two thinkers. In order to do so, we must, in effect "understand understanding," not through a regression back to some ultimate ground, but, on the contrary, by heeding the precedent which is already given within the Greek horizon: namely, the figure which embodies the direction and trajectory of understanding, i. e., message-bearer or "Hermes" as the "go-between," intermediary and emissary. The "Hermes" points to the linchpin of understanding, its anchor, the interposing of different levels of determinateness from which the outline of "meaning" first arises. Understanding develops by expanding the horizon in which it unfolds and unravels its own presuppositions, thereby enriching and deepening what emerges as "meaningful." In turn, the development and unfolding of "meaning" occurs through a process of "interpretation," which continually unravels the intial presuppositions which beforehand orient and guide our understanding. Interpretation, however, is not an activity in addition to understanding, but instead is its fruition or its concrete enactment in and through the emissary of "Hermes." In this way, interpretation harbors the deeper ground from which understanding arises, along with its potential for deepening or radicalization; and correlatively, equally allows for its "diversion" into a narrower "theoretical" form of knowledge.

Given this "crossing," theoretical knowledge equally depends upon, and reconstitutes itself through a form of "intermediary," in Kant's case the connective of the (a priori) synthesis forming the "bridge" between knower and known. Thus we witness a second stage of "translation" in which understanding as Kant views it (and its pure concepts) is to be reconstituted through the figure of an intermediary, the configuring of a horizon within which knower and known reside. For Kant, obvious analogue for intermediary, which emerges within his own epistemic problematic, is *imagination* and its distinctive capacity to mediate between pure concept and the given of empirical intuition, the unity of thought and its object or *schematism*. Heidegger's attempt to make imagination and schematism the focal points of this radical retrieval of Kant's philosophy is well documented. Yet, scholars have not sufficiently recognized that imagination assumes this crucial role because it occupies the position of an "emissary." Through its creative capacity of "schematism," imagination serves as a wellspring and medium to engender and interweave new distinctions by which the pure concepts can acquire the measure of determinates to define objects. Imagination becomes to theoretical knowing what interpretation is to understand, that is, the catalyst of its development and creativity. When recast in this guise as a throwback to "Hermes," imagination emerges not only in its role in schematizing the pure concepts, but also as a *methodological linchpin* to establish ontological counterparts for otherwise epistemic terms. This methodological shift, which brings the thrust of the "pre-ontological understanding of being" or the entire nexus of the "hermeneutical situation" into play is the crucial maneuver and predirective which governs Heidegger's retrieval of Kant.

Heidegger thereby receives clearance to re-establish the Kantian problematic an a new and original ground, that is, from the counterpoint of terms conversant with his own hermeneutics: e. g., facticity for the receptivity of intuition, projection for the a priori of the pure concepts of understanding, transcendence for the relation between knower and known, openness (*Spiel-Raum*) for the creative dynamic of imagination, and, finally, ecstatic temporality for the constriction of time. To develop this counterpoint of his own hermeneutic terminology, however, is to undertake a "translation" of the first *Critique*, rather than for Heidegger to reduce Kant's philosophy to his own. As we follow out the thrust of this translation, and continue to unfold its "keys," we begin to see that strategy by which Heidegger's transforms Kant's epistemic problematic into an ontological one. In other words, in converting Kant's concern for the finitude of knowledge into the question of the possibility of understanding being (*Seinsverständnis*), Heidegger does not proceed wantonly and arbitrarily. Instead, he undertakes a "crossing," which is designed to interject his own thinking squarely into the entire history of philosophy and the corresponding translation of its key concepts and terms.

Indeed, the preliminary, and easily ignored step in Heidegger's "translation" of the first *Critique*, lies precisely in this: safeguarding Kant's own place as participant within the dialogue. By the same token, in initiating this dialogue, it is just as easy to overlook the importance of Heidegger's parallel translation of the key terms of his own philosophy from their deepest roots in the tradition. The historical crucible of this debate provides a further catalyst for Heidegger to undertake from his side an "intralingual translation" of those terms which acquire a more radical "meaning" (through his own thinking), over against their conventional use throughout the philosophical tradition. The dialogue, then, induces a reciprocal transformation of Heidegger's own thinking. By answering the challenged posed of translating Kant's writings, Heidegger simultaneously accepts an invitation for Heidegger to radicalize his own hermeneutics. If we revisit Heidegger's key remark quoted above, "the confirmation of the accuracy of the path which I took in my search" lies precisely in this *venture* of intralingual translation. That is, Heidegger uncovers the key parallels between himself and Kant as a result of this venture, rather than the reverse. For the attempt to establish the synergy, for example, between his own sense of finitude and Kant's, always occurs within this space of translation, the translating of the key terms of Heidegger's philosophy as they give new expression to the significance of such a monumental work as the *Critique of Pure Reason*.

The translation is a "rejoinder" (*Erwiderung*) with the origins of the most basic terms and a "retrieval" (*Wiederholung*) of those roots, revisiting and reconnecting with the "first beginning" of philosophy. Put simply, the act of saying the "unsaid" is such a reciprocal rejoinder, which speaks from this origin and coordinates the inquiry into being with the originative saying (*Sage*) of the most basic philosophical terms. In this regard, the "crossing" joins new connotations of basic terms intimated from out of the future, with the original meanings held in reserve in the past. At the jointure of this crossing, the translation draws upon the "play" of innovation, in order the reignite the power of the most basic philosophical terms, idioms, and concepts? In retrospect, Heidegger's radical new way of interpreting the first *Critique* stands apart from all other commentaries precisely by fueling this innovation.

In the title of his 1927/28 lecture course, *The Phenomenologial Interpretation of Kant's Critique of Pure Reason,* Heidegger reveals the double problem of translation. On the hand, he distinguishes his hermeneutic strategy or tactic (e. g., in the guise of "interpretation") for redefining the key motif in the title of Kant's epoch work, its occurrence not only generically, i. e., as reason/understanding (*Vernunft/Verstand*), but also its individualized enactment (*Verstehen*), i. e., the projecting of possibilities and uncovering of "meaning"(*Sinn*) through them. On the other hand, Heidegger identifies the "phenomenological" directive that guides his explication of the Kantian text, namely, the mandate to "return to the thing itself," that is, to the question of being itself. Given the concreteness of his hermeneutic-phenomenological approach, Heidegger can transcribe the nexus of relations that Kant presupposes in his explication of the finite structure of *human* knowledge: what is known, the conditions of knowing, and, ultimately, the constitution of the knower as such. Kant, however, only indirectly addresses the latter through the temporal-spatial conditions that the knower displays in the act of knowing. Heidegger, on the other hand, can address the origin of finitude itself as emerging directly from the capacity that human begins display for self-understanding, as arising from their "thrownness" into a situation, their inhabitation of a world, and ultimately, from the finality of the horizon of death. Indeed, *Being and Time* testifies to the power of hermeneutic to question and thematize the elements of the constitutions of being-in-the-world, including the disclosedness of the "there," in a way never fathomed by Kant. Given the wider compass of his hermeneutics, Heidegger can also show how the key steps in Kant's account of "synthetic a priori knowledge" can provide the *mirror image* of the possibility of understanding being (*Seinsverständnis*). In other words, Kant's transcendental redistribution of the priorities of knowledge, away from the object, to the conditions of knowing, to the finitude of the knower can provide a profile of the parallel phenomenon Heidegger seeks to outline in hermeneutic terms: what is understood in understanding, its character as a projection, the reciprocity between the being (i. e., Dasein) who understands itself and thereby displays a potential to understand being as well.

Yet here is the *decisive* point in Heidegger's destructive-retrieval of Kant's philosophy. The initial strategy for undertaking this task, as outlined above, is not fixed. Rather, its implementation changes with the new challenges posed by the confronting Kant's thought. Thus, the basic components that are integral to Heidegger's hermeneutics in *Being and Time* require further development, insofar as his own concepts are sharpened on the razor of confronting the epoch text, *Critique of Pure Reason.* Within the unity of finite transcendence as being-in-the-world Heidegger encompasses the relation between knower and knower, which Kant had divided on the premise of the subject-object dichotomy. For Heidegger, the structure of (finite) knowledge can no longer be construed piecemeal, but must be reassembled out of a more primordial wholeness that originates from a deeper ground. That ground, as transcendence, opens forth into the area of world, in such a way as to redefine the relation between knower and known in ontological terms, that is, the manifestation of the latter (i. e., beings) to the former, (i. e., the preunderstanding of being distinctive of humans). Put graphically, the contrast between being and beings establishes the new "ontological" coordinates to map out the landscape of knowledge and to re-establish its basis on the deeper ground of transcendence (rather than split between subject and object). Conversely, Heidegger radicalizes his own task by explicitly characterizing the distinction between being and beings explicitly *as* the ontological difference.

Yet, while he intimates as such in *Being and Time*, Heidegger does not explicitly mention the ontological difference within the published portion of that text. The fact that he develops this terminology and nomenclature in *Kant and the Problem of Metaphysics* provides important evidence of how the challenge of appropriating transcendental philosophy exacts a reciprocal development of Heidegger's own thinking. In other words, the task of "translating" the *Critique* (into ontological terms) is not a one-sided endeavor, but instead implies a mutual transformation and reciprocal rejoinder on Heidegger's part as well. Kant's transcendental perspective and Heidegger's hermeneutic-phenomenological perspective are not mutually exclusive, but instead "cross" at an important juncture. Allow me to offer a simple example of this jointure. For Kant, due to its finitude human knowledge depends upon the "givenness" of the object in order for it to be known; that givenness presupposes the parallel capacity for "receptivity" on behalf of the knower. For Heidegger, human finitude always involves Dasein's thrownness into, and situatedness within, the manifestation of beings in the whole; Dasein can experience the diversity of beings because it itself is always *a* being that belong to within this wider compass of manifestation (as ultimately measured by the horizon of world itself). Conversely, for Kant, in order for the object to be an object "for us" must be able of being determined beforehand by a set of pre-specifications (i. e., the pure concepts) of our understanding — the outline of an "a priori synthesis." For Heidegger, Dasein's pre-understanding of being yields in advance the horizon within which the manifestation of beings can occur — the world as the horizon of finite transcendence.

The impact of Heidegger's reciprocal rejoinder with Kant becomes evident as much as he sheds the external artifice of the latter's architectonic, as in reinterpreting the key motifs of transcendental philosophy. The discipline that in modern philosophy has been included under the agency of reason, or "logic" must itself undergo transformation. For Kant's attempt reconcile knowledge with the conditions of human finitude and its "sensory" mode of experience, has repercussions, also, for redefining what, or for that matter, "who" reason is. In the

Analytic portion of the first *Critique*, Kant contrasts his own "transcendental logic," which grounds the pure concepts through their role in synthesizing objects, with a "general logic," which reveals the origin of these concepts as categories or forms of predication. By the same token, brings into question the place that "logic" has within his own phenomenology, albeit conceived more originally through the Greek understanding of *logos* rather than the modern notion of reason. In *The Metaphysical Foundations of Logic*, which parallels his reinterpretation of Kant, Heidegger proposes a "productive logic," which seeks a more radical ground to develop its understanding of being and prepare the way for its expression in words. "Philosophy can be characterized only from and in historical recollection. But this recollection is only what it is, is only living, in the moment of self-understanding, and that means in one's own free, productive grasp of the task harbored in philosophy."[76] A "productive logic" addresses the singularity of the manifestation of being, and seeks a corresponding *logos* to express this historically distinctive manner of self-showing.

Ultimately, phenomenology becomes ontology when it can it develop a *logos* in concert with its theme, i. e., being itself. In this way, what is already intimated about being in our everyday understanding can be brought to the level of explicit articulation. Just as the test of knowledge is the ability to express what one knows, so the possibility of articulating what we already understand about being constitutes the task of ontology. The new coordinates of ontology establish its ground, although in a way which re-opens it to the novelty of its own question, giving momentum to it by calling the inquirer itself into question. Such is the grounding of finite transcendence, which thrusts the inquirer into the openness and allows that happening (*Geschehen*) to indicate what gives definition, determination, and even the possibility of expression to our understanding of being, i. e., the ontological difference. Kant's plan for a "science" of metaphysics comes to fruition through Heidegger's formulation of a fundamental ontology, which projects forth the possibility of understanding being. Conversely, through his reciprocal rejoinder with Kant, Heidegger's phenomenology undergoes a transformation that lands ontology on a completely new footing.

This new footing arises through the inquirer's executing a "leap" (*Sprung*). Whereto? As Heidegger suggests in the Chapter Three of the second division of *Being and Time*, the leap catapults the inquirer into the "circle" (*Zirkel*) of understanding. The circle insures that the search for clarity, determination, and even "meaning" is never complete, but instead unfolds in stages of development where a return to origins always prefigures any forward advance. For Kant, as well,

---

76 GA 26, p. 9; tr. 8.

human knowledge must make a certain concession: namely, that "possible experience" circumscribes the domains of objects to which pure concepts can refer and acquire their validity. The "circumscribing movement," to which Kant alludes in the only in subtlest way, shows that there is no Archimedean point on which to ground human knowledge. Indeed, the impact of Kant's celebrated Copernican revolution is precisely this: that the possibility of human knowledge must ultimately turn on the axis of its own finitude, in which case its pure concepts all derive their significance from this finite origin. In his lectures from the winter semester of 1925/26, Heidegger makes the observation that we must look upon Kant's categories anew with an eye to how they implicate the circular character of human understanding in general. As we follow the contours of human knowledge, rather than what can be determined objectively through it, we discover that the pure concepts of understanding and the principles, they articulate become examples of "hermeneutic indication" (*hermeneutik Indikation*).[77] Amplifying the implicit sense of *logos* which is echoed in Kant's transcendental logic, Heidegger states:

> Thus true to its inner core, thinking proceeds in a *roundabout way*; thinking moves through the determining representation; thinking is a *running through — is discursive*. The *finitude* of thinking gets manifested in the character of thinking as roundabout and discursive, i. e., in the fact that, as a function of understanding, judging is a representation of a representation, a mediated representing.[78]

Given its circuitous path, human cognition receives its capacity for determination through a "figurative synthesis," by which time inscribes new distinctions within the categories. These (temporal) distinctions share a common idiomatic form, which can "communicate" the principles of the understanding (*Verstand*) in universal, albeit concrete terms, i. e., in compliance with "possible experience." If by themselves the pure concepts lack content in their own right, and depend on a "intermediary" to acquire the power to signify (the generic features of) objects, then it is by a radical "procedure" (*Verfahren*) for generating them anew around a common root. In order to generate the pure concepts from this common root, specifically, time, this procedure must supply the "index" of our finitude. This index interposes the "for us" as the *prefix* for establishing the single precedent from which the twelve pure concepts derive their usage, i. e., the specific determination distinctive of each. Kant calls this procedure "schematism," which yields a new precedent for the (linguistic) usage of the pure concepts by "indexing" them to the conditions of our finitude to provide a nexus of interlocking patterns of

---

77 GA 21, p. 410.
78 GA 25, p. 172; tr. 118.

signification. Because the formulation of its principles rests upon this deeper linguistic dimension, understanding is receptive as well as spontaneous (just as sensibility is spontaneous as well as receptive). When transformed through this figurative synthesis, the categorial synthesis of understanding becomes a power to determine something as something, not derivatively through a linear model of predication (apophantic-as), but originally through the dynamic circumscription of what can be understand. The constellation of meaning on this pre-predicative, semiotic level (*semiotische Ebene*)[79] points back to a more primordial enactment of understanding (*Verstehen*) through "lived-experience" (*Erlebnis*).

To be sure, only on rare occasions does Heidegger punctuate his dialogue with Kant with references to hermeneutics. Yet in the process, Heidegger suggests how a methodological parallel may also harbor the basis of a common "thematic" concern, that is, despite Kant's reluctance to address this topic. The understanding, particularly as pertaining to something presumably as elusive and even as "general" as "being" requires such a counter pole to shape its manifestation, its disclosure, and even potential for determination through language. As a result, a place is reserved for what is pre-articulated, as well as pre-understand, such that an instance of manifestation can become an emissary of the entire horizon of understanding and thereby harbor the gestures to elicit as pervasive a concern as "being." Most of all, being expresses itself through an emissary, and what is conveyed as a result has the potential for novelty, manifoldness, and valences, i. e., "meaning." The wedding of "*logos*" with "Hermes" allows "meaning" to emerge into the forefront as giving shape and definition to the question of being. Thus, the question implies a distinctive language, which takes as its measure the dynamic which spearheads all understanding, i. e., "possibility," "making possible," "conditions of possibility": how being "can" be understand and its meaning be expressed in words. A "language of possibility" characterizes the expressions which arises from, and develop in concert with the broadening of the horizon of understanding and its potential for disclosure.

Ironically, in this distinctive nuances of this "language of possibility," Heidegger discovers that Kant provides a clue of how to express "being," even if he never formulates that theme explicitly. The hint of this insight, however faint and tantalizing as it may be, ultimately draws Heidegger into his dialogue with Kant. As Heidegger had already begun to recognize, what we say concerning "being" hinges as much on the "how" of the saying, that is, in a way which mirrors the

---

79 See La Rocca, "Schematismus und Anwendung", pp. 89–90. For early attempts by J. G. Herder and J. Hamann to address the issue of language, and the implications for developing a "Metakritik" of Kant's project, see Jere Surber, *Language and German Idealism*, pp. 13, 20–21.

dynamic of its manifestation, rather than simply on what is said. For example, Heidegger's preference for the verbal form "to be" (versus the nominative, substantive form) becomes the decisive illustration of how the dynamism intrinsic to our words yields the clue to how we formulate, understand and interpret the questions of all questions. When viewed in this light, the language of possibility serves as the "go-between," the preferred "messenger," to transmit the theme of ontology or express the "meaning" of being in words which mirror its unique dynamic.

The "elemental words," as Heidegger calls them, are themselves historically rooted, preserved within the sediment of the philosophical tradition. As such, their recovery belongs to, and is a key component of, the overarching task of a destructive-retrieval of the entire tradition whose cornerstone is Kant's account of temporality and schematism. Why does Kant occupy this center stage? Because, as Heidegger emphasizes in the second part of his "Introduction" to *Being and Time*, "The first and only person who has gone any stretch of the way towards investigating the dimension of temporality or has even let himself be drawn hither by the coercion of the phenomena themselves is Kant."[80] Here we discover the first indication of how Heidegger's search for a way to express being governs his destructive-retrieval of Kant, despite the fact, ironically, that latter seemingly displayed little insight into the nature of language as such. Yet Heidegger does not simply contrive an etymology in his effort to explore the "roots" of the key philosophical terms. On the contrary, his simultaneous inquiry into temporality — spearheading his *Auseinandersetzung* with Kant — directs Heidegger's search for these roots, insofar as they are shaped by the grammar of the "verbal" form, i. e., "to be." The emphasis on the "verb" illustrates why temporal idioms yield the preferred avenue for expressing the "meaning" of being and cultivating its question-worthiness.

Driven by a response to the *logos*, the new "logic" of being necessarily includes a moment of "recollection." In honoring its most elemental origins, philosophy then pays homage to the figure of "Mnemosyne." In this way we discover that the historical path on which the destructive-retrieval of Kant's thinking is necessarily circular. Through his destructive-retrieval of Kant, Heidegger then expands the radius of the hermeneutic circle. Because of his historical orientation, hermeneutics necessarily includes an archaeology of the key philosophical terms. We now see more clearly how "translation" marks the jointure between Heidegger and Kant. that is, the "crossing" where being comes to expression through the most basic idioms, i. e., those etched in the fabric of temporality.

---

80 GA 2, p. 32; tr. 45.

Insofar as Heidegger's "decision" to engage Kant centers on temporality, which in turn emerges through the latter's portrayal of schematism, may it also be case that this problematic is couched in a further enigma concerning language? Indeed, perhaps latent in Kant's celebrated "transcendental" turn there is also the vestige of a parallel "linguistic" turn. Indeed, uncovering this possibility would go a long way to explaining why Heidegger's exchange with Kant occurs as a reciprocal rejoinder that illuminates the former's path of thinking as much as the latter's. From a hermeneutical perspective, that common setting is none other than the crucible of history itself, which interposes the area of conflict pitting one thinker against another and allowing a critical exchange, an *Auseinandersetzung*, to occur between them. Heidegger's seminal insight into this "betweenness" which joins as well as divides Kant's and his own distinguishes his creative "reading" of transcendental philosophy.

Accordingly, we must keep in mind that Heidegger's decision is also a schism which, while it may highlight certain motifs, may not necessarily follow through in tracing their development from all corners of Kant's Critical philosophy. Indeed, the common criticism voiced by Cassirer and others is that, in profiling the importance of schematism, Heidegger neglects the systematic unity of Kant's thought including its culmination in the *Critique of Judgment*. In heeding that precaution, can we identify a juncture in the first *Critique*, if not in its Analytic portion as least in the Transcendental Dialectic, where a nascent concern for language suddenly erupts and sparks the possibility of a "linguistic turn?"

## 2 The Tribunal of Reason and the Practice of Language

What is "unsaid" in Kant is never simply expressed, but, to employ a motif that Heidegger introduces in *Contributions to Philosophy*, punctuates the silence of language as an "echo" across the deep chasm of the philosophical tradition. By the same token, the overall strategy he employs in his destructive-retrieval of transcendental philosophy perhaps may never be fully articulated, but become evident only as crowning moments in the development of his own "reading" of history of philosophy. In Heidegger's decisive attempt to supplant the supremacy of reason, and cultivate imagination in its place, the key words of philosophy simultaneously evoke a deeper level of meaning. For the etymology of the word *logos* (λόγος) reveals what is hidden in its subjective (modern) characterization as reason: namely, that the dispensation of order is not simply a human product, but rather is the result of a "self-gathering" that is both the source of intelligibility in language and of the participation of humans with one another (e. g., through dialogue). The etymology of the word "*logos*" shows that, while we can distinguish these facets, we cannot separate them from their unity and onefoldness. For the power of human beings to speak is always part of an "openness," which first draws them forth into a world and lends intelligibility to the wide spectrum of their endeavors. Heidegger's foremost student, Hannah Arendt, perhaps stated this matter most simply and eloquently: "With *word and deed*, we insert ourselves into the world, and this insertion is like a second birth ..."[81]

If we follow Heidegger's own lead, and try to hear the subtlest intonation of a text whose title bears the key word "reason," we must ask an important question: are then any loose threads of Kant's discussion of the finitude of knowledge that point back to, and are vaguely reminiscent of, a profounder determination of reason as a "ground" (*Grund*) — either as the source of intelligibility or as the activity of speaking among fellow humans? Does Heidegger's subversion of reason in favor of imagination unlock a further "memory," a "Mnemosyne," which elicits a deeper grasp of Kant's plan of establishing human finitude as the new axis of human knowledge and its expression in the guise of synthetic a priori judgments? The attempt to answer these questions will lead us to consider parts of the first *Critique* that recede into the background of Heidegger's reading of Kant, for example, the discussion of the "ideas of reason" in the Transcendental Dialectic, as well as those parts which occupy the forefront, e. g., the section on schematism in the Transcendental Analytic.

More than anything else Heidegger teaches us to maintain an interrogative posture, to extend the arc of questioning necessary to ponder the meaning of being. But if only due to excessive familiarity we tend to ignore the import of Kant's own question – the enigma as to how synthetic a priori judgments are possible – particularly when we are quick to incorporate his thinking within the scope of Heidegger's hermeneutics. In simplest terms, such judgments qualify as "synthetic" when they extend our knowledge about things in the world and do so by seeking their determination in conformity with pure concepts derived from thought (the "a priori" element). Unlike analytic judgments, synthetic knowledge has as its disposal a content pertaining to the emergence of natural phenomena. In order for this content to be rendered determinate, its pattern of organization must be raised to explicit articulation through the various forms of unity imposed by pure concepts. Not only is it necessary to outline this discursivity in terms of the various predicative acts which stand for or "signify" (the characteristics of) objects; but as an essential component of the "critical" enterprise, it is also crucial to trace the derivation, delimitation, and development of these conceptual patterns insofar as their application implicates the capability of the knower itself, the

---

**81** Arendt, *The Human Condition*, pp. 176–177.

constraints of its finitude. Whether we wish to make this concern for finitude an addendum to a larger ontological question, as Heidegger does, it is still incumbent upon us to consider how the categories can illustrate through their own deployment the discourse by which the self-examination of reason can proceed. At stake is the perplexing "meta-issue" overarching the *Critique of Pure Reason*: namely, how the determination, not of the objectivity of knowledge, but of the finite conditions which make it possible, can achieve expression, so that the self-reflexivity of the critical enterprise can be articulated within the scope of transcendental philosophy.

Hegel and Heidegger each respond to the problem of the self-reflexivity of the critical enterprise in his own way, the former through the method of dialectic, the later through that of hermeneutics. Because Heidegger traces all ontological questions to a pre-articulated level, the capacity to speak about the inquiry in which he/she engages is already implicated in the capability for speech (*Rede*) practiced by the inquirer. Ironically, to the extent that this level of linguistic practice is already operative within his own hermeneutics, when he proceeds to reinterpret transcendental philosophy in hermeneutical terms, he assumes the corresponding relevance of this form of practice in Kant. Accordingly, Heidegger then points to temporality (*Temporalität*) as providing the key to the determinateness of all human understanding and hence as prefiguring the articulation of what is understood, including "being." Because Kant also anchors the human capacity to know in time, Heidegger distinguishes it as that intermediary through which we gain access to the "manifestness" of things, the prelude to all ontological understanding. But how time, which for Kant is originally non-discursive, can facilitate a process of manifestness, which for Heidegger is tied to language, poses something of an anomaly.

Missing in this puzzle is how transcendental philosophy accomplishes a shift in the axis of discursivity so that time can contribute to the development of pure concepts, the key to their determinancy. But does not this shift already reverberate with the implications of Kant's Copernican revolution in philosophy? Indeed, it does. Yet the issue is how to interpret this revolution, as well to establish it as the linchpin in Kant's development of a new kind canon to govern the application of pure concepts to objects, a "transcendental logic." As the hallmark of his radical appropriation of transcendental philosophy, Heidegger construes the Copernican revolution in ontological terms; that is, the axis of knowledge shifts to include a relationship to which both knower and known belong, and whereby things manifest themselves to us in direct proportion to our capability to surpass toward them (transcendence).

According to Heidegger, the Copernican revolution prefigures a topographic change, which relocates the axis of cognition along the coordinates of the world

and thereby overcomes the solipsistic model of the subject-object dichotomy.[82]
The Copernican claim of the object's pre-conformity to the antecedent conditions
of finitude, however, requires demonstration of its own: Kant's doctrine of schematism. Because this demonstration constitutes the crux of overcoming the subject-object dichotomy, Heidegger places the greatest weight on schematism in
reinterpreting transcendental philosophy. In simplest terms, the schema stands
as the intermediary between the content of intuition and its determination by the
signifying act of the category. Insofar as time is essential to the formation of this
intermediating bridge, and the category's applicability to objects hinges on its
"translation" into temporal terms (i. e., schematism), Heidegger argues that schematism charts the trajectory of finite transcendence. But if schematism is to
assume this ontological role, then it must not only re-establish time as the chief
component of the a priori synthesis. Indeed, schematism must also implement a
new form of linguistic practice. Such a practice would attend to the dynamism of
the object's manifestation, upholding an axis for the constellation of meaning or
the genesis of new conceptual patterns.

The question of whether the first *Critique* could be reduced to the doctrine of
schematism, and the dimension of finitude imprinted on reason in its various
uses, was the controversy which triggered much of the debate between Heidegger
and Cassirer in the seminar at Davos.[83] Perhaps it is too easy to dismiss Cassirer's
criticism as reflecting someone within the mainstream of Kantianism who did not
truly appreciate the innovative spirit pervading Heidegger's reading of transcendental philosophy. If not explicitly, however, the sharpness of Cassirer's opposition points to a concern easily overlooked in Heidegger's construal of schematism
as a problem exclusively of "ex-istence," temporality, and finitude.[84] Specifically,
how do we preserve the concern for the articulation of knowledge in a synthetic a
priori judgment, and yet at the same time recognize that the schemata — as the
spawning of new conceptual patterns — deploy another grammar than that which
can be exacted from the operation of traditional logic?

But would not such a grammar be necessary only if the schemata hinged on
the cultivation of new meanings whose root stemmed from the opposite spectrum
of sensibility, rather than from thought? Indeed, because thought can no longer
rely exclusively on its own canon to determine the grammar of judgment there is
a need — in lieu of the schemata as yielding a set of cognitive principles — to
consider a new "precedent" of linguistic usage. What distinguishes this prece-

---

**82** GA 3, pp. 188–191; tr. 132–133. Also see GA 25, pp. 392–403; tr. 267–273. See Dahlstrom,
"Heidegger's Kant-Courses at Marburg", pp. 293–308.
**83** GA 3, pp. 274–296; tr. 193–207.
**84** Ernst Cassirer, "Remarks on Martin Heidegger's Interpretation of Kant", pp. 138–142.

dent, however, is that it must borrow from a vocabulary steeped in the wealth of everyday discourse, employing words whose meanings, while deriving from a pre-philosophical context, lend concreteness to the linguistic role of the categories as predicates which "stand for" the definitive characteristics of objects of possible experience. Through this new precedent of usage, the categories serve as signifying acts which can designate the "third something," i. e., a relation to the object, and thereby "speak to" the diversity of experience and the dynamism of natural events. And what then is to provide the root from which a new precedent of linguistic usage is to be derived via the schemata, supplying a content whose specificity can only by determined in accord with nuances (of meaning) adopted from everyday language? In originating on the side of sensibility, only to be adapted to facilitate the binding character of the predicative acts of thought (rules), this root can consist in nothing other than time. Yet time must be conceived more radically in terms of a distinctive "procedure," which graphically depicts the conformity on any possible object to the conditions of human finitude. Kant called this procedure "schematism."

If knowledge could organize itself strictly around an axis of identity, as in the case of analytic judgments, there would be no need for schematism. But because synthetic judgments require a standard of truth beyond that of the law of non-contradiction, it is necessary to locate a new topography for truth at the intersection between knower and known — a scenario as we have seen Heidegger recognizes above all. To mark this interface, Kant devises a novel procedure which can bring the structure of thought in concert with the specifications of an object. In order to acquire the precision to determine an object, the predicates must be circumscribed in accord with "possible experience" as providing a new context for their usage. "This formal and pure condition of sensibility to which the employment of the concept of understanding is restricted, we shall entitle the schema of the concept. The procedure of understanding in these schemata we shall entitle the schematism of pure understanding" (A 149, B 179).

Since schematism is not a given, it must be implemented as a process where a distinctly new meaning can be assigned to each category. To "schematize" the categories is to ascribe to them those determinations which derive from the same condition on which the givenness of all appearances depends, namely, time. Schematism, then, is a way of reconfiguring the categories — of adjusting their precision and scope of application — according to a procedure harmonized with time. In turn, time must be construed more basically as constellating the form of human awareness through which anything can be given in experience. Just as schematism restricts the categories' employment, so it broadens the purview of time to include its partnership with transcendental imagination. In its transcendental deployment, imagination induces the creation of patterns which permit the synthesis of a sense manifold in compliance with the predicative acts of thought.

In this more radical guise, time re-emerges as the creative ingredient by which imagination graphically displays the pattern for the category to delineate a content in accord with what is given through sensuous intuition. The creativity in question parallels a degree of discretion left to a (determinate) judgment in seeking the key or code, i. e., the schema, to exhibit (the meaning) of the category *in concreto* in conjunction with the content of sensibility. "Transcendental philosophy has the peculiarity that besides the rule (or rather the universal condition of rules) which is given in the pure concept of understanding it can also specify a priori the instance to which the rule applies" (A 135, B 175). In acknowledging this unique power, Kant describes judgment as a "peculiar talent which can be practiced only, and cannot be taught" (A 133, B 172). It is because of this appeal to a deeper source of creativity (in time) that the corollary of judgment, or imagination, constitutes a "blind but indispensable function of the soul" (A 143, B 183).

In developing the power of judgment (*Urteilskraft*), schematism depicts time "figuratively" through an imagination synthesis. Time emerges as the "figure" or intermediary which differentiates and assigns limits to an otherwise intellectual organization. As a figure and intermediary, the imaginative synthesis of time outlines in advance a field of determinations or what we might simply call a context of meaning. "But the figurative synthesis, if it is to be directed merely to the original synthetic unity of apperception, that is, the transcendental unity which is thought in the categories, must, in order to be distinguished from the merely intellectual combination, be called the transcendental synthesis of imagination" (B 151). In its figurative role, imagination represents what is "not itself present" (B 151).

The idea of meaning (*Sinn*) proves to be somewhat problematic for Kant, because it is not a concern he explicitly addressed. To equate "meaning" with the capacity of the category to determine an object, and hence in its role in establishing a "referent" for a judgment, is not so much wrong as it is having the issue backward. Because what we cognitively describe as the object (and hence linguistically as the referent coinciding with it) achieves determination only in conformity with the synthetic unity of the category, its "meaning" hinges on what qualifies it as a condition of the knower, e. g, its translation into temporal terms via the schema. Hence Kant locates the origin of meaning in the schema rather than the category itself. "The schemata of the pure concepts of understanding are thus the true and sole conditions under which these concepts obtain relation to objects and so possess significance (*Bedeutung*)" (A 146). The schemata enables the pure concepts to determine objects in a restricted way for us, i. e., as appearances. And it is this delimiting activity which contributes to the formation of meaning by introducing specificity in how the categories can "signify" or "stand for" (the determinations of) objects. This specificity in turn hinges on the contribution that the intermediary of time, via transcendental imagination, makes in suggesting a new precedent of usage for the category. In other words, the schemata fill out the categories according to a richer tapestry of distinctions stemming from a common temporal root. Hence, each of the twelve categories receives its "new" meaning from a locus of determination they all have in common, and their employment in standing for or signifying (the constitution of) objects sets a new precedent for their usage. As "transcendental determination[s] of time (*Zeitbestimmungen*)" [A 139], to use Kant's locution, the schemeta set this new precedent. Thus time delimits the categories' capacity to signify or stand for something else, and the process of schematism then circumscribes their context of meaning.

As the creative vortex to schematize the categories, time spawns new distinctions and thereby a vocabulary to spell out the content of the categories. For example, in its skeletal form, substance involves identity. But when schematized, that pure concept acquires the additional connotation of continuance, in such a way that the schema, as the key for "transliterating" the category into a more graphic mode of expression, sets a new precedent for its usage. In its schematized form, the pure concept of identity acquires the concrete meaning of "permanence of the real in time" (A 143, B 183). As Kant states in the *Logic*, a schematized category provides "a distinctness in intuition in which through examples an abstract concept is exhibited and explained in concreto."[85] A more graphic context emerges, in order that the knower can designate the articulated pattern by which to spell out the constitutive feature of an object in a synthetic a priori judgment (and make it binding on everyone as a rule).

In Kant's refutation of the ontological proof in the Dialectic, as well as in the Postulates of Empirical Thought in General, we find another importance of schematism in the category of existence. As he emphasizes, existence is a peculiar kind of "predicate," insofar as it does not yield an additional determination to a concept. In providing the synthetic unity of a manifold, the category of existence establishes how can object can stand in relation to a knowing object, its way of appearing through a corresponding sensation. In supplying this synthesis, the category of existence means presence in a determinate time (A 145, B 184). The schema of the present lends determinancy to what is otherwise indeterminate, the copula "is." The meaning of the "is" as a "connective" cannot be given in any ostensive act, since logically speaking the word "is" describes only the copula of

---

85 AA 9, p. 39; tr. 43.

a judgment (A 598, B 626). When redefined through the context of time, however, the word "is" can acquire a deeper significance, and, as Heidegger subsequently illustrates, can still have ontological import even though it does not refer to anything.[86] The category of existence assumes the meaning of "presence" insofar as it originates within the same context from which the other categories derive their signifying power. Here lies one instance where an otherwise elusive word acquires significance through an intricate nexus of determinations — the "transcendental determinations of time" — which comprise a single universe of discourse. To be sure, it would be anachronistic to attribute to Kant's thinking a distinction between "sense" and "reference."[87] And while for him the determination of the former remains primarily a function of the latter, the preliminary circumscription of "possible experience" as the horizon of significance also allows the arc of reference to be completed.

What still remains problematic in these examples is the grammar by which the imaginative synthesis extracts from time a vocabulary for articulating the content of the category, e. g., "permanence." General logic presumes that the common ancestry each of the categories has in thought provides the basis for its grammar. The procedure of schematism, however, demonstrates this commonality by uncovering time as the one source from which the categorical determinations of objects spring. When schematized through time, the categories form a nexus of significations, which as a whole delineates the constitution of objects standing in opposition to a knower. Linguistically speaking, time emerges as the root to generate a new set of "synonyms" whose meanings exhibit the common ancestry of all the categories. Moreover, this condition of synonymy distinguishes the *link* between the proof of the categories' "objective validity" or their transcendental deduction, and language. Schematism graphically delineates the meaning of the categories, allowing the cognitive content of thought to unfold in partnership with the word. The word is not an arbitrary sign. Instead, the word brings with it an ancestry, a common root of synonymy, which provides the grammar — the precedent of usage vis-à-vis the establishment of a new context of meaning or universe of discourse — for articulating the content of the categories. The grammar defines the linguistic side of knowledge by which the categories, in synthesizing the manifold of intuition, stand for or signify the definitive characteristics of an object in order that a judgment about its constitution can be formed. Given this grammar, synthetic a priori judgments can then be articulated according to a

---

**86** Heidegger, *Pathmarks*, pp. 337–363. See GA 24, pp. 35–107; tr. 27–76. Also see Schalow, "Position, Place, and Language: Revisiting Heidegger's Final Essay on Kant", pp. 57–69.
**87** See Hanna, "Kant's Theory of Meaning", pp. 47–59.

vocabulary which speaks to the diversity and dynamism of experience, including the events of nature.

Through schematism, the linear structure of predication from general logic gives way to the development of various layers of meaning, a vocabulary carved from a nexus of distinctions (i. e., transcendental determinations of time). We might describe this layering effect as a "semiotic level" (*semiotische Ebene*) which allows a knower who is immersed in the flux of experience to communicate its structure as a whole. Referring back to Heidegger's remark cited at the outset, the knower is not known in a pure Cartesian act of self-reflection, but instead only emerges through the performance of its ability to know, the exercise of the "I can." As Kant stresses in the B-deduction (which ironically Heidegger downplays in favor of the A-deduction), the analytic unity of apperception or the "I think" accompanying all my representations presupposes the synthetic unity of apperception (B 135–138), or the "*I can*" as the activity of synthesizing the manifold of intuition. The contextualization of the activity of knowing in terms of its finitude, the *declension* of the "conditions of the possibility of experience," dictates, in Kant's terms, that the unity of the knower becomes explicit only indirectly as a correlate to what its synthetic activity accomplishes in determining the unity of an object (B 135). Because the "can" of the ability of knowing co-determines the "I think," the key to the Kantian project hinges on what first and foremost embodies this "performative" dimension, i. e., schematism. This is the case not only because, as Heidegger stresses, schematism provides the clue to the finitude of human understanding, but because, as we have seen, it implicates the participation of the knower as a performer of and *participant in* speech. Speech thereby becomes the activity from which thought arises, in such a way that the critical enterprise itself becomes an *enactment* of reason whose linchpin in anchored in the dynamism of time. Thus, the delimitation of the categories in terms of time, or schematism, *gives the direction for the basic activity by which the self-examination of reason can unfold and achieve expression through the discourse comprising the first* Critique. By making explicit this performative dimension, we confront the perplexing methodological issue overarching the *Critique of Pure Reason*: namely, how the determination, not of the objectivity of knowledge, but of the finite conditions which make it possible, can achieve expression, in such a way that the self-reflexivity of the critical enterprise can be articulated within the scope of transcendental philosophy. The further unraveling of this enigma will lead to an aspect of Heidegger's interpretation of Kant which, while not as visible as his account of the Transcendental Analytic and its portrayal of the finitude conditions of human knowledge, also speaks to that finitude, namely, the Transcendental Dialectic.

Insofar as Heidegger accentuates the analysis of schematism from the Analytic, it is in the Dialectic's complementary attempt to trace the activity of reason in circumscribing its boundaries (*Grenze*) that we discover a nascent concern for language. In the Analytic, language is for the most part reduced to its capacity to "refer" (to something [*etwas*]) through the categories' employment in determining objects of knowledge. Kant tacitly expresses this viewpoint in a brief remark from the "Amphiboly of the Concepts of Reflection": "For we can understand only that which brings with it, in intuition, something corresponding to our words (*Worten*)" [A 277, B 333]. But the Dialectic poses a scenario in which, because of the refusal of any object to which the categories can refer (lacking a sensible intuition), the reflection upon what the limitations of this refusal implies a discourse whose theme derives directly from the activity of reason itself. The grammar of the "itself" distinguishes the element of reflexivity which yields the counter pole to the discussion of reason's concern for the a priori constitution of objects. As Heidegger briefly remarks in the Kant-book, the "ideas of reason" suggest a synthesis of the "whole" or "completeness," which, while admitting no corresponding object, provide a complementary way to depict our finitude to that of the figurative (temporal) synthesis of the imagination.[88] In this respect, the "meaning" of this "complementary" discourse can reside in nothing else than the *example* (e. g., the "figure") set by reason's fulfilling its own critical design, e. g., in resolving disputes on a transcendental plane (such as antinomies) otherwise believed to be unresolvable by relying exclusively on the formal canon of the law of contradiction. And since this resolution does not hinge on the assertion of any new propositions, but, if anything, on the reverse, then the discourse lies in the performance of its role in mediating and unraveling these disputes.

At the beginning of Transcendental Logic, Kant contrasts the Analytic as a "logic of truth" with the Dialectic as a "logic of (the critique of) illusion" (A 63, B 88). But while it may be the case that, bereft of any relation to an object, illusion constitutes "non-sense," the exposure of illusion must still imply some kind of "significance." Perhaps Kant did not fully reflect upon this incongruity. Nevertheless, the criticism which is practiced in the Dialectic has its impact because the observance of the failure of attaining an object still has relevance for suggesting, by contrast, distinct markers as to the scope of knowledge. As Kant suggests in the "Conclusion" to the *Prolegomena*, the determination of the bounds of pure reason, which the legitimate employment of the transcendental ideas delineates, still comprises a "cognition" in some sense.[89] No longer is it an empirical intuition which fills out the cognition and, via the schema, supports the discursivity concerning it (about an object). In place of this form of corroboration, there is

---

88 GA 3, p. 152; tr. 107.
89 AA 4, Pr, p. 361; tr. 109.

instead only "negative evidence." Or put another way, determinateness must now include negativity as a chief ingredient, such that reason can still allow the observance of omissions and dislocations (in the presumption of absolute cognition) to serve as the graphic depiction or illustration marking its own boundaries. The procedure of schematism is not then re-implemented in the course of the Transcendental Dialectic. Rather, the new axis of meaning which is opened up by this procedure sustains a discourse, i. e., a *logos*, whose theme coincides with the parameters of human finitude itself.[90]

The most noteworthy case in point is the conflict between freedom and necessity in the third antinomy. When left to its own resources, reason cannot resolve this conflict because each side of the debate can equally be demonstrated according to its supreme canon, the law of contradiction. Only given the ability to acknowledge negative evidence, as it were, can reason shift the dispute to a transcendental plane and discover a "third way," otherwise precluded within traditional logic, to resolve the conflict. By distinguishing two distinct realms of jurisdiction, one belonging to freedom and the other to nature, reason can establish compatibility whether there was previously only irreconcilable conflict. The resolution hinges on demarcating new boundaries of reason, which separate each faction into a "heterogenous" relation whereby there can be an extension of a spontaneous causality only by the proportional restriction of the natural chain of cause and effect.

Univocity can no long serve as the standard of meaning, since the resolution of the dispute hinges on developing a complementarity (of terms) whereby each becomes relevant only as it marks the terminus of the other. At this juncture where a relation to an object breaks off another dimension of speech must arise, which can distinguish the reciprocity between complements. What is "meaningful" is not simply defined as the outcome of a cognitive process, i. e., the referent of an object, but instead arises through the activity in which reason engages in carrying out its own self-examination. The axis of meaning thereby shifts from its ideational content to the character of its enactment. But in that enactment we discover that what is relevant is a task which is on-going — the re-appropriation of specific boundaries governing us — rather than a fixed set of determinations or propositional forms. Where Kant does not explicitly address the operation of reason in this guise, the basic thrust of Heidegger's phenomenology, as ontologically motivated, is to characterize this enactment of meaning as a task which our finitude always sets before us. Thus the implementation of Kant's critical enter-

---

**90** For a further discussion of this topic, see Schalow, "Reinscribing the *Logos* of Transcendental Logic: Kant's Highest Principle of Synthetic Judgments Revisited", pp. 195–205.

prise defines one permutation of that finitude. But while this side of Heidegger's destructive-retrieval of transcendental philosophy is obvious, he does not as explicitly outline its converse: that the need to convey this finitude poses to language its utmost challenge, insofar as it is by heeding this finitude that language acquires the complexity of its expression – the coordination of contrary poles of meaning.

If language bears an affinity with time, as the analysis of schematism suggests, then would a transformed concept of language which outstrips predication also imply a more radical notion of time? While his unique rendition of schematism reinstates the centrality of time and imagination, Heidegger also recognizes that temporality in Kant's sense is limited by its relying on an Aristotelian vision of presence (*Anwesenheit*). But if Heidegger's destructive-retrieval of Kant is to be complete, he must also show how Kantian schematism spawns dislocations later in the *Critique* which open the way for displacing this Aristotelian concept of presence. From our previous discussion, the missing step would consist of establishing how there is a "linguistic turn" in the Dialectic which anticipates the need to expand the transcendental conditions of time in order to include the opposite side of presence. In other words, the tension inherent in expressing the polarity of meaning void of any object — whose denotation hinges on transcendental determinations of time — must invite the participation of an opposite temporal dimension, or absence, as co-determining (the givenness of) the present (*Gegenwart*). We can no longer envision time as a linear movement that segments and compartmentalizes our experience into its simplest parts. Instead, we must construe time — through the oscillation between presence and absence — as a vortex that joins opposites, thereby eliciting subtler nuances of meaning at a boundary which functions both as a zone of demarcation and an expanse of openness.

In publishing *Kant and the Problem of Metaphysics* in 1929, Heidegger sought to discover in the *Critique of Pure Reason* a prefigurement of his own project of "being and time." Not only does a concern for human finitude prevail in both inquiries, but, insofar as being becomes intelligible at all, it does so through what shapes the horizon of ontological understanding, namely, time. Indeed, temporality becomes prominent because it admits the determination of being according to one of its dimensions, the present; but, more primordially, temporality also enters the forefront because it can convey a "meaning" which entails a dynamism of manifestation, unconcealment and discovery, whereby what is present emerges by inviting a contrast with absence. Thus the so-called "meaning of being" can never be univocally defined, since any "nomenclature" appropriate to it can arise only by incorporating the tension of its unfolding on two adjacent fronts: presence/absence. Six years later in *An Introduction to Metaphysics* (1935), Heidegger accentuates this linguistic side of the ontological problematic when he undertakes an etymology of the word "being" in order to recover its active, verbal dimension.[91]

Heidegger directs his attention to Kant in the late 1920s' in order to find in his emphasis on finitude and temporality an entrance to the inquiry into being. But would it not be ironic that the more radical side of Critical philosophy lies in its potential to spawn a "linguistic turn," as well as in its transcendental orientation? We discover the implications for this possibility in the third *Critique*, when Kant's provisional interest in the "performative" character of language takes root in his appeal to the "*sensus communis*," the universal communicability of an aesthetic experience.[92] Language emerges as the lived dimension which introduces its participants to a "world" (*Welt*), to their co-existence (*mitsein*) with others from which Critical philosophy's forum of disputation first becomes possible.[93]

As Heidegger unfolds the hermeneutical situation of his philosophy in the late 1920s, the emphasis on the cultural dimension, which is more reminiscent of Dilthey, and the appeal to transcendental conditions of temporality, which is more reminiscent of the tenets of Kant's first *Critique* than the third, appear to be polarized. To be sure, Heidegger later alleviates the incorrigibility of this tension with his subsequent portrayal of language as a hearing which prefigures speaking, as a response to the differentiation of being through the interplay of presence-absence. And yet, in retrospect, the obstacle which he had to leap in order to reach this more radical orientation of thinking may not stem from having "turned" to Kant in the first place, as some scholars have argued,[94] but, on the contrary, from a failure to map his own project of "being and time" upon all the permutations of Critical philosophy.[95] Had Heidegger done so, it would have been easier for him to clarify two premises which underlie his destructive-retrieval of transcendental philosophy: 1) the hermeneutic shift to a pre-predicative level of understanding (*Verstehen*) and disclosedness (*Erschlossenheit*); and 2) the displacement of the proposition as the fundamental locus of truth in favor of disclosedness, *including that enacted through the play of imagination*. Indeed, only

---

**91** GA 40, pp. 60–65.

**92** AA 5, KU, pp. 238–239; tr. pp. 75–76. See Arendt, *Lectures on Kant's Political Philosophy*, p. 4. For a discussion of "performative" dimension of speech, of language as "deed," as important jointure between Heidegger and Kant, see Sallis, *Echoes: After Heidegger*, p. 1. For a further development of the concern for praxis, see Sallis, "Free Thinking", pp. 3–12.

**93** For one of the most insightful applications of the Kantian view of language, see Arendt, *The Human Condition*, pp. 198–200.

**94** Theodore Kisiel, *The Genesis of Heidegger's Being and Time*, p. 457.

**95** GA 25, pp. 426–427; tr. 289.

because the vocabulary required to articulate being has its root in temporality, which in turn yields the possibility of disclosedness, can the meaning of being be put into words that uncover and amplify, rather than disguise and leave indeterminate.

When we bring the concern for language into the forefront of a destructive-retrieval of transcendental philosophy, we discover the clue to how temporality can serve as the emissary for being's transmittal and articulation – the intermediary of hermeneutics – because it provides the root for an ontological vocabulary which is inherently disclosive. The intermediating role of transcendental imagination in schematism can then be seen to mirror the hermeneutical role of interpretation, insofar as both appeal to the *medium* of time to "translate" (the meaning of) being into terms that disclose rather than conceal. Ironically, could it actually be the case that Heidegger's difficulty in developing a sufficiently radical language[96] to address being may have stemmed from "too little Kant" rather than from "too much" — at least as far as exploring the nascent concern for language that underlies transcendental philosophy? The formulation of this question, which points ahead to Chapter Three, holds to key to why (the retrieval of) imagination forms the cornerstone of Heidegger's *Auseinandersetzung* with Kant.

## 3 The Doubling of Imagination

Let us reconsider the title of Heidegger's lecture course from the Winter Semester of 1925/26, which signaled his dramatic turn in the direction of Kant. Through his phenomenological approach, Heidegger circumvents the preconceptions that traditionally have governed logic, first and foremost, the linking of truth with its expression in the form of propositions. By contrast, question truth is to examine its occurrence as a phenomenon, e. g., the "lived experience" of truth, prior to its characterization as a standard of "correctness" for evaluating theoretical claims. Yet this phenomeno-logical inquiry does not simply dispense of the traditional framework of logic, but, as its namesake suggests, instead yields to a even more "radical" directive. That directive resides in the way that language as *logos* elicits its own measure of "determinateness," in concurrence with the uniqueness and singularity of what manifests itself and which can simultaneously be "experienced" by the inquirer, e. g., Da-sein. In this regard, Heidegger's attempt to challenge the supremacy in the Kant-book can be viewed as a kind of litmus test,

---

**96** Heidegger, *Pathmarks*, pp. 249–250.

as it were, for the initial hypothesis how, on the one hand, we can have access to truth independently of reason, and, how, on the other, that access presupposes a deeper origin of language than the theoretical form of the proposition.

When looked at from this wider perspective, Heidegger's controversial attempt in the Kant-book so supplant reason in favor of imagination occurs on two fronts. First, truth must be traced back to its origin in the inquirer's concrete access to it, in disclosedness, and ultimately, through the historical precedent set through the Greek experience of *Aletheia*. Secondly, the shifting away from the proposition as the traditional locus of truth implies, conversely, that language derives its power from this primordial impetus toward "unconcealment." The fact that language depends upon truth, and not the other way around, marks the transformation of what has traditionally gone under the heading of "logic." Even the advance that Kant makes in the name of "transcendental logic" over general, "formal" logic, presupposes this more radical possibility. Yet if the Kant-book Heidegger begins to map this new landscape, how does the retrieval of imagination make explicit the *phenomenon* of language as well as truth?

In seeking this more primordial ground, Heidegger introduces the principles of his own hermeneutics, in whose very employment emerges Wilhelm Dilthey's insight into the historically situated, lived dimension of understanding as *Verstehen*.[97] In his radical rendition of Kant, Heidegger thereby allows the common thread of the German root to play out these two distinct permutations of understanding, one that is cognitively couched in (Kant's) theoretical reason (*Verstand*), the other which bears the more inclusive seeds of (Dilthey's) hermeneutic tradition. Not only must reason in its theoretical employment, and its concepts (*Verstehen*), be traced back to a more primordial origin, e. g., imagination; but, human cognition as Kant outlines it in the Transcendental Analytic of the *Critique of Pure Reason* must implicate the capability of *Verstehen* in projecting open a horizon of possibilities.[98] The concrete enactment of this power to differentiate and unfold various levels of meaning — which remains implicit for Kant — Heidegger ascribes to "interpretation." Rather than simply being interchangeable with imagination, interpretation is its existential analogue, the origin of its root in the disclosedness of care itself. While on the surface imagination may appear as a free-floating phenomena, it harbors the capabilities of disclosedness as the avenue for projecting open a horizon of possibilities. In the Kant-book, Heidegger accentuates the creative power of the "productive" imagination in constituting

---

**97** See Sallis, *Echoes: After Heidegger*, p. 146. Also see Nelson, "Begründbarkeit und Unergründlichkeit bei Wilhelm Dilthey", pp. 7–9.
**98** Kant, *Critique of Pure Reason*, A 136 / B 175.

the "play-space" for the enactment of temporality through its power in throwing forth the horizon of finite transcendence.

In providing a strategic linchpin between understanding and sensibility, between spontaneity and receptivity, imagination epitomizes a uniquely "synthetic" power. But implicit in its exercise, if only as suggested by its own namesake as image-producing, productive imagination is also a "figurative" mode of expression. As Heidegger states in his 1927/28 lectures on Kant: "Thus *pure* power of imagination must bring the *pure manifold* of time into the form of a *pure* image. Productive synthesis forms "an image"; it offers productively a *figura*. Hence [Kant] also calls productive synthesis *figurative synthesis*."[99] When annexed to understanding and its pure concepts, imagination draws upon a new nexus of distinctions which a common ancestry in time. In producing transcendental schema, then, the imagination yields explicitly a temporal distinction for every pure concept, providing for each one a more finely etched, "transcendental determination of time."[100] The imaginative inscription of these temporal nuances constitutes the hallmark of schematism. Insofar as time provides the common root around each new nuance develops, e. g, "presence," "permanence," "succession," a new "idiomatic form" arises to express the "meaning" of the pure concepts. But what do we "mean" by "meaning" in this case?

While there are twelve categories, they share a common root of synonymy by deriving their specific connotations from time. Given this common root, a single universe of discourse dictates the use of the twelve categories, according to new "precedent" which is set by the corresponding (temporal) schemata., e. g., "presence," "permanence," "succession." The categories do not have unlimited applicability, but instead their scope must be restricted in compliance with our finitude nature, i. e., to "possible experience." The pure concepts achieve their legitimate use, and their power to stand for or signify the constitution of objects, only when restricted to this sphere. But what is Kant emphasizing with this qualification "possible experience?" He suggests that there is no isomorphic relation between the signifier and the signified, the referential act and the referent (e. g., the constitution of the object). On the contrary, an object *qualifies* as such when it can be given in accord with the preconditions of experience, in such a way that this givenness is "contextually bound" by the limits which the schemata outline. The circumscribing of this context is not itself objective, but allows everything else that appears within it to be considered as such, that is, to be determined

---

99 GA 25, p. 415; tr. 281. Heidegger cites Kant's *Critique of Pure Reason*, B 151.
100 Kant, *Critique of Pure Reason*, A 138 / B 177. See Schalow, "Imagination and Embodiment: The Task of Reincarnating the Self from a Heideggerian Perspective", pp. 151–165.

*as* something. If in Kant's terms we can best describe this process as "transcendental exposition," then its enactment outlines the entire circumference of human finitude as an example of a sphere of relevance or "meaning."

The horizon of meaning that is created through this act of transcendence is not an indeterminate whole, however, but rather is the potential for determination. As a declaration of finitude, the horizon implies boundaries whose demarcation gives the preliminary contours to whatever can be defined and even thematized. As shaped as much by the tendency toward withdrawal as appearing, this backdrop yields the expanse for all that can be understand, the "farthest" (i. e., the *worauf*) from which springs all the points of reference and nexus of relations as the harbinger of intelligibility as such. We can thereby describe the horizon as a prearticulated whole of meaning, while also recognizing its infusion with the power of *logos*. For the self-gathering of the *logos* itself is already enacted in the pre-verbal gestures, signs, indications, icons, etc., whose specific enunciation and vocabulary may still only be vaguely housed in the nascent syntax of expression. By the same token, the power of the words themselves that emerge in connection with this syntax, that is, in actual speech and conversation receive their ability to convey "meaning"in and through this "prearticualted whole." Indeed, the "signifying power" of the actual words must always be connected with the projecting-open of this "expanse," of this "horizon" of intelligibility.

By contrasting an enactment of language which discloses with another which merely defines what is already disclosed, Heidegger provides the cornerstone for a key phenomenological distinction. Specifically, he distinguishes between two difference fulcrums or "as-structures" of determination, the "hermeneutic-as" and the "apophantic-as." The apohantic-as is a derivative mode of determination which restricts the manner of self-showing to what can appear within a predicative model, including the pure concepts of the understanding (*Verstand*).[101] By contrast, the "hermeneutic -as" pertains to the how understanding (*Verstehen*) as a concrete instance of being-in-the-world allows beings to be disclosed in their being, a 'practical' (rather than a 'theoretical') context, e. g., within a compass of involvements of using equipment. The importance of the "hermeneutic-as" lies not only in opening up the intelligibility of our being-in-the-world, but also allowing for "being" itself emerge in its potential for determination, i. e., *as* a phenomenon, *as* different from beings. Only in this way can an inquiry target the possibility of understanding being and make it the explicit theme of ontology.

As simple as Heidegger's allusion to the hermeneutic-as may be, it becomes critical for his reinterpretation of Kant's schematism of the understanding. While

---

101 GA 2, p. 210; tr. 201.

Heidegger has in view an understanding which targets "beings" in the most encompassing way, the Kantian view of the same pertain to what can be determined generically (e. g., "beingness") about a region of beings according to the preset specifications of twelve categories. As a result, an inescapable ambiguity arises. On the one hand, Heidegger suggests that the role of schematism is to demarcate understanding in the first sense, in a manner implying a (temporal) "horizon"within which being can become manifest. On the other hand, he recognizes that understanding in this second, strictly cognitive sense, is slanted toward a regional ontology of 'nature.' As a result, the power of signification which Kant's schematism secures for the categories can only define 'being' in a derivative manner, that is, as a mode of "nature being extant," i. e., as "presence-at-hand."[102] Heidegger's way around this ambiguity is to suggest that the "hermeneutical-as" has a place within schematism on a deeper level than the actual categories themselves, in such a way that the temporal activity of imagination provides a "pre-predicative" backdrop of intelligibility.[103] When the fulcrum of understanding shifts from (the theoretical cognition of) beings to the wider concern for "being" (*Seinsverständnis*), the axis of truth also shifts from the propositional model of "correctness" (the apophantic-as) to the pre-predicative dimension of "disclosedness" (the hermeneutic-as).

Once having made established this jointure between Kant's transcendental philosophy and his own fundamental ontology, Heidegger characterizes imagination in terms of disclosedness (*Erschlossenheit*). That is, imagination equals the "play-space" of the manifestation as such. Heidegger thereby establishes the fulcrum around which his entire reinterpretation of transcendental philosophy revolves. He thereby allows the dominant concerns for his own hermeneutics — of Dasein, temporality, and horizon of world — to accentuate the corollary motifs of Kant's transcendental philosophy, human finitude, imagination, the domain of possible experience. The privileging of key motifs of Kant's thought at the expense of others defines the both the ingenuity and "violence" of Heidegger's radical rendition of transcendental philosophy, insofar as he transposes an epistemic enigma (of how synthetic a priori judgments are possible) into an essentially *ontological* problem (the possibility of understanding being [*Seinsverständnis*] in relation to time).

In centering the problematic of "being and time" in transcendental philosophy, Heidegger arrives at the title of his seminal book, *Kant and the Problem of Metaphysics*. This title presents an irony to the Neo-Kantian account of Kant,

---

102 GA 25, p. 427; tr. 289.
103 GA 3, p. 42; tr. 30.

which Heidegger vehemently opposed.[104] The popular view of Kant suggests that a "theory of knowledge" precedes any attempt to develop a "metaphysics." But to make the concern for metaphysics the key to addressing the limits of knowledge, on the other hand appears to reverse Kant's philosophical priorities. Of course, that reversal may not be seem so peculiar if we follow an ancillary hermeneutic thread which weaves its way through Heidegger's analysis, namely, that the as-structure of interpretation supplants the apophantic-as, in such a way that the constitutive elements of the knowing process which Kant's outlines assume the richer texture of the "anticipatory," "projective" dynamic of understanding in its existential form. In this way, the role of the a priori synthesis as mediating between the knower and its object becomes a proxy for an existentially rooted "temporalizing" movement of "surpassing to" or "transcendence."[105] Transcendental philosophy thereby receives its name, not because it addresses an epistemic concern, but, on the contrary, because it provisionally poses the ontological problem of finitude transcendence, i. e., temporality. The heart of that problematic is the difference between being and beings, the ontological difference, which becomes explicit in the act of transcendence.

Due to the shift in favor of the hermeneutic-as, and only because of it, an interesting reversal occurs in which Kant's transcendental philosophy reverts into a "postscript" to *Being and Time*, which is designed to map out the presuppositions or "hermeneutical situation" of that project as a whole.[106] When in a lecture course from 1935/36, Heidegger alludes to the "ambiguity" in the title of his earlier book ("the *problem* of metaphysics"),[107] he may well have recognized that the line between own his thinking in *Being and Time* and his exposition of Kant's transcendental philosophy had begun to blur. By unraveling this hermeneutic situation, Heidegger develops another side of his reciprocal rejoinder with Kant. That is, the rejoinder is the recoiling of the question of being itself from the root of its own historical origin. When recast within this wider historical orbit, the key motifs of Kant's philosophy becomes occasion to re-enact the understanding which is concealed is the basic concepts of all metaphysics: that whatever (conceptual) determinations can be attributed to "being," (these, e. g., "presence," "permanence,") still depend on a prior allusion to a temporal origin. Thus, Kant's own thinking is transformed into a kind of precursor of Heidegger's own attempt to re-enact the historical projection of being upon time.

---

**104** See Dahlstrom, "Heidegger's Kant-Courses at Marburg", pp. 293–308.
**105** GA 3, p. 236; tr. 135. Also see GA 24, pp. 459–461; tr. p. 423.
**106** See Part IV of the Kant-book, GA 3, 238–243; tr. 167–170.
**107** GA 41, p. 127.

But, why, then, should Kantian imagination become so focal to this "re-enactment?" Is it simply because imagination is inherently temporal? Yet, but only if we develop this claim in light of the need to develop an accompanying *logos* of being, to articulate, and specifically, through the medium of temporality as spawning the requisite (ontological) vocabulary. In this regard, the task which Heidegger undertakes in "translating" the *Critique of Pure Reason* couples with the "intralingual translation" of the "elemental words" of philosophy, that is, to direct the search for a "*logos*" of being. Let us consider two passages in which Heidegger undertakes the intralingual translation of the word "being." First, in his discussion from the 1925 lecture-course text *Plato's Sophist*, he claims that time determines the "grammar" of a distinctive linguistic practice, the declension of the verb "to be" as a "time-word" (*Zeitwort*).[108] Secondly, in his 1929/30 lecture-course text, Heidegger succinctly summarizes the correlation between the enactment of our speech and our understanding of being: "The two essential elements characterizing the verb are that it also refers to time, and in its meaning is always related to something that the discourse is about, namely to beings. This indicates that all positing of being is necessarily related to time. In keeping with this, in German we therefore call the verb a time-word (*Zeitwort*)."[109] In prioritizing the verbal form, the intralingual translation of the word "being" shifts the fulcrum of concern to the "and" designating the grammar of its connection with time.[110] The focus of philosophy is no longer on being or time considered separately, but, through the guidance of intralingual translation, the grammar of the "conjunction" assumes prominence according to the heading "time and being."

When we consider imagination as (temporal) medium, and its schemata as sculpturing out a pre-articulated whole of intelligibility, we see can see why Heidegger took particular interest in this problematic. In this regard, Kantian schematism becomes a prelude to Heidegger's own "intralingual translation" of the key terms (i. e., through the medium of time) which facilitate being's manifestation as well as the articulation of its meaning in words. Heidegger's retrieval of imagination, then, becomes a springboard for addressing being through the intimacy of its relation to time, that is, for outlining a new problematic in which temporality provides the key for understanding being and expressing its "meaning." Where Kant had first described the schemata as "transcendental determinations of time," Heidegger shows how temporality can transmit the meaning of being and fosters its disclosure in words. Temporality intercedes as the emissary,

---

108  GA 19, p. 592; tr. 410.
109  GA 29/30, p. 465; tr. 321.
110  See Schalow, "Attunement and Translation", pp. 295–296.

the interposing of the hermeneutic-as, which allows for meaning of being to be understood thematically, yet in a way that reconciles the singularity of its manifestness (our experience of it) with the universality of its expression (the *logos*). The dynamism of this reconciliation is the key to schematism as the hallmark of the creative power of imagination.

While the concern for imagination does not disappear in Heidegger's subsequent writings, it does recede — only in on rare instances coming to the forefront. Indeed, in responding to a remark from Jean Beaufret in a 1973 seminar at Zähringen, Heidegger describes the key expression of imagination, or schematism, as "the Kantian way of discussing being and time."[111] In this regard, we see how the imagination continues to provide a signpost for Heidegger, despite his reluctance to address its variation as a vehicle of aesthetic "play" in Kant's *Critique of Judgment*.[112] In a brief passage from *Contributions* (1936–1938), Heidegger provides one of the few instances in which he revisits the theme of the imagination:

> Indeed: *As thrown projecting-opening grounding, Da-sein is the highest actuality in the domain of imagination*, granted that by this term we understand not only a faculty of the soul and not only something transcendental (cf. Kantbook) but rather enowning itself, where all transfiguration reverberates.
> "Imagination" as occurrence of the *clearing* itself.[113]

In this remark, Heidegger offers an even more radical view of the power of imagination than he did even in the Kant-book. Rather than merely a productive power of synthesis, imagination re-emerges through the tension which holds between its creativity and the occurrence of unconcealment itself. Insofar as in the mid-1930s Heidegger turns to the work of art in order to identify the key instance of truth, his circuitous path back to imagination shows that philosophy, having forsaken the artificiality of Kant's rational architectonic, must resurrect another form of *technē*, namely the "craftsmanship" of thinking. Ultimately, we practice this craft by safeguarding the word (*Sorgsamkeit des Wortes*), by caring for language, particularly as the "place" for the unconcealment of being.

By showing how Heidegger's retrieval of imagination harbors the topic of language, we uncover the hermeneutic thread, which weaves its way through Kant's disparate discussions of knowledge, as well as art, beauty and the "sublimity" of nature. As a result, we discover that Heidegger's *Auseinandersetzung*

---

111 Heidegger, *Four Seminars*, p. 69.
112 See Sallis: *Echoes: After Heidegger*, pp. 185–187.
113 GA 65, p. 312; tr. 219.

with Kant, which begins by making imagination the "centerpiece" of human knowledge,[114] unfolds through an "ellipsis" in which the search for "figurative" modes of expression, rather than a linear model of predication. The leading edge of Heidegger's exchange with Kant can now be expressed most simply this way. To follow the path of "translating" the *Critique of Pure Reason* is to reach the arch of a crossing, the *trans-literating, iconic power of imagination through* which time emerges as the figure to transcribe (the "meaning" of) being into words.

By following this elliptical path, we can expand the circumference of the hermeneutical circle, allowing it to unfold within the wider orbit of language. Let us now plot the precise coordinates by which Heidegger extend his dialogue with Kant, in order to locate its place within the wider scope of the philosophical tradition.

---

114 GA 25, p. 421; tr. 291. See Schalow, "Heidegger and Kant in Conversation", pp. 338–348.

# Chapter Three
# Turnings: Of Time and Being

Frequently viewed today as the greatest work of twentieth century philosophy, many questions still swirl about the "completeness" of Heidegger's task, the unpublished portion of his *magnum opus*. This concern, along with the fact that he alludes to a "turning" in his thought, have created controversy about the "genesis" and development of his philosophy. But much of the ambiguity surrounds the fact that scholars have failed to emphasize that the turning is multifaceted, blending various dimensions together. And so, while it is often argued that the turning leads Heidegger away from Kant's transcendental way of thinking, the mirror image is equally compelling: that Heidegger's turning carries a self-testimonial about how we do philosophy which is largely reminiscent of Kant's Copernican revolution. At stake in either case is a dramatic change in the style of how to practice philosophy, the relocation of the center — a radical dislocating and de-centering, as it were — around which the orbit of philosophy can revolve. In Heidegger's terms, which may be roughly Kant's as well, the matter of thinking determines this center as to the novelty of how one thinks, i. e., the zero-point around which thinking gravitates. But what does this mean? When a thinker comes upon a simple motif, like temporality, which can provide the key to reformulating a highly complicated, albeit perennial topic like being, a radical transformation of thinking occurs. The thinker initially sees him/herself as in pursuit of this novelty, as pioneering change, when, in terms of the actual dynamic, the topic in question requires that change. Thus the turning, as Heidegger characterizes it, has the ambiguity both as a pursuit he undertakes and as a transformation he undergoes. And the tension of the ambiguity is precisely why there appears a "glitch" in Heidegger's thinking, which can be located at the problematic formulation of the unpublished division three, Part I of *Being and Time*, to be titled "time and being." Here we find a curious anomaly that overshadows the litany of the scholarship on the Heidegger-Kant connection: that despite the fact various studies address the importance of time, the role which this *exchange plays in facilitating the "turning" around of the question itself, from "being and time" to "time and being,"* has been almost totally lacking. This omission is puzzling given the fact that, as Charles Sherover observes, Heidegger clearly saw that the destructive-retrieval of transcendental philosophy held the key to radicalizing the problematic of *Sein und Zeit*.[115]

---

115 See Sherover, *From Kant and Royce to Heidegger*, p. 111.

We can gain a sense of this emerging problem (of the "turning" of the question) when we ask how well the motif of temporality, despite the lucidity of Heidegger's analysis of it, advances us along the path of unraveling the perennial riddle of being. Indeed, no matter how directly Dasein's temporality casts a spotlight on being, we still remain largely in the dark about its "meaning." How promising a "clue" to the perennial enigma of philosophy is it to show that time constitutes the possibility of any understanding of being? Given the ascent of his inquiry to the apex of this possibility, Heidegger can confirm his claim only by identifying a specific instance where the philosophical tradition conceives of being, no matter how uncritically, in terms of time. In the *Basic Problems,* Heidegger makes the following remark while emphasizing the priority of the problematic of temporality: "within the ontological sphere the possible is higher than anything actual."[116] But it is really the opposite which is up in the air as far as the need for confirmation goes: that the possibility of understanding being, according to the preconditions Heidegger sets down, must be met with an actual example, if only in a faulty and distorted way. And thus, while the *Basic Problems* may carve an important path along which Heidegger's inquiry may *proceed*, it does so only by housing a twofold problematic. First, it is necessary to show how the tradition's tendency to grasp being in temporal terms — beginning with the ancients — sets a precedent for subsequent attempts to thematize or conceptualize its "meaning." Once ancient philosophy sets this precedent, its uncritical acceptance by both Medieval and modern philosophy leads to the accumulation of distortions through which the question of being remains concealed. Second, it is necessary to counteract this errancy, transforming indifference toward being into genuine questioning, that is, by uncovering the original presumption by which the tradition assumes the link between being and time.

Heidegger begins to work out this twofold problematic in the concluding pages of Part IV of the Kant-book. But what special place does Kant occupy in the philosophical tradition, such that a critical exchange with him could point the way back to the original presumption and simultaneously leave a trace as the *possible relevance time* has to formulating the question of being? By serving double duty to highlight how indifference and vigilance constitute two sides of the same question, Kant's thought occupies a special place in the tradition. This becomes evident when, for example, the need arises to clarify the presuppositions of his task, Heidegger then turns to Kant, because he emphasized the centrality of human finitude, in contrast to Hegel.[117] Even though critics have argued that

---

116 GA 24, p. 438; tr. 308.
117 GA 32, p. 212; tr. 146–147.

Heidegger's exchange with Kant is somewhat one-sided, the irony is, as Dennis Schmidt points out, Heidegger treats Kant much more sympathetically than he does Hegel.[118] And while the cursory judgment is that Heidegger does most of the "talking" in his dialogue with Kant,[119] the opposite possibility is more compelling: Heidegger heeds the grounding-attunement, as we addressed in the beginning of Chapter One, which allows us to *listen* to what Kant says for the first time. As Heidegger remarks in his 1935/36 lecture(s) on Kant:

> The further task of this lecture thus becomes very simple. We need not report in broad surveys and general phrases "about" the philosophy of Kant. We put ourselves within it. Henceforth, only Kant shall speak. What we contribute, from time to time, will indicate the sense and the direction so that, en route, we do not deviate from the path of the question. The lecture is thus a kind of signpost. Signposts are indifferent to what happens on the highway itself. They emerge only here and there on the edge of the road to point out and to disappear again in passing.[120]

I will begin this chapter by outlining the pivotal importance that Heidegger's discussion in Part IV of the Kant-book plays in both addressing the question of the reciprocity between time and being, as well as initiating the task of a "phenomenological destruction of the history of ontology." I will then address the enigma of the turning as Heidegger first construes it as the turning around of the question from "being and time" to "time and being." In the next section, I will address the central role that imagination assumes in Heidegger's attempt to think the hidden reciprocity between being and time, that is, by redefining temporality as an interplay of presence and absence. Finally, I will show how, after the Kant-book, Heidegger brings his appropriation of Kant's thought within the wider orbit of the history of philosophy as a whole, and thereby emphasizes his *distance* from Kant, as well as his proximity.

## 1 Errancy and the Forgottenness of Being

To contrast two different stances toward the question of being, Heidegger employs the terms primordial and derivative. These terms are not mutually exclusive, but rather occur across the spectrum such that the detection of the latter provides a signpost to the former. We are a "signpost that is not yet read,"

---

118 Dennis J. Schmidt, *The Ubiquity of the Finite*, p. 207.
119 For a development of Kant's counter reply, see the concluding chapter of this book, *which addresses the importance of the third Critique in raising the question of language.*
120 GA 41, p. 55; tr. 56.

Heidegger remarks in *What Is Called Thinking?*, in alluding to how our neglect for the question of being provides an inroad to its mystery.[121] Conversely, what is original arises only in contrast to its opposite, because truth is always enjoined with untruth. These distinctions are not arbitrarily, since they are enacted in Dasein's understanding, including how it can understand itself, as owned or disowned. Paraphrasing Hegel, the power of the negative, of the "not," once again becomes prominent, insofar as Dasein is especially prone to misunderstand itself. As we discover, Dasein's vulnerability in this regard may also impede its ability to re-ask the question of being. Indeed, in the course of its everyday activities, Dasein may be as much disinclined to engage in questioning as inclined to do so. In fact, the self may be so immersed in its everyday interactions within the world that, to undertake philosophy, is to engage in a pursuit that requires swimming upstream.

If Dasein can so easily misunderstand its own being, then it would appear that it is placed at somewhat of a disadvantage when the opportunity arises to pose the question of being, to engage in philosophy. It is not due to a frailty that Dasein may be misguided in its philosophical efforts. On the contrary, whatever errancy philosophy may fall prey to through its long history has its roots in, and is prefigured by, the fallen (*Verfallen*) mode of misunderstanding that typifies Dasein in its everydayness. At stake is not much a causal influence, but the fact that the misunderstandings which creep into Dasein's everyday understanding, e. g., its tendency to refer to itself in the grammar of the first person pronoun as an "I" set over against others and things, gets recapitulated at the thematic level in such philosophical locutions as Descartes's "*cogito, ergo sum.*" Though whatever these philosophical miscues may be, and we should not underestimate them, they become evident only given the critical perspective that only history can provide.

A "phenomenological destruction of the history of ontology" becomes necessary, in order to undo the accumulation of misunderstandings which occur throughout the tradition. Along with the first stage of undertaking an *Auseinandersetzung* with Kant, the second and third stages of the *Destruktion* involve criticizing Descartes's *cogito* (as mental substance) and Aristotle's identification of being with *ousia* (as permanent substance). As a solipsism that overlooks the self's unity with the world, Descartes' thinking creates the basic metaphysical dichotomies — mind versus body, freedom versus nature, values versus fact — which encumber modern philosophy and exacerbate the forgottenness of being. But overshadowing the continuity of the *cogito* is a metaphysics of presence that

---

121 GA 10, pp. 17–18. For an earlier English translation, not based on the *Gesamtausgabe* edition, see Heidegger, *The Principle of Reason*, p. 11.

leads from Medieval philosophy back to Aristotle. Yet, as the case with Kant, Aristotle's philosophy harbors a unique ambiguity because, on the one hand, he masks the tension of the ontological difference by postulating an exemplary entity, the "unmoved mover"; on the other hand, he recalls the early Greek experience of *physis* as "self-emerging presence,"[122] as well as restores the balance between theory and practice.[123] Even if Heidegger never explicitly implemented his plan of *Destruktion*, there is a distinctive logic to it. Indeed, the critique of the Western tradition and the errancy it exposes arise historically, not of course by an accident, but because Dasein's understanding already unfolds through history and hence the question of being is inherently historical.

Dasein's understanding is historical, however, because it is shaped through a temporal dynamic in which the self develops possibilities from the future, returns to itself from the past, and addresses its situation in the present. One might then assume that Dasein arrives at philosophical concepts which are equally steeped in history, but, nothing could be further from the truth. Indeed, in concert with Dasein's tendency to misunderstand itself, philosophy falls prey to philosophical abstractions as to the eternality of the soul and the divine origin of the world. Moreover, these abstract formulations not only fly in the face of temporality, but, almost paradoxically, harbor a presumptuousness that seems to be almost oblivious of its own history. Hence, a certain dogma of ahistoricism arises which, as an extension of Dasein's misunderstanding of its temporal origin, weaves another web of confusion into the philosophical attempt to understand being. In an enlightening passage from the *Basic Problems*, Heidegger indicates the complex tension whereby Dasein both overlooks its temporal nature and presupposes the relevance that temporality has for formulating philosophical concepts of being:

> Faulty interpretations, misunderstandings, put much more stubborn obstacles in the way of authentic cognition than a total ignorance. However, these faulty interpretations of transcendence, of the basic relationship of Dasein to being and to itself, are no mere effects of thought or acumen. They have their reason and their necessity in Dasein's own historical existence. In the end, these faulty interpretations *must* be made, so that Dasein may reach the true path by correcting them ... It would run counter to the sense of philosophizing and of every science if we were not willing to understand that a fundamental untruth dwells with what is actually seen and genuinely interpreted ... Even the basic act of the constitution of ontology, of philosophy, the objectification of being, *the projecting-open of being upon its horizon of understandability*, and precisely this basic act, is delivered up to uncertainty and stands continually in danger of being reversed, because this objectification of being must

---

122 See McNeill, *The Glance of the Eye*, pp. 53–54.
123 See Brogan, *Heidegger and Aristotle*, p. 151.

necessarily move in a projective direction that runs counter to the everyday comportment toward beings.[124]

This statement provides us with the key to uncover the presuppositions which governs Heidegger's inquiry in *Being and Time* and thereby confirm the radicality of his point of departure. Heidegger begins *Being and Time* with an analysis of everydayness, the life-situation where Dasein tends to misunderstand itself Rather than assume Dasein's interest in philosophy, he affirms the opposite, that is, the everyday individual's indifference toward philosophical issues. But is this point of departure radical? We cannot answer this question until we take Heidegger's insight from the *Basic Problems*, as to the horizon for the understandability of being; and then project it open against the tradition's tendency to neglect it (i. e., the primordiality of time) or confront the "danger of its being reversed." Given this projection, an apparently accidental tendency of Dasein's oversight turns into an inescapable historical trend, the *forgottenness* of being vis-á-vis its affinity with time.

We will return shortly to consider Heidegger's reference to the preceding "danger," which overshadows the entire history of philosophy. But where in his own inquiry does he bring his earlier discussion of everydayness under the umbrella of the larger attempt to counteract the neglect of the question of being, such that the roots of the former can be graphed upon the latter and thereby, in the guise of "forgottenness," become a necessary ingredient in the Western *experience* of being. But what is it about everydayness as to be so ubiquitous as to suggest a pattern which we may typically experience being, even as philosophers? The pervasive characteristic of everydayness is a desire for complacency, for the status quo. Everyday Dasein, then, avoids questioning at all costs in order to secure a refuge for itself, regardless of what it does, understands, or interprets, in what is most obvious. The immersion in an everyday routine, for example, breeds a familiarity that makes it easy to forget, the appointment to which one would rather not go or even the whereabouts of the car keys that would allow one to drive to such a destination! And the familiarity of our involvement with the ready-to-hand is so emphatic, that it is only when the equipment malfunctions that we cast an eye in the direction of its being, the equipment become "un" ready-to-hand. And what this ease of neglect, indifference, and forgetting means is that, because of its ubiquity as pertaining to each and every being (*Seiende*), being (*Sein*) itself slips into an "obviousness" by withdrawing from consideration and short circuiting any need for inquiry.

---

**124** GA 24, pp. 460–461; tr. 322–323 (translation modified).

This obviousness becomes like the veil of being, which, in its withdrawal, shifts the focus of philosophical attention to beings (in their beingness) and relegates the former to simple forgottenness. At the close of section 42 in Part IV of the Kant-book, Heidegger brings into view the historical importance of inquiring into Dasein's finite transcendence (temporality), as the task of fundamental ontology, by stating: "The finitude of Dasein — the understanding of being — *lies in forgottenness.*"[125] Heidegger must have sought to capture with this statement, since he sets it off as comprising a single paragraph. He then remarks in the opening line of the next paragraph: "This [forgottenness] is nothing accidental and temporary, but on the contrary is necessarily and constantly formed."[126] But despite this parallel between Dasein's everydayness and what transpires in the philosophical tradition, why are the actual features of "obviousness" such that, one the forgottenness of being begins to take place, it becomes a downward spiral (*Absturz*) after that? And how does Heidegger's inquiry into temporality speak to this obviousness and begin to counteract the inertia of the neglect for the question of being?

We would be mistaken to attribute to Heidegger a privileged insight into the origins of Western philosophy. His strategy is instead to extrapolate from the magnitude of the contemporary neglect of the question of being to the historical circumstances from which an ambiguity, if not a confusion about being, both originates and sets a precedents for subsequent (mis-)interpretations. Indeed, whatever may have been the various scenarios for addressing being at the inception of Western thought, relative to its influence on the subsequent tradition, one approach in particular assumes prominence: Aristotle's concept of *ousia* as permanent presence. And, while some scholars argue that Heidegger simply rejects Aristotle's interpretation of being, his criticism targets instead the ambiguity surrounding the birth of the ancient concept of *ousia*. What exactly is this ambiguity? In conceiving of being as permanent presence, the ancients implicitly allude to time, but they do not question why this linkage should be so inevitable. But once the ancients forgo this initial line of questioning, the *first* level of neglect for the question of being arises. Given the lack of insight into the inevitable conjunction of being and time, the ancients then "fall" victim to a *second* level of neglect when the occasion arises to address the constitution of temporality. Rather than make concern for time the antecedent to any inquiry into being, the ancients proceed in the reverse order: they adopt an understanding of being that is already thematized through time, and then, once being has

---

**125** GA 3, p. 233; tr. 163 (translation modified).
**126** GA 3, p. 233; tr. 164 (translation modified).

been conceived as permanent presence, redefine time, as if by an afterthought, on the basis of this permanence.

But how does this dissimulation subsequently impact the genesis of the traditional concept of time? The problem with preconceiving being as permanent presence is that it "prejudices" any subsequent view of time in terms of the single temporal ecstasis to which it gives rise, e. g., the "present." "The being of beings obviously is understood here as permanence and constancy [*Beständigkeit und Ständigkeit*]. What projection is to be found in this understanding of being? The projecting upon time; for even "eternity," perhaps taken as the "*nunc stans*," is only thoroughly graspable as the 'permanent' 'now' on the basis of time."[127] On the basis of a preconception of being in terms of permanence, a controversy then irrupts as to which temporal model can best salvage the priority of the present: the continuance and constancy of the present under the ideal of eternity, or, in, recognition of the coming to be and passing away of nature, the opposite concept of transitoriness. Eternity and the "immediate and always present" [*gegenwärtigen*] are two sides of the same coin.[128] As the flip side of this vision of eternity, a linear concept of time as a sequence of "nows," which segments the movement of time into "before" and "after," is born. The philosophical tradition must then juggle two conflicting views of time, as stasis and transitoriness, each of which, however, stems from the same derivative root of time that privileges the temporal dimension of the "present." Once this dichotomy between the eternal and the transitory opens up, the tradition becomes hopefully entangled in a confusion about the origin of time which becomes increasingly difficult to resolve. For without the preliminary inquiry into time, and the prejudice in favor of permanence, the intimacy of our affiliation to time that could point back to its emergence through us, that is, its *finitude*, becomes obscured.

Without the reference back to finitude, the circular movement of temporality as conjoining future and past together in the tension of the present, gets lost in favor of the linear privileging of the "now." Once the finitude of death, for example, ceases to uphold the future as the primary direction from which temporality originates, the continuity of the present, in the name of permanence, then provides the occasion to erect the opposite as an ideal in the name of the "infinite." And then a further backlash to this distortion arises in which the eternal intervenes to sustain an idealized view of being, for example, Aristotle's unmoved mover or St. Thomas Aquinas God as the First Cause. And, to summarize

---

127 GA 3, p. 240; tr. 168.
128 GA 3, p. 240; tr. 168.

the levels of dissimulation, uncritical acceptance of the time's contribution in defining being as permanent present, the first distortion, then lead to a derivative (linear) concept of time on the basis of this faulty ontological interpretation, the second distortion. Given the tradition's entanglement in the second level of distortion, a dangerous situation emerges in which the forgottenness of being in terms of its link with temporality gives rise to an equally derivative view of time, in short, to a forgottenness of (our) forgottenness, a double dissimulation. In Part IV of the Kant-book, Heidegger provides as clear an account as anywhere in his writings of this double dissimulation:

> This [ancient] projection betrays the fact that: being means permanence in presence [*Anwesenheit*] ...
> But where is the *ground* for this spontaneous and self-evident understanding of being on the basis of time? Have we likewise only attempted to ask — in the sense of a problem which has *already been worked out* — why that is so and why it must even occur?
> The essential nature of time as first put forward by Aristotle in the way that has proven decisive for the subsequent history of metaphysics gives no answer to this. On the contrary: it can be shown that precisely this analysis of time was guided by an understanding of being that — concealing itself in its action — understands being as permanent presence and that accordingly determines the 'being' of time from the 'now,' i. e., on the basis of the character of time which is always and constantly presencing [*anwesend*], i. e., which strictly speaking *is* in the ancient sense.[129]

In the forgottenness of this forgottenness, Heidegger locates the precise historical point where Western *metaphysics* is born. Notice the title of the book that forms the cornerstone of our study, *Kant the Problem of Metaphysics*. According to the title, the possibility of metaphysics as such hangs in the balance, in regards both to the ambiguity surrounding its historical inception as an endeavor distinctive of Dasein. Metaphysics includes a positive connotation as an inquiry which challenges Dasein to engage in its own self-questioning, and a negative connotation as an historical discipline which spearheads the forgottenness of being. In the Kant-book, Heidegger plays both of these connotations off against each other, if only to illustrate the complexity involved in making the transition from the forgottenness of being to its recollection. While most of the Kant-book takes this positive direction, the detour toward the negative highlights the outcome of the tradition's "reversing" the temporal projecting-open of being. Specifically, when these dynamics are "reversed," the focus of "metaphysical" inquiry shifts from the dynamic of being's manifestation to an instance that epitomizes what is accomplished in the process, that is, *a* being. The subordination of being to a

---

**129** GA 3, pp. 240–241; tr. 168–169 (translation modified).

being, then, marks the inauguration of metaphysics as an historical occurrence. To describe the birth of metaphysics from this derivative origin, Heidegger points to the ontological difference as that which harbors the possibility for, and gives impetus, to the forgottenness of being. As an historical occurrence, the forgottenness of being then takes shape through the forgottenness of the difference between being and beings.

If metaphysics "begins" with "reversing" the projecting-open of being upon time, then the concealment of the ontological difference, which occurs simultaneously with that beginning, configures each and every subsequent "misinterpretation" throughout the entire history of philosophy. This fine distinction, between the birth of metaphysics and the transmission of its origin through the constellation of various historical periods, becomes important it we are to appreciate Heidegger's strategy for counteracting the forgottenness of being. For that forgottenness translates into various depictions of "being," each of which champions, in the name of the greatest philosophers, different conceptual formulas that to a greater or lesser extent distort its "meaning." But what all of these faculty interpretations have in common is the initial "errancy" or illicitness of the initial way of projecting being, such that the search for an exemplar of perfect presence dominates the entire history of philosophy. In this search, the activity of presencing becomes detached from what within the sphere of beings stands out most as abundantly present, and, as the recipient of all superlatives, occupies alone the privileged position of eternity. The supreme being (creator), as that from which everything else with beings derives its ability to become present (creation), then becomes the analogue of "being" (*Sein*).

In this way, Heidegger explains the various incarnations of being that thread their way throughout the entire history of philosophy. Ontology then becomes onto-theo-logy. But the fact that this transformation happens naturally and inevitably, however, does not diminish in any way the actual conflict which philosophers endure as either defenders or detractors of the Divine. A battle inevitably erupts in metaphysics, not simply between atheism and theism, but rather over the domain, whether supersensible or natural, eternal or transitory, from which "being" can best be determined. How can we justify and ground either domain? Appealing to a line from Plato's *Sophist*, Heidegger alludes to the "gigantomachy," the battle between and gods and the giants over the meaning of being. The passage from Plato's *Sophist* which opens *Being and Time* serves not as a decoration, but rather as an indication of the fact that in ancient metaphysics the gigantomachy over the being of beings had broken out. In this battle, the way in which being as such comes to be understood — however generally and ambiguously the question of being may have been posed there — must already be visible."[130] Throughout the history of philosophy, the battle wages on as philosophers assume different sides of a dichotomy, for example, of advocating the ideal realm of "being" or the natural realm of "becoming."

As these oppositions play themselves out throughout the history of philosophy, the ontological difference becomes increasingly forgottenness. Given the interpretation of being as permanent presence, the idealization of being in the figure of Aristotle's Unmoved Mover, or the Neo-Platonic One, or St. Thomas Aquinas's God, or even, in the modern shift toward the subject, the self-certainty of Descartes's *cogito*. When we arrive at Humean empiricism, the emphasis on the flux of impressions emerges as an extreme version of the ancient doctrine of becoming. We cannot discount these periodic swings to the other side of pendulum, even if the philosophers who propose them are adamant against metaphysics. And the fact that in the nineteenth century Hegel emerges to incorporate the dynamics of process into the a concept of the paraousia of Absolute Spirit, the mediation of time and eternity, only testifies to how entrenched the dichotomy between being and becoming is. Indeed, the supreme metaphysician and system-builder envisions the Absolute qua God as the apex of an historical process which unfolds through humanity's experience of conflict and its resolution.

Even when time seems to have a say in the metaphysical equation, as it does in Hegel's case, its dynamics are still sacrificed in favor of the determination of a being, of the Absolute Spirit in its infinitude. Thus, the locus of temporality through the individual's experience of finitude remains concealed. For all of his advances, Hegel, by rejecting Kant's emphasis on the limits of reason, retards than radicalizes the inquiry into being by disguising its connection to the problematic of human finitude. In section 45 of the Kant-book, Heidegger suggests that Kant's appeal to human finitude becomes like an echo bouncing off the corridors of Hegel's elaborate metaphysical system, which, while recalling a different path to investigate being, tends to fall on deaf ears. Indeed, Heidegger's way of opposing Kant to Hegel is an uncanny reminder of the risk that inevitably surrounds the inquiry into the meaning of being.

> What does the struggle against the "thing in itself," which started with German Idealism, mean, other than the growing forgottenness of what Kant struggled for: that the inner possibility and necessity of metaphysics... are preserved through the more original working-out and increased preservation of the problem of finitude?[131]

---

130 GA 3, p. 239; tr. 168.
131 GA 3, p. 244; tr. 171 (translation modified).

Because of its dependence on the dynamics of temporality, the forgottenness of being began as a flight away from and rejection of our finite natures. If we are created by God, and thereby possess an eternal soul, then our proper destination lies in shedding the mortal coils of transitoriness in favor of everlasting life. While serving only as an offshoot of metaphysics, this ideology of personal salvation nevertheless provides a huge obstacle to recovering the origin of temporality, as arising from the future and not merely the present. For the doctrine of the eternal soul obscures how temporality originates from the self's projecting-open its mortality (being–toward–death). And thus, as in Heidegger's case, the way back to the question of being, insofar as it can "turn-around" this tendency toward forgottenness, lies in initiating his inquiry from a point of departure that can show how falling into the tendency to flee death goes hand in hand with an indifference toward questioning one's being, and, conversely, how projecting-open one's death (temporality) recalls the clue to formulate the question of being.

> On the way to this goal of fundamental ontology, i. e., together in the service of the working-out of human finitude, the existential interpretation of conscience, guilt, and death becomes necessary. The transcendental interpretation of historicality on the grounds of temporality should at the same time give a preconception of the mode of being of that happening which happens in the retrieval of the question of being.[132]

Let us then consider Heidegger's strategy for "turning-around" the tradition's reversal of the relation between being and time, which goes under the controversial heading of "time and being."

## 2 The Overlooked Linchpin in Heidegger's Problematic

In titling the unpublished third division of Part I of his *magnum opus*, "Time and Being," Heidegger already implies some kind of change in the direction of inquiry, a "turning" (*die Kehre*), as it were. The turning, then, would enact a change in the priority of the two phenomenon that bear the title of his *magnum opus*, from "being and time" to "time and being." And yet in the intervening years, the amount of attention this "turning" has attracted, coupled with the confusion which has been generated by the scholarship on it, proves to be remarkable. Propelling much of this confusion is an easy criticism to advance, namely, that Heidegger never completed his task according to the plan he outlined at the close of the second introduction to *Being and Time*. Heidegger himself

---

**132** GA 3, p. 245; tr. 170–171.

lights the fire of this controversy when, in his "Letter on 'Humanism,'" written two decades after the publication of his *magnum opus*, he comments on how the "language of metaphysics" inhibited his ability to proceed along the path of this "turning" (to time and being).[133] Though the controversy which Heidegger scholarship tabbed "the turning" spirals out in many directions, the enigma itself originates with the aforementioned reference to "time and being." We are thereby led back to what might be called the "linchpin" in Heidegger's whole task.

Whether this linchpin can be found, a dichotomy emerges in the scholarship in which one side argues that Heidegger, through a mosaic of his writings, provides the missing pieces to "complete" *Being and Time*. Citing Heidegger's prefatory remark to the *Basic Problems*, Pöggeler points to its role in "'providing a new conception to the third division of Part I of *Sein und Zeit*.'"[134] And the other side argues that the "incompleteness" of his *magnum opus* bears the symptom of a fatal flaw, dooming his task from the start. In "Heidegger's Completion of *Sein und Zeit*," Michael Zimmerman appeals to the *Basic Problems* to trace the steps by which Heidegger expands his hermeneutics in order to address the "temporality of being" (and not just that of Dasein).[135] In "The De-struction of being and time in *Being and Time*," Charles Scott argues that Heidegger not only failed to complete *Being and Time*, he could not have done so, because the task was fatally flawed due to its reliance upon "transcendental-horizonal" thinking and its subjectively based conception of temporality.[136] By definition, Scott criticizes Heidegger's allegiance with Kant, although with the problematic implication that the "turning" would seemingly dismiss, rather than confirm, the importance of Heidegger's exchange with his predecessor. More recently, in "The Demise of Being and Time: 1927–1930," Theodore Kisiel argues that Heidegger took various stop-gap measures — of which *Basis Problems* is the foremost example — to complete a work whose transcendental premises doomed it to failure from the start.[137]

As divergent as these interpretations are, none explores how Part IV of the Kant-book outlines the historical setting within which we can *experience* the turn to time and being. That is, the turning transposes the focus of questioning from two distinct terms, "being and time," to the reciprocity between them, "time *and*

---

133 GA 9, p. 328; tr. 250.
134 Pöggeler, *Martin Heidegger's Path of Thinking*, p. 270.
135 Zimmerman, "Heidegger's Completion of *Sein und Zeit*", pp. 537–560.
136 Scott, "The De-struction of being and time in *Being and Time*", pp. 91–106.
137 Kisiel, *The Genesis of Heidegger's Being and Time*, pp. 189–214. For a critique of Kisiel's position, see Kalary, "New Access to *Being and Time*: Focusing on Friedrich-Wilhelm von Herrmann's Commentary on *Sein und Zeit*", pp. 183–195.

being," as echoed in the grammar of the conjunctive "and." Indeed, most scholars have overlooked the importance the Heidegger's that exchange with Kant plays in *tracing the turning around of the question itself*, and concomitantly, its re-emergence from the darkness of forgottenness into the light of recollection. And while the controversial "turning," as Heidegger addresses it in his later writings as well as preoccupies subsequent scholarship on this topic, takes on various permutations, the concern for the turning around of the question receives its most explicit formulation through Heidegger's exchange with Kant. Indeed, in his "Preface to the Fourth Edition of the Kant-book,"[138] Heidegger alludes to the unpublished division of Part I ("Time and Being"), as well as the task of "*Destruktion*" in Part II, calling special attention to the conclusion (Part IV) of the Kant-book.[139] At stake in these rather oblique references is not only the positive repercussion of retrieving Kant's task, but also the example which the corollary undertaking of its "destruction" provides for developing the historical character of the question of being and radicalizing Heidegger's hermeneutic task. The fact that in the "Preface to the Fourth Edition" of the Kant-book (1973) Heidegger 1) alludes to the "real question" left open in the third division of the first part of *Sein und Zeit*, and 2) singles out the importance of "Part IV" of the Kant-book for outlining the historical character of the question of being, underscores the significance of his destructive-retrieval of transcendental philosophy: "*Beiträge [Contributions to Philosophy]*: beginning to a new beginning (*Anfang zu neuem Anfang*)."[140]

Yet there is another issue pertaining to the incompleteness of *Being and Time* that is easily overlooked, namely, an indication not of its inadequacy or failure, but instead the loophole which is left open to misinterpret Heidegger's *magnum opus* as an existentialist work. The omission of the section devoted to the "temporality of being," as well as the Part II pertaining to the destruction of the history of ontology — of which the Kant-book offers one third of the puzzle — allows the existential themes to overshadow the larger ontological problematic of re-asking the question of being. As Dahlstrom points out, "The first book [Heidegger] published after *Sein und Zeit*, and presumably the first installment towards the projected completion of that torso, is *Kant und das Problem der Metaphysik (1929)*."[141] In *Mindfulness* (1938–39), Heidegger identifies this difficulty:

However, in the first presentation of *Sein und Zeit*, the actual "systematic" section of "Time and Being" proves to be inadequate, while external circumstances (such as the enlargement

---

**138** See Sallis, *Echoes: After Heidegger*, pp. 103–104.
**139** GA 3, p. xiii; tr. xvii.
**140** GA 3, p. xiii; tr. xvii.
**141** Dahlstrom, "Heidegger's Kantian Turn" p. 329.

of the volume of [Husserl's] yearbook) fortunately hindered the publication of the section in which, considering its inadequacy, I had placed little confidence. This section was destroyed, but it was immediately approached anew in a more historical manner in the lecture-course of the Summer Semester 1927 [*Basic Problems of Phenomenology*].

Nevertheless, viewed from the standpoint of these retrospective observations, "Time and Being," that totally inadequate section would have been at the end quite important if it were to be printed. This publication would not have let the misinterpretation of *Sein und Zeit* as a mere "ontology" of man and the misconstrual of "fundamental ontology" go as far as these misinterpretations have gone and are going.

... [t]he inquiry in the withheld section of "Time and Being" could have shown nevertheless what *Sein und Zeit* accomplishes, although what this work strives for is often enough *said* in what is communicated. For the inadequacy of the withheld section on "Time and Being was not because of an uncertainty concerning the direction of the inquiry and its domain, but because of an uncertainty that only concerned the appropriate elaboration.[142]

Does Heidegger then "complete" *Being and Time*? The answer lies in the fact that there is no simple completion or even failure of a work, but rather the tentativeness of taking up the task of thought and allowing that to become the occasion for the "turning." And so when we allude to the "turning," we speak of Heidegger's participation in a controversy historically handed down to him, in which he accents the interdependence between being and time which the tradition neglects. If the tradition assumes the fact of being's projection upon time (i. e., as "permanent presence") and then, given this assumption, misconceives time on this basis (as either the constancy or passing of the "now"), then a double neglect occurs. According to Heidegger, insofar as the tradition "reverses" the priority of the relation between being and time, then it is by undoing this "reversal" that the historical relevance of his own task comes to light. Beginning with the designation "being and time," Heidegger's own inquiry invites the change whereby the two terms are granted anew through their reciprocity with each other. Since the terms themselves remain the same, but the focus of priority is different, the radicality of that shift can only emerge by *transposing the relation between* these terms in the guise of "time and being."

Insofar as the reversal of the priority of the relation between being and time takes the form of forgottenness, the undoing of the reversal of those terms, reconnecting them in a more radical way, constitutes "recollection" or "remembrance." In this way, as Otto Pöggeler suggests, Heidegger raises the question, "at the end of the Kant-book, of how "error belongs to truth."[143] In two key passages from section 44 (Part IV) of the Kant-book, Heidegger makes explicit recollection

---

142 GA 66, pp. 413–414; tr. 366–367.
143 Pöggeler, *Martin Heidegger's Path of Thinking*, p. 75.

as a crucial stage in singling out the uniqueness of his task, not to mention as constituting a key stage in the history of philosophy.

> Rather, if the interpretation of Dasein as temporality is the goal of fundamental ontology, then it must be motivated solely by the problem of being as such. With that, however, the fundamental-ontological sense — i. e., the *only* guiding sense in *Being and Time* — of the *question* concerning time is first opened up.
> The fundamental-ontological laying of the ground for metaphysics in *Being and Time* must be understood as retrieval [*Wiederholung*].[144]

Toward the conclusion of this section, he then adds:

> On the basis of the philosophizing "remembrance" of the concealing projecting of being upon time as the innermost happening in the understanding of being for ancient and subsequent metaphysics, a task arises for a retrieval of the grounding-question of metaphysics: to carry out the going-back into the finitude of human beings which was demanded by this problematic so that in the *Da-sein* as such, temporality as transcendental primal structure, becomes visible.[145]

We might best characterizes this transition from forgottenness to recollection, at least as Heidegger outlines it at the close of the Kant-book, as a turning around of the question itself, the "dynamic of 'being and time' and 'time and being.'"[146] Although this characterization does not in any way exhaust the "turning," we can say that it stands out as a first indication of the turning's unique dynamics. What specifically transpires in this turning, as far as determining the "meaning" of being goes, still remains worthy of questioning. For what first comes to light is the emphasis on the conjunction "and." For it is grammar of the connective that directs questioning back to the "giving" of each, being/time, in its reciprocity with one another, as enunciated through the most primeval of all gestures: "there is/it gives" (*es gibt*) being, and, correlatively, "there is/it gives" (*es gibt*) time. These locutions help to carry out the turning as Heidegger describes it, by allowing an attunement to language to intervene and introduce the basic *experience* by which being can first become "understandable" to us and we can participate in its openness. There is understanding only in connection with such experience, because the former is predicated upon an openness that can only be granted through the latter. And that predication is simply the self-gathering of language, in and through expanse of openness, which we participate in due to our temporal

---

144 GA 3, p. 239; tr. 168.
145 GA 3, p. 242; tr. 169.
146 Emad, *On the Way to Heidegger's Contributions to Philosophy*, p. 112.

*natures*. As Heidegger states in his 1930 lectures on Kant: "The question of being (the understanding of being), and the question of time, are both questions concerning man, or more precisely, they are questions concerning the ground of his essential nature. This is especially so when we inquire into the co-belongingness of being and time, i. e., into the '*and*'."[147]

In a subtle way, language begins to make its impact and gradually enter the forefront of questioning. We should not be surprised by that, however, because the basic thrust of Heidegger's attempt to thematize the meaning of being is to call upon time as the key for developing the proper vocabulary for its expression. But what does proper or original imply in this context? We have in mind only the conjuring of the basic idioms which, because of their affinity with time, convey a dynamic to promote the disclosure, rather than the covering up, of being. Once again, the grammar of expression provides somewhat of a microcosm of this problem, insofar as the dynamics of being's disclosure imply a turn away from the nominative form in favor of the verbal mode. To be sure, a gap emerges between Heidegger's discussion of the temporal lexicon of being in the Kant-book and his inquiry into language in *Unterwegs zur Sprache*. Nevertheless, the explicit plan, as he later notes, for working out how time can provide the "preliminary name for the truth of being," becomes concretely executed through his ingenious retrieval of Kantian schematism.[148]

*The Kantian legacy is such that conceptualization of being must always be linked to the experience thereof, with temporality serving as the "go-between," the middle point of intermediation.* With time as the backdrop upon-which to project-open being, history emerges as the horizon within which Heidegger can re-enact this projecting. The circle of hermeneutic interpretation extends further to implicate, through the orchestration of Heidegger's exchange with his predecessors, the relevance that time has in determining the historical character of the question of being. But is being's disclosure through time, on the basis of Dasein's temporality, more than just accidentally related to history? If there is indeed a necessary connection, it is because the historical movement which is implicated in Heidegger's destructive-retrieval of the tradition also incorporates Dasein's innermost finitude.[149] Rather than following a model of linear progress, any advance which history makes is predicated upon a return to the origins. Only by returning to the origins, and appropriating them, can we anticipate again the possibilities hidden within them as they re-emerge from out of the future. History can then provide an

---

147 GA 31, p. 126; tr. 87 (emphasis my own; translation modified).
148 GA 9, p. 377. For an earlier translation, not based on the *Gesamtausgabe* edition, see Heidegger, *Pathmarks*, p. 286.
149 GA 3, p. 216; tr 151.

avenue of disclosedness, because it enacts a cyclical dynamic, which preserves who Dasein is only by placing it in service of a past still to be rediscovered in the future. By implicating the transitoriness of Dasein's sojourn in the world, history extends the expanse of openness by which we can *experience* that dynamic precisely in tension with its opposite, of the unconcealment occurring in tandem with concealment.

Insofar as history can stage this play of unconcealing-concealing, the arc of temporality widens in such a way as to annex the extreme poles of forgottenness and recollection, to juxtapose them as two possibilities which arise from the same origin. History chronicles the emergence of one possibility through another which, in the guise of the philosophical enterprise, allocates a period in which forgottenness reigns, reserving an occasion, however, for the pendulum to swing in the opposite direction and pave the way for recollection. Heidegger's thinking is not exempt from this historical conflict. Instead, it receives its impetus from, and guidance through, its immersion in history. Accordingly, Heidegger can *experience* the turning only as he pulls upon the thread which interweaves his own inquiry with history, the finitude of his own task. The turning provides the momentum whereby his inquiry can overcome the inertia of the forgottenness of being only given his "thrown-projection" into history. Thus, Heidegger's inquiry into being first becomes possible only when it is subordinated to this historical "claim" of a "thrown-projecting," and, ultimately, being's "enowning throw" (*der ereignende Zuwurf*).[150] His historical re-enactment of the question of being, then, has as its counter focus the locating of his own thought within history itself. An important transformation, that withdraws even from Heidegger's thought, becomes evident: namely, that the enactment of temporality can occur only in conjunction with a "place" (*topos*).

Indeed, history harbors its own presupposition about its linkage to a situation, the constellation of site (*Ort*) of disclosedness. And here a troubling, but nevertheless inevitable query looms large in Heidegger's re-interpretation of Kant, namely, that no matter how much we emphasize the priority of time, its ecstatic unfolding seems to be implicitly conjoined with space. Can an "un-Kantian" problematic be looming in the background of Heidegger's appropriation of transcendental philosophy? Or instead does an implicit allusion to space challenge us to undertake a further step in this destructive-retrieval of Kant? These questions will become increasingly prominent throughout the remainder of our study.

---

**150** For a discussion of this "enowning throw," see Emad, *On the Way to Heidegger's Contributions to Philosophy*, p. 159. For a clarification of this phrase, see von Herrmann, *Wege ins Ereignis: Zu Heidegger's "Beiträge zur Philosophie"*, pp. 18, 24, 30, 33, 36, 40, 56, 59, 62, 70, 77, and 92.

# 3 The Unthought Dimension of the "Play-Space"

Does the Kant-book provide any indication of this attempt to recast space according to the dynamic of time, even if the two are not yet thought in their essential interdependence and unity?

Perhaps we need look no further than that whose unfolding spearheads the destructive-retrieval of transcendental philosophy, the imagination. Indeed, to distinguish its *versatility* in both generating time through human finitude and then reconciling whatever can become manifest to these temporal dynamics (e. g., as the predicates of existence qua presence in time, substance qua permanence, and cause/effect qua necessary succession), Heidegger refers to the "*Spiel-raum*" of imagination. Literally, the word means "play-space," although it is sometimes translated as "free-space."[151] In either case, the emphasis on "space" points, however ambiguously, to coordinates which give breath and depth to Dasein's disclosedness. If only because of its own ambiguity, Heidegger appeals to imagination in order to mark the occurrence of this play-space. Imagination emerges as that extra-rational source which, not only implicates temporality, but does by embodying its capacity for disclosure and allowing language to serve this potential. Imagination can emerge as this play-space, because it provides an economy in which linguistic, disclosive, and temporal forces all converge and come into their own through their reciprocity with each other. Through this economy, imagination brings into play all the powers which are alternatively implicated in the hermeneutic exercise of interpretation.

The tasks reserved to hermeneutics and imagination, however, are not interchangeable, despite the fact that each may bridge the gap between concept and experience. As we will discover, imagination provides hermeneutics with a wider circle of possibility within which it can cultivate diverse interpretations of the meaning of being. In the *Critique of Pure Reason*, Kant identifies transcendental imagination as the power to "schematize" pure concepts, that is, to exhibit their meaning in concrete terms of temporality. As we have already seen, Heidegger deploys imagination in a more explicitly strategic role than even Kant does, that is, to chart the topography in which to uncover the historical possibilities for understanding being. By outlining imagination's creative potential, we can underscore the opened-ended character of interpretation. Indeed, interpretation assumes this form by forsaking one-dimensional ontological concepts in favor of diverse possibilities of being's disclosure. Thus imagination and interpretation remain distinct insofar as the former anticipates the change in contexts in which

---

151 See Churchill's translation of the Kant-book, p. 81.

the latter develops more nuanced philosophical concepts, for example, at the crossroads between thought and poetic expression. In these paradigms shifts we discover the contemporary relevance of re-examining the issue of imagination.

While interpretation presupposes an historical situation which houses what is pre-understood, imagination measures the breaks and ruptures in which the possibilities of understanding dormant in one historical period can re-emerge as prominent in another. Imagination, then, occurs at the cusp of the expansion and contraction of an horizon of possibilities, allowing for their appropriation and transmission in novel ways. In the Kant-book, Heidegger downplays the "reproductive" imagination as the ability to recall the previous stages in a synthetic act. On the contrary, it is due to its creative power to anticipate possibilities shaping the future that the "productive" imagination can supply the organization stem of finite knowledge, the a priori synthesis. As Heidegger emphasizes in identifying the root of the threefold synthesis of human knowledge: "Thus the third mode of synthesis [i. e., the future] also proves to be one which is essentially time-forming ... If the transcendental power of imagination itself forms time — i. e., allows time to spring forth — then we cannot avoid the thesis stated above: the transcendental power of imagination is original time."[152] The ability of imagination to shape the horizon of knowledge provides the clue that futurity is the primary temporal ecstasis, which determines the arc along which the other temporal ecstases of past and present arise. As an emissary of the future, imagination coincides with the projective movement of temporality, and thereby forms the horizon for understanding being.

In conformity with human finitude, temporality graphs the potential to understand upon the horizon of world, by schematizing new patterns of meanings as they translate the origins of the past into the possibilities of the future. If we associate the preservation of these origins with "tradition," then tradition is formed through their retrieval and appropriation. It is out of the place we occupy in tradition, and our involvement in transmitting/handing down (*Überliefern*) this heritage, that we first *experience the cyclical dynamic of temporality*. Due to its elusive character, temporality exemplifies the circular path of hermeneutics, animating the process of interpretation. In its mode of retrieval and repetition, the encircling dynamic of temporality, brings the act of interpretation into its own, rooting it in its finitude. As Heidegger recognized, however, temporality cannot be objectified and thematized. Rather than saying that "time is," it is necessary to employ such round-about locutions as "there is" temporality. This linguistic shift yields the path to a more radical development of hermeneutics, the doubling of its interpretive role in a way which fosters an original relation to language.

---

152 GA 3, pp. 188–189; tr. 131.

By enacting the movement of temporality, interpretation yields to the disclosive power of the word, graphing new levels of meaning on each other the roots of which reside in the ineffable, creative power of the word. The prospect of introducing innovation into language, the creative wellspring of imagination, already appears interwoven into Dasein's temporality. Innovation is not just novelty for novelty's sake. Rather, it involves transmitting and appropriating origins through their retrieval in those possibilities that re-emerge from the future. Even when these possibilities seem to remain latent, they still temporalize in the sense that their incubation sets the stage for rediscovering their relevance in still undisclosed ways. The singular, if not unexpected character of this disclosure, determines the novelty in question. And this dynamic of temporalization provides the soil for the fertility of language by commissioning the word to serve new possibilities for disclosure. By practicing hermeneutics, we becomes candidates for participating in being's possibilities for disclosure. Specifically, the act of interpretation allows what has been withdrawn previously to re-emerge and establish the relevancy of what we are addressing, or being, in order to convey the full depth of its meaning. As Heidegger states in his 1930 lectures on Kant, *"All philosophical interpretation is destruction*, confrontation, and radicalization."[153]

Hermeneutics can be radicalized only given a pre-understanding which allows what is "unsaid" throughout the philosophical tradition to invert and dislocate the expression of its own conventional wisdom.[154] Given this historical orientation, hermeneutic phenomenology opposes any attempt to present truth in univocal concepts. In his inaugural lecture upon assuming the chair at Freiburg in 1929, Heidegger emphasizes that his questioning can never be reduced to the more narrow aims of scientific method or positivism.[155] Yet a turn to sheer equivocity through an anarchical denial of all signifying patterns may not prove any more viable. Is a third path still available? From Heidegger's early interest in Medieval philosophy and Aristotle, we can recall the importance that the role of analogy plays in developing clues to articulate the manifold senses of being out of the context of factical life.[156] In light of radicalizing his hermeneutics, the relevance of analogy would lie not so much in providing a recipe for thinking, as in suggesting a "thought" experiment" within the overall strategy of destruction. In his 1930 lectures on Kant, Heidegger distinguishes the intersection between

---

153 GA 31, p. 168; tr. 118 (translation modified).
154 For a discussion of the importance of the "unsaid" and the "unthought," see Kovacs, "The Unthought at the Limit of Heidegger's Thought", pp. 337–355.
155 GA 9, pp. 113–120.
156 van Buren, *The Young Heidegger*, pp. 75–110.

hermeneutics and de-construction: "*Philosophical confrontation [Auseinanderset-zung] is interpretation as destruction.*"[157]

Such analogy would not be confined to the shadow of forgottenness, but would instead accentuate the tension of the double questioning of being. As hermeneutics circumvents conventional designations of meaning such as *cogito* and substance, the enigma remains how a stereotypical use can be displaced in favor of another which still points to the same theme (i. e., "being"), though with an unprecedented degree of subtlety. When discharged through this process of doubling, a traditionally signifying act is not locked into a linear line of reference; instead, such an act re-appears in the proximity to a limit which permits the emergence of a second, complementary meaning. In this way, the questioning that is in force allows language to carry the connotations of the conventional meaning but only *as* deficient. The coupling of a second meaning can then arise. This second meaning doubles in relation to the first; but now it indicates the same theme from another angle and with the addition of new nuances that avoid the narrowness of the first way of signifying.

We might characterize this approach as a "double analogy," or what has also been called "analogical differentiation" in light of Heidegger's early hermeneu-tics.[158] Most simply, analogy is a way to cross pairs of terms which seem unre-lated, only to allow the overlaps between one pair of complements to provide the bridge to establish the reciprocity between two other terms. Within this attempt at "destruction," a double analogy traverses the *chiasmus* between concepts estab-lished through conventional understanding and the retrieval of alternative mean-ings hidden within that metaphysical context. Mattéi describes this process as one of a "crossed articulation" of meanings.[159] A new, post-metaphysical context thereby emerges to break down metaphysical dichotomies which univocally fixate meanings. The change in contexts include more permeable boundaries in which alternative conceptual patterns can arise.

The transposing of these contexts — of the metaphysical and the post-meta-physical — explores alternatives for expression that previous thinkers have ignored. But are we, in the process, assuming a relation between truth (disclosed-ness) and language, as enacted through Heidegger's task of destructive-retrieval? In serving like an earthquake to loosen the layers of philosophical sedimentation, Heidegger's approach is inherently violent, as he first notes in the Kant-book. But his tactics also encourage a flair of philosophical creativity which breathes new

---

157 GA 31, p. 292; tr. 198 (translation modified).
158 van Buren, *The Young Heidegger*, p. 111.
159 Mattéi, "The Heideggerian Chiasmus", pp. 44–45.

life into worn out concepts. Such creativity is not capricious, however, but seeks a precedent which exalts in the possibilities of manifestation of the "thing itself." For Heidegger, the novelty of the occurrence of truth would yield such a precedent, and relocates the boundaries of meaning in a way that defers in favor of the self-showing of the theme or being as such. Under the auspices of destructive-retrieval, a double analogy emerges through the play of imagination, which circumvents the tendency to impose univocal structures or what Heidegger later describes as representational thought (*vorstellendes Denken*).

In opposing the same adversary, the innovation of double analogy and the play of imagination seems to complement each other. But if this is the case, then there must be some reciprocity between the powers discharged by each. While imagination is not inherently discursive as Kant realized, it nevertheless can contribute to the process of configuring new patterns of meaning. In Heidegger's case, the most overarching meaning of all — that pertaining to being and its disclosure — receives its outline through the movement of primordial time, which arises from imagination. We thereby discover an inevitable tension in Heidegger's retrieval of imagination in the Kant-book, of his attempt to follow out the dramatic implications of imagination as usurping the supremacy of reason. On the one hand, he approaches imagination as a synthetic power mediating between concept and intuition in an act of finite transcendence. Yet, his overall plan of dismantling transcendental philosophy is to point to two analogically related "meanings" of being, relative to the explicitness with which either is "translated" into temporal terms, e. g., as "permanent presence," versus the dynamic of presencing arising from its opposite, or absence. Thus, temporality's role in configuring the meaning of being develops not just on a single front of showing its emergence from time, but also on the adjacent front of implicating how temporality can provide for being's withdrawal or "non-presenc(ing)." Precisely because an interpretation of being builds upon the omission found in the other, there must arise on the abground of dismantling a kind of "place-holder" of negativity. In Heidegger's destructive-retrieval of Kant, imagination emerges as such a candidate, uncovering the horizon of transcendence to project-open the meaning of being and to overthrow reason as a traditional superstructure to fixate that meaning. In playing out this opposition, imagination ceases to be only a synthesizer and re-emerges as an "innovator," i. e., as a spring for developing new conceptual patterns and nuances of expression. Through its "play-space," imagination spawns new idioms beyond the traditional constraints of reason; and hence the openness sought in the play of imagination comes to fruition more profoundly in the receding depths of language.

How does the innovative play of imagination radicalize the hermeneutic question to translate the meaning of being into temporal terms? Most simply, imagination allocates a wider expanse of possibilities in which variations in being's potential to manifest itself can unfold. Through its encircling, ecstatic movement, time supplies the further impetus toward differentiation, which allows beings to be grasped thematically rather than vaguely understood in a pre-ontological way. The propensity of time to differentiate various conceptual patterns can be compared to an index which collects together the plurality of possibilities for articulation and expression. Interpretation (*Auslegung*) no longer entails only our meaningful comportment toward beings, but also includes a thematic level which outlines the boundaries of understanding (i. e., the "upon-which") as the field to articulate what arises still higher up, namely, being in its meaning(s). This interpretation evolves into Interpretation (*Interpretation*).[160]

By the same token, imagination emerges as the spring of the hermeneutical project, the stimulus to interpreting the meaning of being in new ways to match its diverse manifestations. Imagination thereby supplies the matrix of possibility from which interpretation receives its *open-ended* character. But are not then using the term meaning in an ambiguous way, that is tied as much to the semantic as to the ontological? What then, is the "meaning of meaning?" Once again, imagination provides the clue to how *meaning can maintain its ontological roots in disclosedness*, and yet exhibit a linguistic dimension as accenting different connotations of words. Given its emergence in a temporal spiral or ellipsis, imagination upsets any linear sequence of order in favor of blending possibilities "old" and "new." What we call "meaning" is a development which conjoins many different levels at once, allowing their intersection to unfold in both scope and depth. Meaning attains an "elasticity" in which the subtleties, permutations, and variations arise, not arbitrarily but by inscribing new levels of differentiation in the cyclical, retrieving movement of "stretching forward" and "stretching back."[161] The creative power of imagination thereby provides the occasion whereby "being" is lifted from its confinement to the proposition in the form of the copula ("is"), and transposed into a new relation in which the word occurs in partnership with unconcealment.

## 4 Reestablishing Distance within Proximity

In Heidegger's retrieval of transcendental philosophy, we find a concerted effort to wrench the question of being from its entrapment in modernity and to recast

---

**160** GA 24, p. 461; tr. 322–323.
**161** Schalow, "Imagination and Embodiment," p. 166.

that question from the wider parameters of its Greek, albeit, pre-Socratic begin-ning. For him, imagination marks the paradigm shift, the "crossing," from the inhibiting aspects of modern subjectivity to the liberating possibilities of a lan-guage beyond representational thought. Beginning with Descartes and culminat-ing in Hegel, representational thought rises on the shoulder of a specific disci-pline that becomes detached from its roots in the Pre-Socratic experience of *logos*, namely, logic. Logic attempts to capture the organizational structure of reason in rules and principles that already implies a platform of permanence that is anchored in a derivative concept of being as permanent presence. To challenge the supremacy of reason is also to supplant the discipline, namely, logic, that allows the rationality of human subject to monopolize the meaning of *logos*. The *logos,* is thereby divested of its power to disclose, truncating the nuance, ambi-guity, and richness of speech in favor of a presumption of order, uniformity, and representation. If the force of Heidegger's destructive-retrieval of Kant is to resurrect the imagination, then its resurrection must also signal the inevitable downfall of that the need for that discipline devoted to (the study of reason) or logic. At the close of Part IV of the Kant-book, Heidegger subtly points to the importance of this transformation: "This [retrieval of imagination] thus rattles the mastery of reason and the understanding. 'Logic' is deprived of its preeminence in metaphysics, which was built up in ancient times. Its idea has become ques-tionable."[162]

In the next paragraph, Heidegger then adds:

> Kant must have anticipated something of this collapse of the mastery of logic in metaphysics if you could say of the grounding character of being, of possibility (what-being), 'actuality' (which Kant called 'Dasein'): 'Possibility, existence [Dasein], and necessity can be explained in no other way save through obvious tautology if we intend to gather their definitions solely from pure understanding.'[163]

This is one instance where Heidegger quotes an intriguing, albeit obscure state-ment from Kant's first *Critique*, and then allows that obscurity to stand without much an attempt at clarification. Kant's remark, the quote within the quote, points to a perennial enigma about the meaning of existence/being and whether, as a pure concept, that determination can be drawn exclusively from reason, or whether it instead requires an allusion to that which bestows the power of signification upon all our concepts, namely, time. Kant, of course, elects the latter alternative, within the larger context of establishing the impossibility of proving

---

**162** GA 3, p. 243; tr. 170–171.
**163** GA 3, p. 243; tr. 171.

God's existence. When schematized, the pure concept of existence means to be "present" in time, in such a way that whatever cannot be potentially present – as given within a time-space continuum – recedes from the realm of knowledge.

Philosophers have often appealed to the modalities (possibility, actuality, and necessity) as avenues to address being, and yet for the most part these modalities have remained as obscure as they are important. For Kant, the modalities are especially hard to grasp because they are not explicitly discursive as categories, but are only indirectly so in conjunction with our intuitive natures. In this regard, Kant deviated from the canons of traditional logic, which reduce the modalities to structures of rationality, e. g., what is "possible" is simply what does not defy the law of (non)-contradiction. And precisely because of this "transcendental" strategy, Kant could criticize reason's presumption to know objects that lie beyond possible experience, and expose the illusions that rational metaphysics generates in transgressing these limits. Kant exposes these illusions, including the pretense to proof God's existence, throughout the Transcendental Dialectic. And yet perhaps it is ironic that the Transcendental Dialectic, which frequently occupies a backseat in studies of Kant, should provide the focus for one of Heidegger's most subtle readings of transcendental philosophy: "Kant's Thesis about Being" (1962).[164] Though Dahlstrom alludes to Heidegger's "Kantian decade" as the period between 1926–1936,[165] we cannot underestimate the continuation of Heidegger's exchange with Kant, and specifically the importance he himself attributed to the 1962 essay. The concern for being as existence, as Kant formulates it, questions whether existence is another predicate. Contrary to St. Anselm, who originated the ontological proof of God's existence, Kant argues that existence is not another attribute, but instead is the "positing" of an object (with all its attributes), as corresponding to the concept we have of it. As Heidegger summarizes the matter: "Kant's thesis contains two assertions. The first is a negative one, which defines to being the character of a real predicate ... In accordance with this, the positive assertion of the thesis that follows it characterizes being as 'merely the positing.'"[166]

While sparingly addressing the Dialectic throughout his many rejoinders with Kant, Heidegger remains true to a conviction he espoused in his 1929 conversation with Cassirer at Davos: "On the grounds of my interpretation of the Dialectic as ontology, I believe that I am able to show that the problem of being [as appear-

---

**164** GA 9, pp. 445–480. For an English translation, not based on the *Gesamtausgabe* volume, see Heidegger, *Pathmarks*, pp. 337–363. See GA 24, pp. 34–107; tr. 27–76. Also see GA 41, pp. 237–241; tr. 238–242.
**165** Dahlstrom, "Heidegger's Kantian Turn," pp. 330, 334.
**166** GA 9, pp. 447–448; tr. 339.

ance] in the Transcendental Logic, which for Kant is only negative in the form in which it appears there, is [actually] a positive problem ..."[167] That is, the Dialectic illustrates that even in the spurious pursuit of rational metaphysics reason still yields examples (e. g., antinomies) to articulate its boundaries and thereby implies another language to exact its own form of self-criticism.[168] With the exception of his account of freedom in his 1930 lectures on Kant,[169] Heidegger does not emphasize the resolution of the antinomies as such. He instead uses the strategy of destructive-retrieval to allow the exposure of specific errors in metaphysics to point the inquiry in the opposite direction, i. e., through the "modalities," in order to address being in its *difference* from beings. If only because of their inherent obscurity, Heidegger views the modalities as occasions to address how time contributes to our understanding of being, allowing for its articulation in terms of the ontological difference.

For Heidegger, the modalities (possibility, actuality, necessity) are crucial, albeit elusive, dimensions for distinguishing the *meaning* of being. In the Appendix to *Mindfulness* (1938–39), he cites his discussion from *Die Frage nach dem Ding*, pointing out that the modalities are like unfulfilled promises in the attempt to understand being.[170] Yet if the modalities are to direct us to this "meaning," no matter now obscurely and obliquely, the question becomes not only what they tell us but also "how." Indeed, they direct us not as explicit determinations of being, but rather as "gestures" that issue from the enactment of language itself, stemming from the roots of its grammar. For possibility, actuality, and necessity are themselves harbingers of the tenses by which conjugate verbs, of future, present and past. Kant has a vague inkling as such when, in his section on "Schematism," he identifies the schema corresponding to each pure concept, for example, of necessity as "existence ... at all times," that is, in a way that allows the significance of the past to pervade the entire spectrum of time.[171] Given the importance of schematism, Kant prefigures the need for thought to think being in terms of these three tenses that shape its expression, and hence always in connection with the dynamism of temporality. Ultimately, the modalities that Kant addresses are instances of these tenses, and, thus, because of their proximity to language, the most difficult to think. "We use 'being' to name it [the most elusive concern of thought]. The name names that which we mean when we say 'is' and

---

**167** GA 3, p. 275; tr. 194.

**168** See Schalow, "Kant, Heidegger, and the Performative Character of Language in the First *Critique*", pp. 91–106.

**169** GA 31, pp. 193–200; tr. 132–139.

**170** GA 66, p. 424; tr. 375.

**171** Kant, *Critique of Pure Reason*, A 145/ B 184.

'has been' and 'in the offing.' Everything that reaches us and that we reach out for goes through spoken or unspoken 'it is.'"[172]

Heidegger's reference to "being" in the title of his 1962 essay — which speaks to the Neo-Kantians who maintained Kant had no such "thesis" — may perhaps be somewhat of a misnomer. For the thesis is really about the ubiquity of time as it circumscribes the limits of determination and thinking as such. As Ted Klein remarks, "Heidegger's interpretation is right up to a point in his effort to establish that Kant's thesis can be defended on ontological grounds."[173] Yet it is just as important to realize that Heidegger is not defending Kant as much as showing how, by detecting omissions in his approach to being, we can still uncover a more primordial way to understand being through its reciprocity with time. Seen in this light, "Kant's Thesis about Being" is Heidegger's attempt to radicalize the "dialectical" strategy that Kant implements, in order to find in the exposure of transcendental illusion the clues to redirect thinking (*Denken*) to its proper boundaries. In order to link Kant's discussion of the modalities to a concern for being, however, it is necessary to establish a parallel between the critical task of the Transcendental Dialectic and Heidegger's own inquiry into being. As pertaining to Heidegger's question, the Dialectic places the power to understand/think within specific limits, providing an example of how the inquiry into being — including the possibility of our understanding of it — turns along the orbit of human finitude. When we question back to the Pre-Socratic origins of philosophy, the between being and thought are conjoined through a dynamic tension. Since modernity, however, the relation between being and thinking becomes particularly difficult to fathom; unlike for Parmenides, who first spoke of that sameness, the terms that comprise the relationship are equally opaque. "The guiding question for the metaphysical determination of the being of beings, 'being and thought,'does not so much pose the question of being, let alone find an answer."[174] The finitude of temporality that shapes human ex-istence, to which Heidegger appeals in order to re-ask the question of being, must also, when recast in light of the legacy of the Pre-Socratics, also yield the parameters of thinking. Within the context of a dialogue with the Pre-Socratics, as well as Kant, the Transcendental Dialectic speaks to the second issue, just as Heidegger's "phenomenological interpretation" of the Transcendental Analytic speaks to the first issue. In either case, the grammar of the three tenses yields the clue to the finitude of our ontological understanding, the need to understand being in relation to something else (e. g.,

---

172 GA 9, p. 445; tr. 337.
173 Klein, "Being as Ontological Predicate: Heidegger's Interpretation of 'Kant's Thesis about Being'", p. 50.
174 GA 9, pp. 479–480; tr. 363.

time). As a result, the counter focus of otherness, the "reserveredness" of the truth of be-ing, always retains an element of mystery in whatever insight we are able to attain.[175] *By reaffirming the problematic of finitude from that standpoint of thought as well as existence, Heidegger comes full circle to radicalize the strategy that Kant employs in the Transcendental Dialectic*: the reallocation of boundaries to define the possibility of understanding being. Language thereby emerges as the linchpin to connect two distinct axes simultaneously, of "being and time" and "being and thought." Heidegger's thinking thereby proceeds from a "being-historical per-spective," in which his *distance* from Kant becomes the focal point in his dialogue, as his proximity to Kant was initially.

By tracing philosophy back to its Pre-Socratic origins, Heidegger outlines the shift from truncated view of being as the copula or logical "position/positing" (*Position oder Setzung*) between subject and predicate in a judgment, to the transmission of its meaning through language as the abode for thought — as the self-gathering of a "place," i.e., for being's unconcealment. And insofar as language governs all thinking, any insight into being erupts through the transi-tory proclamation of the word. For this breakthrough to occur, thinking must continually cultivate the creative power of language, the unfolding of new idioms of expression in which to reinscribe the most perennial of all concerns, "being." "Kant's Thesis about Being," then, becomes less a reformulation of transcenden-tal philosophy as an exercise in how thought anticipates its return to the origins of philosophy, which as buried in the past can only re-emerge from the future. In concluding his essay, Heidegger ask about the status of presence as the tradi-tional "name" for being:

> What does presence mean here? The present? Where does the determination of such things come from? Does an unthought character of a concealed essence of time here show itself, or more exactly, conceal itself?
> If that is the situation, then the question about being must come under the heading "Being and Time."[176]

And what role does imagination continue to play, as we experience the turning from being and time to time and being, and, correlatively, the *historical distance* between Heidegger and Kant becomes more and more pronounced? Imagination resides at the crossing of hermeneutical inquiry into the meaning of being and the emergence of language as the abode of thinking as such. We must emphasize, however, that imagination cannot be a substitute for thinking (*Denken*) or super-

---

**175** See Emad, *On the Way to Heidegger's Contributions to Philosophy*, p. 64.
**176** GA 9, pp. 479–480; tr. 363.

cede its unique task. On the contrary, the role of imagination lies in developing the *versatility* of thought or its ability to unfold in new historical contexts. For example, Heidegger appeals to adjacent domains of religious and artistic experience in order to arrive at more innovative ways to address issues which have become congealed in rigid categories. Thus, the spiritual activity of *Gelassenheit* (Eckhart) suggests a more radical enactment of freedom as "letting be," while the work of art yields a clue to the dynamic event of truth as unconcealment.

As a blending of the old and the new, philosophy as a hermeneutical task of retrieval (*Wiederholung*) continues to evolve by honoring its beginnings. The appeal to imagination brings into play the most remote dimensions of future and past in a way that redistributes the boundaries of the philosophical task, that is, which charts a "topography" for the question of being. Because each historical age constellates a new set of issues, every thinker must face the dilemma of seeking meaning within the void of meaninglessness. Accordingly, imagination continues to have special allure for thought by recalling the conflict that breaks out in Pre-Socratic philosophy between the mythic forces of chaos and order. This conflict is one that has special importance to Heidegger, as he seeks to define what lies behind the interrogative spirit of philosophy, that is, freedom as a venture with and a leap toward openness. To address the ownmost (*eigentlich*) character of freedom, we must consider, not simply how it yields the impetus to act, but also how it sculptures out the arena of praxis, reclaiming it as a basic *modality* of our experience of being. How does this concern for freedom provide a new point of departure for Heidegger to re-implement his exchange with Kant? What do the issues of praxis, and its corollary, ethics, have to do with charting the landscape of philosophical inquiry, the *topography* that is born through the interdependence of time and space, i. e., "time-space"?[177] Let us now address the importance of these questions.

---

177 For Heidegger's discussion of this topic, see GA 65, 379–389; tr. 264–271.

# Chapter Four
# Praxis and the Experience of Being

The more we pursue the radicalization of Heidegger's project under the heading "time and being," the more explicitly we encounter the issue of language. The same might be said about the topic of ethics which, except with a few scattered references to Kant,[178] seems to withdraw into the background of Heidegger's hermeneutic phenomenology of the late 1920s. Is it more than an accident that Heidegger's apparent disinterest in ethics throughout *Being and Time* parallels the minimal degree to which language enters the forefront of his inquiry? And may it not also be the case, conversely, that only when his inquiry has explicitly shifted toward language can ethics also become prominent? If this is so, then perhaps we can locate a hidden path of ethical inquiry at a juncture where Heidegger addresses the disclosive power of language. By showing how these two avenues of inquiry intersect in Heidegger's destructive-retrieval of Kant, we will discover to what extent the practical, i. e., praxis, can contribute to our experience of being.[179]

I will begin by identifying the origin of Heidegger's concern for ethics, particularly as he addressed the foundation of morality which Kant sought to provide. Foremost in this regard is how the former pointed to the enactment of "self-responsibility" as the cornerstone of our moral obligation to others. Then I will unfold the implications, which a parallel inquiry into our "inhabitation" of language has for radicalizing ethics, i. e., by fostering our capacity to dwell on the earth. Finally, I will show how Heidegger's analysis of human freedom (as developed in his 1930 lectures on Kant) provides the key to translate Kant's concept of autonomy into the more concrete terms of self-responsibility, the initial step toward developing, an "original ethics." By recasting the *question of ethics* in this way, we will take the initial step toward outlining historical arena of the political as emerging along the *cusp of human freedom*.

## 1 Metontology and the Ethical Turn

As we follow the development of Heidegger's thought in the late 1920s and early 1930s, the tendency is to marvel at the brashness of his insights — emerging after

---

178 GA 24, pp. 199–201; tr. 140–141. Also see GA 26, p. 199; tr. 157.
179 For an excellent discussion of this topic, see C. Esposito, "Kausalität als Freiheit: Heidegger liest Kant", p. 101–125.

the so-called "break" in *Being and Time* — and yet be equally as *perplexed* at how he arrives at them. On the one hand, there is a tendency among Heidegger scholars to fall into complacency and accept the inevitable: that given the faultering of his own project, Heidegger had no other recourse than to abandon his hermeneutic strategy in favor of a more radical, albeit obscure, style of thinking. On the other hand, critics exploit this complacency in order to suggest that Heidegger compromised his philosophical mission in behalf of "turning" to a mythic-poetic brand of mysticism. But this is where the Kant-book allows us to question back (*rückfrage*) to the presupposition of fundamental ontology itself, the spark of the inquirer's interest in that enterprise, given the ubiquity of *everyday* Dasein's indifference toward philosophical questions. Within the context of Heidegger's exchange with Kant, to clarify this presupposition amounts to explaining what the latter took as self-evident, namely, the source of our "natural predisposition" to engage in metaphysics. What Kant in part construes negatively, Heidegger seeks to re-establish positively as a possibility which, *by placing the inquirer him/herself into question, speaks to his/her essential finitude.* As Heidegger states in Part IV of the Kant-book: "genuine philosophizing will only then be able to come upon the question of being if the question belongs to the essential nature of philosophy, which is itself only a decisive possibility of human Dasein."[180] As a possibility of human existence, philosophy finds its distinctive path by rediscovering its origin in freedom, that is, in the corresponding openness in which the inquirer participates by asking the question of being.[181]

How is Dasein, then, drawn toward this "natural predisposition" to engage in metaphysics, as it were, and propelled thereby, from the root of its finitude, to place itself in question? For Kant, there is a universal interest in philosophy, but that universality is assumed on the basis that each of us possesses reason as a natural endowment. Lacking throughout Kant's *Critique of Pure Reason* is the inquirer's own testimony of the relevance that philosophical questions have. Heidegger addresses this omission by directing his inquiry from Dasein's everydayness, in order that he can trace the emergence of a philosophical understanding from its pre-philosophical roots. Not only must the relevancy of the philosophical task be discoverable by each of us, rather than abstractly assumed; but that discovery must pose to the individual on a personal level, that challenge which philosophy already prepared itself to meet, in other words, the confrontation with the limits of finitude itself. Thus, in the second division of *Being and Time*, Heidegger illustrates the life (and death) situation in which Dasein not only

---

180  GA 3, p. 225; tr. 158 (translation modified).
181  See McNeill, *The Time of Life*, p. 76.

confronts its finitude, but testifies to its ability to do so. In the process, he also describes the catalyst of self- transformation, which prompts the individual to raise those philosophical questions that both address, and testify to, its finitude. Philosophy then takes the form of the question "why?", because that is the perplexity by which the individual first proclaims his/her finitude and attests to its willingness to take over its individuality. In addressing our ability to fulfill obligations, or the "can" corresponding to the "ought," Heidegger states in Part IV of the Kant-book: "Whosoever asks: What can I do? betrays thereby a finitude. Whoever comes wholly to be moved by his innermost interest in this question reveals a finitude in the depths of his essential nature."[182]

These various references to testimonials and attestations imply a relation to language that Dasein develops in conjunction with, and in service of, its own-edness (*Eigentlichkeit*). Such a relation would not simply give Dasein the ability to "parrot" words and maintain its relation to the status quo; but, on the contrary, would direct it toward possibilities by which it can discover its individuality and place its conformity to the status quo in question. Can we then identify a primeval act whereby the self, in the sway of its everydayness and yet in criticism of it, comes to be endowed with language? In response to this question, Heidegger points to the phenomenon of the "call of conscience" to distinguish the primary instance by which the individual first experiences language's capacity for disclosure. As one scholars states, "The call of conscience, which lies at the heart of human beings, is a showing-forth (*epideixis*) of this heart, a rhetorical revelation par excellence, whereby a call for ... decisive action is announced."[183] Specifically, conscience is the self's testimonial to its acceptance of the inevitability of its being singled out to confront death. The candidness of this testimonial, in disclosing the self, removes the presumption of Dasein's conformity to social expectations, to the dictates of the "they." The "they," however reinforces its position as representing the status quo through an exercise of discourse, namely, "idle chatter." In idle chatter, the "they" promotes the "sensational" character of what is said at the expense of confirming its veracity, sacrificing the disclosive power of language to its employment as an instrument of curiosity and rumor-mongering. By contrast, the call of conscience interrupts this tendency toward shallowness and indulgence, directing the self back to its individuality through an enactment of discourse that defers the penchant to speak in favor of the power to hear.

---

**182** GA 3, p. 216; tr. 151 (translation modified).
**183** Hyde, "A Matter of the Heart: Epideictic Rhetoric and Heidegger's Call of Conscience", p. 95.

As Heidegger remarks in the second division of *Being and Time*, "The call of conscience speaks by remaining silent."[184] The silence thereby commands the self's attention, awakening it to the claim of its own individuality, by cutting through the noise of idle chatter. The call of conscience thereby exercises speech in a primordial way, harnessing its disclosive power by prioritizing listening over saying. By heeding the silent call of conscience, the self becomes awakened to its own individuality, in order to cultivate those possibilities through which it discloses its identity apart from the expectations of the "they." The call signals the change which the self undergoes when it seizes hold of its identity from out of its falling into the "they." Yet we cannot underestimate the extent to which a primordial enactment of speech comes to fruition through the call of conscience. The silence of conscience speaks through one's unique way of standing forth within the "there," i. e., in choosing one's individuality. Through the temporalization of confronting the imminence of one's death in the future, and the renewal of one's commitment to be oneself from the past, Dasein heeds the silent voice of conscience. In this crucial and decisive moment, the caller and the called become self-same. The temporality of self-transcendence — the decisiveness of one's choices and the steadfastness of one's actions — conveys a message which cannot necessarily be said in words. Specifically, the individual who exhibits the greatest reticence can thereby speak the loudest, not through words, of course, but through actions.

While actions can be an alternative to speech, the former cannot simply replace the latter. An action is not simply devoid of intelligibility, for it is the self's way of disclosing its place within the world. Thus, in acting the self already draws upon its place within the network of involvements, i. e., the "wherein" of the world, and thereby projects-open its possibilities against that pre-articulated backdrop of significance, in order that these can be developed for the relevance they may hold (in unfolding) this specific situation. Cultivating those possibilities, which reconcile their relevance for unraveling (the predicament of a situation) with the self's exercise of choice (in owning up to its individuality), defines the interpretive dynamic at the heart of any action. On the one hand, speech or language elicits the presuppositions, attuned responsiveness, which give direction to and harbor the implicit meaningfulness of these actions. On the other hand, language re-enacts the projecting-open of this world-horizon, directing it back to its origin in Dasein's disclosedness itself. The individual's own act of speaking can thereby include, and be governed by, the referential whole allowing the speaker to participate in the larger expanse of what is disclosed. Due to this

---

**184** GA 2, p. 363; tr. 318.

participation, the speaker can exchange places with the hearer, as in the case of the call of conscience. The call of conscience thereby occupies a key place in Heidegger's hermeneutics, because it exemplifies the dynamic whereby the word enters into partnership with unconcealment.

The disclosedness in question both precedes and makes possible the unfolding of the instrumentality of involvements which defines the self's everyday interactions. In this regard, Heidegger distinguishes between the "wherein" of these involvements and the pre-understanding whose projecting-opening discharges the equipmental relations of the ready-to-hand and subordinates them to their relevance "for the sake of" a possibility of Dasein. The axis of understanding sustains the distinction between "owned" and "unowned," and, in respect to the former, the self can grasp who it is through possibilities distinguishing its individuality, that is, from out of the initial projecting of "that for the sake of" or the "can" of its existence. In this way, Heidegger makes explicit the exercise of choice, the "can be," which is presupposed in action. Thus, the self can seek guidelines precisely in concert with its capability of subscribing to them. Rather than simply being coerced by its circumstances, the self can be governed by the admission of those possibilities "for the sake of which" it exists. In light of this "for the sake of," Dasein can then fathom ways of relating to itself and others that circumvent the instrumentality of its use and the manipulation of equipment.[185] In this manner, the self can be bound precisely by those directives that correspond to its capacity for choice, and, indeed, which it "can" impose in its attempt to come to terms with its essential finitude. To paraphrase a statement which Heidegger makes in Appendix II of the Kant-book, Dasein thereby comes to determine who it is "from out of that for which it is freely *capable*, from itself and for itself as an ethical subject."[186]

A reference to the ethical implications of Heidegger's appears unavoidable. What becomes more problematic, however, is whether the similarities that arise between Heidegger account of the self's finite freedom and the Kant's ethics are more than accidental, despite the former's destructive-retrieval of the latter's practical philosophy. Does Heidegger explicitly advocate a Kantian ethic of the categorical imperative? Most scholars would argue "no."[187] At best, he would

---

185 Commentators have often dismissed too quickly Heidegger's interest in the ethical, particularly as it grows out of, his exchange with Kant. Often this oversight is due to focusing on narrowly on isolated texts, without considering the entire spectrum of Heidegger's writings on Kant. See Gordon, *The Heidegger-Buber Controversy: The Status of the I-Thou*, pp. 92–93.

186 GA 3, p. 262; tr. 185.

187 See Hatab, *Ethics and Finitude*, pp. 53–54. Sherover, however, supports a Kantian ethic founded on Heidegger's analysis of human existence. See Sherover, "Heidegger and the Reconstruction of the Kantian Ethic", pp. 527–532.

address the presuppositions for such an ethic, by divulging the individual's capability to be the recipient of, and to be bound by, obligation. In heeding the call of conscience, the self accepts the exclamation of its potential to be "guilty!"[188] The guilt, however, does not distinguish a mere deficiency of action or breach of conduct, but instead points to the self's invitation to own up to its choices, that is, to be answerable for them. The German term for responsibility, or *Verantwortlichkeit*, preserves this dynamic of responsiveness, which is implied in the call of conscience, as a reply to the solicitation to be oneself. Only because it is endowed with this capability, and can adhere to the very commitment it proposes, can the self exercise freedom in a way commensurate with its obligations.[189]

At least initially, exactly what freedom is and how to define, remains somewhat of a mystery for Heidegger, as it was for Kant. Indeed, Kant tied freedom to morality, because we could witness its "factual" occurrence only as the presupposition for a distinctive kind of action made possible through it, that is, the fulfillment of a moral mandate or obligation. In *Being and Time*, we find a similar circuitousness in Heidegger's approach to freedom. That is, the self first experiences it as a capacity by which Dasein can own itself through its actions only by embracing its finitude. The limitations which the self then confronts are not merely obstacles, but instead are avenues by which freedom comes to fruition in precisely those possibilities which speaks to the difficulties (i. e., predicament) posed by a current situation. As Heidegger states in his discussion of guilt and conscience in the Chapter Two of second division of *Being and Time*, "freedom *is* only in the choice of one possibility," that is, in dismissing others and having to do so.[190] While not endorsing a Kantian ethic, Heidegger summarily dismisses other modern theories, including Max Scheler's *Wertphilosophie*.[191] But on the few occasions where Heidegger does broach the topic of ethics, the emphasis on finitude provides the common thread that joins Heidegger's inquiry into with Kant's.

This Kantian influence comes to light, for example, in such statements as the following from Heidegger's 1928 essay, *Vom Wesen des Grundes*: "In this transcending that holds the 'for the sake of' toward itself there occurs the Dasein in human beings, such that in what is ownmost to their existence they can be obligated to themselves, i. e., be free selves. In this way, however, freedom simultaneously unveils itself as making possible something binding, indeed

---

**188** GA 2, p; 373; tr. 326.
**189** For an important discussion of this topic, see Raffoul, *The Origins of Responsibility*, pp. 7–15.
**190** GA 2, p. 378; tr. 331.
**191** See Schalow, "At the Crossroads of Freedom: Ethics without Values", pp. 250–262.

obligation in general."[192] We will wait until the next section to examine Heidegger's appropriation of moral praxis in the Kant-book. Yet, two years earlier in the *Basic Problems*, he provides a clue to his subsequent attempt, by showing how the binding character of the categorical imperative becomes possible through the self's capacity for freedom:

> The imperative [to treat humanity as an end in itself] is categorical, not hypothetical. It is not subject to an if-then. Because there is no hypothesis present here, no *if-then*, this imperative is categorical, if-free. As a moral agent, as existent end of his own self, man is in the kingdom of ends. End, purpose, must be understood here always in the objective sense as existent end, person.
> The *kingdom of ends* is the *being-with-one-another*, the *commericum of persons* as such, and therefore the realm of freedom.[193]

The fact that Heidegger invokes Kant's doctrine of respect for persons, and does so in the context of his third formulation of the categorical imperative, bears noting. In appealing to a realm or kingdom of ends, Kant identifies the specific domain to which the legislation of the moral law, the sphere of freedom, applies. That is, human beings experience freedom through a sphere that they inhabit, which is not determined by a rule of instrumentality or a means/ends continuum. On the one hand, Heidegger rejects Kant's attempt to split freedom and nature into separate realms, the former relegated to eternity and the latter to mere transitoriness. On the other hand, Heidegger argues that transcendental philosophy harbors the vestige of a concept of world, which demarcates the scope of each legislative realm and ensures their complementarity. In his 1928 essay *Vom Wesen des Grundes*, he shows how freedom and world arise equiprimordially together. Two years later in his 1930 lectures on Kant, Heidegger states: "The *problem of freedom arises from and as the problem of world.*"[194] For Heidegger, these two are intertwined, such that we experience freedom only insofar as we occupy a place within, or inhabit, the world.

Does not *Being and Time*, by discussing Dasein's resolute self-choosing and its solicitous concern for others, prima-facie already include a nascent ethic? Indeed, for all his reluctance to discuss ethics, he at least seems to leave the door open for its possibility. His approach to ethics remains inherently ambiguous; for it gravitates around a distinction which we must first clarify in order to arrive at a new point of departure for ethical inquiry. That is, our way of inhabiting the

---

192 GA 9, p. 164; tr. 126.
193 GA 24, p. 197; tr. 139 (translation modified).
194 GA 31, p. 209; tr. 145.

world, and the freedom that allows us to do so, comprises an historically rooted setting for our interaction with others, that is, an "*ethos.*" For Heidegger, then, the traditional discipline of ethics presupposes the *ethos*; and our inhabitation of it can be revealed only through a hermeneutic inquiry of being-in-the-world. In phenomenological terms our experience of freedom, by transporting us into the openness of being-in-the-world, provides us access to the *ethos.* Conversely, the *ethos* constitutes that phenomenon which, paradoxically, traditional ethics cannot gain access. For an offshoot of metaphysics, traditional ethics overlooks the problematic of world and hence adopts abstract concepts about freedom as an operation of the will (e.g., volition) which clashes with natural impulses of desire.

We can arrive at the *ethos*, then, only through a counter movement of inquiry which begins from our thrownness into the world and brings the inquirer him/ herself into question as overwhelmed by the manifestness of beings themselves. In Part IV Four of the Kant-book, Heidegger points to the "moment" of Dasein's entry into the world as a "self-surrender" to the manifestness of beings into which it is thrown.[195] He then makes one of his most provocative statements: "... man is the there [*das Da*], ... the opening irruption into beings[s] so that it can show itself as such for a self. *More original than man is the finitude of the Dasein in him.*"[196] In commenting on this extraordinary passage, Gadamer remarks:

> Already in the book on Kant, which appeared in 1929, the task was no longer of the Dasein of a human being but suddenly of the "the Da-sein in a human being." The question concerning being and its "Da," which Heidegger had gleaned from the Greek *Aletheia* (unconcealedness), could no longer be missed. This was no revival of Aristotle. Rather, this was a thinker who had been preceded not only by Hegel but also by Nietzsche, and who reflected back upon the beginning, upon Heraclitus and Parmenides, because the never ending interplay between disclosing [*Entbergung*] and concealment [*Verbergung*] and the secret of language, in which both idle talk and the 'sheltering' [*Bergung*] of truth occurred, had unfolded before him.[197]

Through its irruption into the "there," the self is transposed into the open expanse of possibilities, thereby acquiring the power to choose in proportion to the unconcealment it serves. To choose, then, is to bring possibilities to bear on a situation, unfolding it within the widest expanse of openness in which self and other can stand, not as separate egos, but in a relationship of reciprocity. The

---

**195** GA 3, p. 160; tr. 229.
**196** GA 3, p. 229; tr. 160.
**197** Gadamer, *Heidegger's Ways*, pp. 116–117.

turning back of the question back into the median of Dasein's stance within beings, "overturning" fundamental ontology, Heidegger calls "metontology."

In his 1928 lectures on logic, which parallel *Vom Wesen des Grundes*, Heidegger summarizes this development by which we allow the question of being to well up in us through the query "why?". "This new investigation resides in the essence of ontology itself and is the result of its overturning [*Umschlag*] ... I designate this set of questions *metontology*. And here, in the domain of metontological-existentiell questioning, is the domain of the metaphysics of existence (here the question of an ethics may properly be raised for the first time)."[198]

Metontology outlines the transformation of fundamental ontology, as it were, the turn within the turning. The axis of inquiry shifts from addressing Dasein's understanding of being to what becomes possible through it, the diversity of being's manifestation. In connection with Dasein's thrownness into a situation, its inhabitation of the "there," Dasein stands both in proximity to and at a distance from itself and others. As Heidegger states in the closing paragraph of *Vom Wesen des Grundes*:

> And so the human being, existing as a transcendence that exceeds in the direction of possibilities, is a *creature of distance*. Only through originary distances that he forms for himself in his transcendence with respect to all beings does a true nearness to things begin to arise in him. And being able to listen into the distance awakens Dasein as a self to the response of the other Dasein in whose company [*Mitsein*] it can surrender its I-ness so as to attain itself as an owned self.[199]

The distance that Dasein traverses in its transcendence brings its self before the freedom of that for the sake of, in order that it can act in behalf of the welfare of others.

Transcendence is essentially a temporal process. Yet as far as its contribution in defining the dynamics of Dasein's interaction with others goes, transcendence implies the deployment of spatial coordinates to outline the expanse of a situation. In the metontological context of the *ethos*, a concern for the allocation of space becomes worthy of question. We might pause to ask why this is so. Rather than appealing to the instrumentality of our use of equipment (ready-to-hand), or even their objectification as theoretic objects of knowledge (present-at-hand), we look to the intricacies of our interaction with others to explore the dynamism of space. In discussing world in Chapter Three of the first division of *Being and Time*, Heidegger addresses the spatiality of circumspective concern by which Dasein

---

198 GA 26, p. 199; tr. 157.
199 GA 9, p. 175; tr. 135.

establishes a nexus of interrelationships in its use of the ready-to-hand. He also distinguishes the derivative character of space conceived physically and mathematically as a determinant of the properties by which scientists formulate universal principles about nature, for example, the Newtonian laws that Kant gives a metaphysical grounding. The practical dimension of the former, or "lived-space" — which forms the basis for the preconception of the latter (as an abstraction) — includes as part of its fabric our engagement with others. We can distinguish this further dimension of practicality as the acting in response to the welfare of others, or praxis as such.

Because space and time are both preconditions of experience, and the initiation of moral action through a spontaneous cause (freedom) seems to originate outside the experiential realm, Kant narrows the descriptions of space, as well as time, to their roles in organizing our experience to physical objects in conformity with Newton's laws. In *Die Frage nach dem Ding*, Heidegger describes this way of pre-establishing the field of experience the "mathematical project" of nature.[200] But, "knowing," as Heidegger argues in *Being and Time*, is a "founded" way of being-in-the-world.[201] This argument proceeds from a different hermeneutic pre-concept that inverts the priority of theory, and retrieves the world as the interactive field of practical involvements (the solicitude of being-with-others and the circumspective concern of being-alongside the ready-to-hand). By making the phenomenon of world primary, Heidegger avoids the modern tendency to reduce space to a theoretical abstraction, for example, as a form of measurement. In stark contrast with Kant, Heidegger then re-examines space in its "practical" dimension as contributing to the dynamic whereby we inhabit the world. Thus, space pertains most fundamentally not to the being of things, either ready-to-hand or present-at-hand, but, on the contrary, to the being of the self and its relation with others. In section 70 of *Being and Time*, Heidegger seems already concerned about problems of following Kant's precedent of privileging time, as the precondition of all mental as well as psychical experience. "If Dasein's spatiality is 'embraced' by temporality in the sense of being existentially founded upon it, then the connection between them ... is also different from the priority of time over space in Kant's sense."[202]

Time and space play off each other in forming a dynamic in which the self reclaims its individuality in struggling again the tendency to become dispersed and fragmented.[203]

---

200 GA 41, pp. 91–97; tr. 90–96.
201 GA 2, pp. 80–84; tr. 86–90.
202 GA 2, pp. 486–487; tr. 418. See Sherover, *From Kant and Royce to Heidegger*, pp. 114–115.
203 In his 1962 essay "Time and Being," Heidegger reflects back upon a parallel difficulty he encountered in his effort to re-think the interdependence of temporality and spatiality: "The

Spatiality distinguishes the "wherein" of this struggle, which allows for these dispersing and fragmenting elements. But spatiality also pertains to the trajectory whereby the self rediscovers its uniqueness, both in the practicality of taking up residence in the world and acting to benefit others. The counterpoint that time "individualizes," as Heidegger suggests, is that it also brings us, in conjunction with space, into a world that we co-occupy with others. "So while time as the horizon of being possesses the broadest breadth, it concentrates the breadth in the question concerning man's individualization. Not man as one of many present cases, but man in his individualization, i.e., in each case the individual as individual."[204] On the one hand, it is only through the differentiation of individuals that we have the possibility of a community. On the other hand, the community provides the fabric in which individuals can experience their intimacy with one another and thereby also pursue their possibility of selfhood.

> Everybody has his time. We have our time with one another. Do we all possesses it in some loose way — our time, my time — such that we can cast it off at will? Or do we each of us possess our own proper portion of time? Do we each of us partake of time, or is it much more that we ourselves are possessed by time? And this not just in the indefinite sense that we cannot take leave of time, that we cannot escape its fetters, but such that time as in each case our time individualizes each one of us to his own self … So long as we do not see that time fulfils its ownmost as temporal only by in each case *individualizing the human being to himself, temporality as the ownmost of time* will remain hidden.[205]

The individuation of time also implies the multiplying of possibilities by which individuals can occupy a world, and hence the distinctness of a space in which to reside, e.g., a house or a farm.

Space is not simply a given, but, in conjunction with time (*Zeit-Raum*), exacts a challenge of making it one's own, of appropriation, as in becoming rooted in a vicinity, in a neighborhood, or in a home. Likewise, the inhabitation of a home is not something we can take for granted. Rather it is a task which, since it evokes a response of ownedness, simultaneously poses the question of how we stand toward being. In his lecture-course from 1942, the *Basic Concepts*, Heidegger begins to think more originally how space defines our potential to inhabit the world, i.e., to be "owned-over" (*Übereignet*) to being through this inhabitation. "We reside in the realm of being and yet are not directly allowed in. We are, as it

---

attempt in *Being and Time*, section 70, to derive spatiality from temporality is untenable." See Heidegger, "Time and Being", p. 23. Also see Thomä, "*Being and Time* in Retrospect: Heidegger's Self-Critique", pp. 217–220.

**204** GA 31, p. 129; tr. 90 (translation modified).
**205** GA 31, p. 129; tr. 90 (translation modified).

were, homeless in our ownmost homeland."[206] Even the self's incarnality, or way of becoming at home through its embodiment, requires ownedness, i. e., a movement of "coming into one's own." As we who are further along in years recognize, health and fitness are not givens, but instead constitute tasks that each of us must undertake with increasing vigilance.

Through its appropriation of space, Dasein first begins to experience the *ethos*, to take up residence within it. But does not the self already reside in the *ethos*? We might ask if the self is already inclined to be ethical? In either case, whatever has been granted to it, Dasein must still grapple with the challenge of taking ownership of its situation, and that means first and foremost administering to the freedom with which it is endowed. Because freedom is finite, the self can as easily relinquish the power with which it is endowed as develop it. Thus the concrete possibilities through which Dasein experiences its freedom expand and contract, in such a way as to anticipate changes in the "wherein" of its situation, giving it both depth and breadth. The "wherein" of Dasein's world is not merely an environment of conquest and survival, but instead is like the environs or surroundings "graphed upon" a "play-space" of expanding and contracting possibilities. A "geo-graphics" then belongs to being-in-the-world as the way in which the self sculptures out a place in which to reside.

An enactment of space is already implied in the ecstatic trajectory of Dasein's transcendence. If only in name, the temporal ecstases themselves suggest vectors of directionality, an outsidedness through which the self can enter the open expanse of possibilities. In *Being and Time*, Heidegger restricts his discussion of space to how Dasein' monitors the availability of the equipment it uses. The environmentally gauged vectors of near and far, of proximity and distance, help to configure the "wherein" of the world as Dasein locates itself in relation to each instrument's position within a nexus of equipment, e. g., hammer, nail, wood. Yet the determination of space through (the field of) Dasein's circumspective concern is an important enactment, but not the only one, thereof. But what about a spatiality that extends breadth not only to the environment in which we use equipment, but also the depth to our interaction with people? Indeed, the possibility of the self's individuation also implies the distribution of individuals within a community, so that each distance and intimacy suggests the locales that people occupy in assuming relationships with each other. And thus it is not only within the environment of using equipment (circumspective concern), as Heidegger discusses in Division I of *Being and Time*, but also the *ethos* of being-with-others (solicitude), that Dasein comes to allocate space through its inhabitation of the world.

---

206 GA 51, pp. 88–89; tr. 75.

Critics like Emmanuel Levinas who question Heidegger for overlooking the importance of ethics, and subordinating it to ontology, may themselves overlook an important ontological corollary of the "metontological turn" in the direction of ethics.[207] By annexing the metontological domain of the ethical, Heidegger brings the importance of space itself into question. Space not only involves the presumption of our existing "alongside" others, the ready-to-hand, and nature. But that alongsideness is only a signpost on the way to a larger question of how we "inhabit" the "wherein" of this world. Such inhabitation implies a task of becoming at home, which colors not only our response to the welfare of others (solicitude), but, through the solicitous administering of the *ethos* as a place of dwelling, our response toward nature (and our animal counterparts) as well. Would it not be ironic if Heidegger, despite all the criticism he takes for discounting the importance of an ethic of the other, *were to sow the seeds for an even richer ethic of the "trans-human?"*[208]

## 2 Saying and Doing

Other than the German ancestry each held in common, an enigma still remains as to why Heidegger found Kant's ethics to be especially compelling. As outlined above, the relevance that a specific situation has for the enactment of finite decisions, much less our manner of inhabiting the world (*ethos*), seems to suggest a problematic quite alien to Kant's. Indeed, in identifying ethics with the *ethos*, Heidegger recalls a Greek origin of which Aristotle would be the best example. The Aristotelian emphasis on habit as a pre-understanding of the good, deliberation as a choice of the proper option, and the "mean"as a way of balancing these two components of action, implies a concrete setting for ethical life. But the concrete development of ethics out of the facticity of life-experience, so prominent in Aristotle's *Nicomachean Ethics*, appears lost in the abstract dichotomies that Kant inherits from modern philosophy — freedom vs. the necessity of nature, mind vs. body, will vs. desire, individual vs. society.

As an Enlightenment figure, Kant struggled with the problem of how human beings could be subject to a moral authority that was not imposed externally from without, e. g., the sphere of religion or politics. For example, even while Kant embraced the precepts of Christian pietism, he did not want to base the legislation on morality upon it. He instead sought an independent, neutral foundation for

---

207 Levinas, *Collected Philosophy Papers*, p. 52.
208 Llewelyn, "Prolegomena to Any Future Phenomenological Ecology", p. 65.

morality in universal principles of reason that would be equally binding on everyone. These principles did not presuppose a Christian theodicy in which, according the narrative of Scripture, the force of good prevails over that of evil. Theist and atheist alike could subscribe to Kantian morality.[209] For Kant sought a direct link between the origin of moral authority, and the ability to submit to it, so that the moral standard and capacity to follow it, could derive from reason. Through his "Copernican revolution in ethics," Kant maintained that the law's capacity to bind each of us equally determines the (concept of) the good, rather than the reverse.[210] Given that the standard of goodness and its legislation would be complementary, the proclamation of morality and the acts which exemplify it would be inherently consistent. Put in simple terms, there would be no deviance between the moral ideals we proclaim and the deeds we perform, no room for hypocrisy.

To be sure, Heidegger may not have been concerned about the social climate which bred hypocrisy. Yet he was acutely aware of Kant's innovation in emphasizing the freedom which disposes us toward the good, apart from religious authority, as the following passage from the *Basic Problems* attests. Paraphrasing a line from the "Dialectic" of the *Critique of Practical Reason*, Heidegger states: "Man exists as an end in himself; he is never a means, not even a means for God; before God, too, he is his own end."[211] In Kant's words, "[man] is never to be used merely as a means for someone (even for God), without at the same time being himself an end."[212] In an analogous way to Kant, Heidegger was interested in how the self could avoid the deceptions inherent in relying upon external authority (whether social or religious), and could instead affirm the possibility of its own freedom. Heidegger's portrait of resoluteness and Kant's account of the self-legislation of the moral law, suggests parallels between each thinker's concept of freedom which, as we have already seen, are more than coincidental. In Kantian morality, Heidegger uncovers a particularly compelling allusion to the "facts," which pertains more to the formulation of moral claims, to the "motives" for subscribing to them, and to finitude to which they attest, rather than to their actual content. What Kant himself saw was a curious "fact" that the actions are themselves declarations of words, because they exhibit the extent to which the self exercises its freedom. And, conversely, the formulation of the maxims by which we act is it itself an occasion of speech, for it is only through their expression that we can weigh the "consistency" of the maxims and evaluate their

---

**209** Kant, *Religion within the Limits of Reason Alone*, pp. 55–72.
**210** See Silber, "The Copernican Revolution in Ethics: The Good Re-Examined", pp. 266–268.
**211** GA 24, p. 192; tr. 136.
**212** AA 5, KpV, p. 132; tr. 136.

legitimacy as "grounds." According to Heidegger, the fact that morality seeks "grounds" for its actions is an insight that both Kant and Aristotle shared, despite proceeding from different premises about human nature. In his 1922 lectures on ancient philosophy, Heidegger suggests that Kant could successfully establish a "foundation for morality" because he, like Aristotle, saw that *language held the clue to the synergy between expressing and following moral principles.* As Heidegger emphasizes in his lecture course, *The Basic Concepts of Ancient Philosophy*, Aristotle recognized that the being who is capable of speaking (*logos*) is also capable of acting.[213] "'This very same determination of human being turns up again in Kant: the human being that can speak, that is, act with grounds.' As Franco Volpi points out in commenting on this passage: "'This very same determination of human being turns up again in Kant: the human being that can speak, that is, act with grounds.' The equation of 'speak' and 'act with grounds' should be noted here — a hint for interpreting the existential called 'discourse.'"[214]

Where Kant more or less assumed this commensurability, Heidegger traces its origin back to the factical, life experience by which the individual occupies its *ethos*. And the self becomes a resident when it is disclosed in such a way that it counters the "hypocrisy" of the status quo, and, in the process, reclaims or "renews" the commitment that leads it to act in the first place. The dynamic of subscribing to what summons us becomes the formal indicator for what Kant upheld as key to the self-legislative employment of the categorical imperative. For Heidegger, the call of conscience performs a "double duty," not to use a Kantian pun, in which to act is to respond, formally indicating the relation which holds between the claim of freedom and the binding character of any moral principle. As Kant emphasizes, it is only through the freedom which allows one to be bound by the claim of oneself that one "can" be prepared to act in behalf of its obligation to others. "Only because Dasein can expressly choose itself on the basis of its selfhood can it be committed to others."[215] What Kant does not himself see, however, is that we occupy an *ethos*, including our being-with-others, insofar as freedom is interwoven with the very proclamation of these claims. Hence our occupation of an *ethos* goes hand in hand with our inhabitation of language. As Steven Crowell suggests, the call of conscience is the formal possibility of *expressing* the binding character of our obligations.[216] That is, we rise to an ethical plane — above the arbitrariness of acting on behalf of expedient ends — through

---

213 GA 22, p. 188 (note 174); tr. 157, 230.
214 Volpi, "*Being and Time*: A 'Translation' of the *Nicomachean Ethics*?", p. 210.
215 GA 26, p. 245; tr. 190.
216 Crowell, "Subjectivity: Locating the First Person in Heidegger's *Being and Time*", p. 134.

the example of the "authority" we ourselves embody in accord with our potential to convey or communicate the grounds or justification for our actions.

Though Kant does not emphasize the *ethos*, its importance nevertheless pervades his entire inquiry into ethics. Where, then, in his ethics do we find an entryway into the *ethos*, the vicinity, as it were, where the other can emerge as someone to whom I am obligated? In light of what allows for membership in the kingdom of ends, my respect toward the moral law, and its translation into respect for others, points to this vicinity. We must also include self-respect, for only when predisposed in this way can the individual honor the moral law and its mandate to treat others as ends in themselves. *This threefold relationship of respect for the law, respect for self, and respect for others, establishes the coordinates to map out the nexus of obligations that constitutes a kingdom of ends.* The kingdom of ends comprises an *ethos* in which all maxims harmonize, allowing for the transitivity of obligation in which each person can stand in a relationship of *reciprocal respect* toward the other. In this way, the other is granted a space in which his/her uniqueness can pose an obligation to me and I, likewise, can heed the welfare of the other.[217] As Heidegger remarks in his debate with Cassirer in Davos in 1929:

> Cassirer wants to show that finitude becomes transcendent in the ethical writings. In the categorical imperative we have something which goes beyond the finite creature. But precisely the concept of the imperative as such shows the inner reference to the finite creation ... The inner relation, which lies within the imperative itself, and the finitude of ethics, emerges from a passage in which Kant speaks of human reason as self-supporting, i. e., of a reason which stands purely on its own and which cannot escape into something eternal or absolute, but which also cannot escape in the world of things. This being-among-[others] is the ownmost dimension of practical reason.[218]

These coordinates or topographical indices of the *ethos* imply an allocation of space which is alien to Kant. Due to omitting the problematic of world, he subordinates the experience of lived-space to a model of geometrical space. In occupying the play-space through the trajectory of its transcendence, the self stands toward itself, or is oriented in this way, as to be inherently spatial as well as temporal. In discussing the self's transcendence in the Kant-book, Heidegger makes another cryptic allusion to the importance of space as a necessary addendum to temporality. The self-relatedness of the individual, or its capacity for to be

---

**217** For a discussion of the reciprocal sense of responsibility, see Nelson, "Heidegger and the Ethics of Facticity", pp. 129–147.
**218** GA 3, p. 279; tr. 196 (translation modified).

"affected" in and by its existence, is such that "like time, space in a certain sense also belongs to the self as something finite, and that this [self], on the grounds of original time to be sure, is essentially 'spatial.'"[219] The affectivity of the self implies the "lived" dimension where it becomes responsive to all that factical elements that pertain to our embodiment, e. g., emotions and feelings. A further radicalization of fundamental ontology, or metontology, is required in order to address the concrete dimensions of live-spaced.

Through the shift to metontology, Heidegger brings the concern for "lived-space" into the foreground, allowing the dimensionality of our occupation of the *ethos* to emerge, which is otherwise concealed in most views of the moral agent as a harbinger of the will. But if it is lived space we are discussing, and it arises in conjunction with the *ethos*, then as situated, spatial beings are we not already embodied? The fact we encounter others means that each of is factically instantiated and differentiated with regard to our thrownness as situated beings. The other stands out in a reciprocal relation to me by virtue of the mutuality of our embodied conditions, that is, as extending the capability to participate in the expanse of openness. And the capacity stems from how the other and I co-occupy a world together, namely, through our common inhabitation of language. In terms of the *ethos*, I allow the other to address me through what simultaneously conveys the finitude of my embodiment, my power to hear. For Heidegger, hearing is not merely an auditory sensation. Instead, it is an attunement that is disposed to heed the other, to stand in reciprocity to him/her, precisely by transposing me into the expanse of openness where I can first answer to myself and become responsible. Thus silence can be the message conveyed in hearing. For example, Heidegger tells the story of how, to his query about leaving his rural home to assume a university position, his peasant neighbor responded by saying nothing. He simply placed his hand on Heidegger's forearm in order to say "no."[220] Hearing, then, is that ecstatic response that allows to stand in reciprocity with the other. In this regard, the characteristic of my "incarnality" which would seem best to reserve my place in the *ethos* is "hearing," rather than "seeing." For Heidegger, seeing harbors too many connotations stemming from a Platonic desire to re-present something through its outward appearance. Hearing, on the other hand, includes a dynamic in which presence arises only in conjunction with absence. According to his scenario, a seeming paradox arises in which silence can convey more than the most eloquent of speeches. It is not seeing the "face" of

---

219 GA 3, p. 200; tr. 140.
220 Heidegger, "Why I Stay in the Provinces?", in *Heidegger: The Man and the Thinker*, p. 29.

the other, as Levinas suggests, which transplants the self into the *ethos*, but instead hearing the other's "voice."

Incarnality is the specific way in which the self takes up and comes to terms with the vulnerability its body poses. As vulnerable in this way, we experience primeval emotions such as love and grief, exaltation and suffering, the range of which is "formally indicated" by Dasein's solicitude. With the exception of a few scattered references in *Zollikon Seminars*, where he participates in a seminar with the psychiatrist, Medard Boss, Heidegger discounts the problem of embodiment. "Bodying forth belongs to being-in-the-world, which is primarily the understanding of being."[221] Indeed, he rarely proceeds beyond this formal level to explore the implications which the metontological turn toward ethics has for addressing the spectrum of human emotions. On the one hand, he claims in *Zollikon Seminars* that the grounding-attunements ground the more common emotions.[222] On the other hand, he seems wary about treating embodiment as a separate problem if only because it points to a preconception of philosophical anthropology that we are divided into a body, intellect and spirit. This is a preconception which, given his divergence from Scheler's phenomenology, Heidegger would soon avoid. In discussing "The Idea of Philosophical Anthropology in Part IV of the Kant-book, Heidegger states: "Anthropology means the science of man [*Menschenkunde*]. It embraces all that is knowable [*erkundbar*] relative to the nature of man as this corporeal, ensouled, spiritual creature."[223] In *Ethics and Finitude*, Lawrence Hatab explores the relation between the phenomenon of care and its expression through our emotions such as empathy: "Empathy is not simply a feeling; it is a mode of disclosure that generates ethical import. In its atmosphere of affective nearness and its being-toward structure there arises the existential 'draw' of the other that can be called the pre-reflective condition for the possibility of, and openness to, important ethical forces, such as responsibility, obligation, conscience and guilt."[224] To be incarnated is not be bound passively by a body, but instead to undertake a venture into the arena of vulnerability where the self grapples with the benefits and drawbacks of its finitude. In this arena, the self experiences the abundance of its possibilities as tempered by a void, in which the pursuit of one possibility is at the expense of another.

The self's incarnality points to the diverse directions from which the self can be disclosed, including through the relationship each has with others. When properly understood, the ownmost, "authentic" dimension of Da-sein — far from

---

**221** Heidegger, *Zollikon Seminars*, p. 200.
**222** Heidegger, *Zollikon Seminars*, p. 139.
**223** GA 3, p. 208; tr. 146.
**224** Hatab, *Ethics and Finitude*, p. 150.

isolating it from others — bestows upon the self its capacity to be free, the "gifting" of all its possibilities throughout the course of its "temporal" sojourn in the world.

There may be various way of illustrating the reciprocity between individual and world, self and community, but one power that brings each within the tension of their "play-space" belongs to imagination. Kant had originally portrayed imagination in cognitive terms as a zone of inter-mediation between the universal and the particular, concept and intuition. But now partnered with the incarnality by which we inhabit the *ethos*, imagination takes its lead from the larger drama of life, the interval of "not" which extends another vista of possibility upon what life already offers. In construing the schematizing power of imagination as an "art concealed in the depths of the human soul" (*eine verborgene Kunst in den Tiefen der menschlichen Seele*),[225] Kant had overlooked, paradoxically, that it is only through its "incarnation" that the "self" or animating, temporal spark, becomes a vessel of imagination. In emerging from this abground (*Abgrund*), imagination provides the "graphics," the temporal-spatial opening, to channel its inherent creativity. Imagination can thereby spawn new patterns of meanings at the crossing between speech and silence. John Sallis points to the link between imagination and language in this way: "As the gift of imagination comes, coming as if from nowhere, hence as free, pure gift, one will say, letting resound an abysmal freedom that is necessity itself: yes, yes. Even as mute, this double affirmation will be almost indistinguishable from the most originary opening to speech as such, to *logos*."[226]

Instead of referring to this development as an "enlargement of mind," as Hannah Arendt does in retaining a vestige of Kant subjectivity, we can characterize the "visiting" which imagination undertakes as a topographical exercise.[227] But the converse is equally important: because of its topographical character, imagination enables us to depict the body as a juncture where many different avenues of communication converge, that is, in its affinity with the "self-gathering" of *logos*, rather than as mere corporeality divorced from meaning. As a result, bodily gestures, like a handshake or a wink of an eye, can signify so-called "higher levels" of spirituality, for example, my friendship and even intimacy with others. Under the sway of this twisting and torsion of imagination, *logos* ceases to be a formal component of rationality, and instead re-emerges as a forum for our exchange with others, as a community of conversation to which we all belong. As

**225** Kant, *Critique of Pure Reason*, A 141.
**226** Sallis, *Force of Imagination*, p. 198.
**227** Arendt, *The Life of the Mind*, Vol. II, p. 257.

an embodied activity, *logos* assumes a double role both as a forum for speech and as the demarcation of the domain of social inhabitation (*ethos*). Through our participation in language, our ethical decisions root the self in its inhabitation of the community, of *ethos*, and perhaps, even the earth. Given this "rootedness," we are not inherently spiritual beings of a supernatural origin. Rather, the self can admit such distinctions as "higher" and "lower" because ek-sistence spawns its own topo-graphical indicators, joining existence from the apex of its transcendence and the roots of its facticity. Imagination allows us to participate in their openness by multiplying the levels of signification words can have, in placing in tension what is proximal as a gesture with what is remote as a determination, thereby playing one off against the other. As a result, the greatest "leap" of imagination lies not in reaching the highest flights of fancy, but instead in arriving at that destination where we already are, in our "earth-boundedness" (Arendt) or as rooted in our incarnality. In this regard, the self's incarnation with a body serves as a singular image as a hyperbolic depiction of its dual origin as both terrestrially and socially rooted. As one scholar states, echoing both Heidegger and Arendt: "The earth ... is that on which humans found their living; it is that into which the arising "shelters back (*birgt zurück*) everything that arises (human, animals, plants, things)."[228]

Not surprisingly, imagination re-emerges as a pivotal motif in the course of addressing the *ethos* from alternating Heidegger-Kantian perspectives. But the emphasis on incarnality, which Heidegger provides in contrast to Kant, allows us to rediscover the factical origin of imagination apart from any "mentalistic" overtones. By extricating imagination from its confinement to such a mentalistic model, we see more clearly why Heidegger turned to imagination as the key to his destructive-retrieval of transcendental philosophy. Conversely, as imagination assumes this kind of prominence, we should be able to outline a more inclusive topography for the question of being that includes as part of its landscape radicalizing the question of ethics.

## 3 The "Administrator" of Freedom

**A**

In attempting to appropriate Kant's ethics from a Heideggerian perspective, we inevitably face one obstacle: the disparity between the atemporal focus of the

---

228 Vallega-Neu, *The Bodily Dimension in Thinking*, p. 92.

former's concept of freedom and the temporal origin of the latter's concept of choice. In the Kant-book, Heidegger seeks to bridge this gap by developing a "sensible practical reason," that is, transferring the power to legislate the categorical imperative back to its emergence from the facticity of the individual's situation.[229] He does so in four scant, yet illumination pages. In his review of the Kant-book, Cassirer characterized Heidegger's brief analysis of Kantian practical reason as a kind of paradox or "wooden iron."[230] Against the backdrop of Cassirer's criticism, I fleshed out the details of Heidegger's appropriation of practical reason in *Imagination and Existence* (1986). In *The Renewal of the Heidegger-Kant Dialogue* (1992), I recast Heidegger's task within the wider context of his *Auseinandersetzung* with his predecessor as a whole and its place in the development of his thinking overall. Spearheading these efforts, however, was a need to bring the question of human freedom to the forefront of any discussion of ethics, as Heidegger outlined in his 1930 lectures on Kant, *Vom Wesen der menschlichen Freiheit*.

Many of the issues which Heidegger addresses in these lectures speak to Cassirer's criticisms, even though the scope of its inquiry is much wider. Ironically, the concept of freedom initially appears as elusive for Heidegger as it was for Kant, although the former will gradually make it the theme of an explicit inquiry. Though we will ultimately seek to establish the intersection between them, Heidegger diverges from Kant by addressing our experience of freedom or its occurrence as a phenomenon. Kant linked experience to the domain of sensible objects insofar as they could be determined by laws of cause-effect relations, the law of causality. He opposed to that sensible domain another realm of legislation, which he called noumenon, from which originates a spontaneous cause or the freedom requisite for obeying the moral law. Given this dichotomy, human beings seem to have no direct encounter with or experience of freedom. But if we cannot directly experience freedom through our senses, we can still, as Heidegger argues, attest to its "influence" indirectly by showing how it is "formally indicated" through the occurrence of a specific action. That is, an action which we can "point to" as illustrating the fulfillment of an obligation — the exercise of the categorical imperative — can serve as an example of the freedom which we assume as a precondition of morality. Because when the self acts morally it does so to fulfill precisely those obligations it could if it were free, the actions themselves stand for, and attest to, the possibility of freedom as such.

Put in simple terms, if something is actual it must also be possible. The fact that such actions occur, whose undertaking alone could have for its "ground"

---

229 GA 3, pp. 158–160; tr. 111–112.
230 Cassirer, "Kant und das Problem der Metaphysik", p. 147.

none other than an "uncaused" or spontaneous causation, i. e., confirms indirectly that such freedom occurs, that is, is actual. Heidegger summarizes this argument in his 1930 lectures: "*The factuality corresponding to the idea of freedom is that of praxis.*"[231] Given this insight, we can arrive at the key to transplanting Kant's ethics on the existential soil of finitude. The way that our actions confirm our capacity of freedom suggests that they qualify as "facts" which provide "proof," if only indirectly, of what cannot be "theoretically" or "logically" demonstrated. But here again an ambiguity arises. For a "fact" in this context pertains not to a sensuous given, to an empirical concept,[232] but to an example that our manner of acting provides, the concrete instance of praxis. With a view to the Greek meaning of action, Heidegger distinguishes two dimensions of praxis. "First the 'practical man' who possesses abilities of a certain kind and who know how to apply them at the right moment; secondly, praxis and action in the specific sense of ethical action, i. e., moral-practical comportment. Kant includes this latter meaning in his concept of practical [freedom]."[233] To designate the actual occurrence of freedom, or its appearance through a concrete instance, Heidegger reserves the term "facticity." For him, facticity points to the concrete enactment of our existence, as developing out of a situation, in exercising its own potential for self-understanding. Factic life-experience can then bring forth the self-signifying character of those experiences, in which a specific instance, for example, of praxis, illustrates the essential element of freedom. Moral praxis then resides in the "facticity of freedom."[234] Through this facticity we can experience the freedom which Kant assumed as a precondition of morality.

By emphasizing this factical dimension, Heidegger brings freedom and our experience thereof into question, not as it is restricted exclusively to moral issues, but as it incorporates the larger concern for the question of being. Conversely, the limitations of Kant's metaphysics, resulting in the dichotomy between freedom and nature, prevented him from addressing freedom in this radical way on a par with the question of being. In this 1930 lecture on Kant, Heidegger poses the question of freedom on two fronts: both as a key for deposing the metaphysics on which Kantian ethics rests and then retrieving the possibility of ethics as it reappears within the wider landscape of the *ethos*. In this way, Heidegger offsets the two levels of forgottenness that occludes Kant's insights into the nature of moral responsibility: 1). the privileging of one dimension of time in order to understand being, namely, the present, so that its ideal form or eternity marks the

---

**231** GA 31, p. 271; tr. 186.
**232** GA 31, p. 269; tr. 184. Also see GA 86, p. 201.
**233** GA 31, p. 196; tr. 136.
**234** GA 31, p. 273; tr. 187.

origin of freedom (i. e., a spontaneous cause or unconditioned will) and 2). the truncation of time as a series of nows in contrast to eternity, in such a way that the realm delimited by the former or nature stands in stark opposition to the domain circumscribed the latter or freedom. "Kant's orientation to causation to being-present, which he equates with actual and existence as such, *means that he sees freedom and being-free within the horizon of the being-present.* Since he *fails to pose the question concerning the particular way of being of beings who are free,* he does not unfold the metaphysical problem of freedom in a primordial manner."[235]

Rather than subordinate freedom to the metaphysics of presence, as Kant does, Heidegger elects to make freedom focal to the question of being; freedom ceases to be equated with a human activity. Instead, in displacing this focus of presence, we experience freedom as springing from a relationship to what is most radically other, that is, which being extends to us in inviting our participation in its unconcealment. In this regard, freedom holds the key to transposing the relationship between man and being, not as subject and object, but as the open expanse of reciprocity and responsiveness. This transposition, however, springs from the momentum of the turning from being and time to time and being. Indeed, the emergence of the practical dimension of the self, in contrast to the theoretical contemplation of the "I think," provides an avenue by which Heidegger dismantles the metaphysics of presence. We consider the topography of the transformation in these terms. The analysis of the self's temporality in *Sein und Zeit* points to the fact that any understanding of being takes shape in terms of time. But once having brought the possibility of Dasein's understanding of being to light, the landscape or hermeneutic situation of the inquiry expands to include the "other side" of this problematic: that the overcoming of the metaphysical concept of being as permanent presence has as its corollary the assignment of "substance" as a derivative characterization of the "being" of the self. Descartes' depiction of the "I think" as a "mental substance" is a derivative concept of the self, and hence buries one layer of metaphysical sediment under a previous layer, i. e., the forgottenness of the temporal presencing of being — the forgottenness of forgettenness. In contrast to the "I think" of fixed contemplation, Heidegger reaffirms the "I can" of the practical self.[236] Where Kant had emphasized that the "I think" must be able to accompany all my representations,[237] Heidegger argues that the enactment of this practical "can" harbors the deeper insight, not only into

---

**235** GA 31, p. 193; tr. 134.
**236** GA 31, pp. 278–281; tr. 190–191.
**237** Kant, *Critique of Pure Reason*, B 138.

the self, but of being as well. Conversely, the "can" of the practical self provides the concrete footing for the enactment of theoretical knowledge: "Only as the constant, free 'I can' does the 'I think' have the power to allow the being-in-opposition of the unity [of knowledge] to stand against itself ..."[238]

As Heidegger states in his 1930 lectures on freedom: "*All interpretation is destruction*, controversy [*Auseinandersetzung*] and radicalization ..."[239] This statement is obviously a throwback to Heidegger's original plan for a phenomenological destruction of the history of ontology. But while the critical exchange with Kant provided the point of departure for this endeavor, the second stage, featuring the destruction of the Cartesian *cogito*, re-emerges in the guise of Heidegger's reaffirmation of the practical self. It is in this light, as I have argued elsewhere, that we must reinterpret the importance of his analysis of conscience.[240] Through the exchange of calling and responding, the self ceases to be defined through a permanent substratum of unity. Rather, its identity is reconstituted through the dynamic of temporality as the interplay of absence as well as presence. Given this temporal enactment, the actions of the practical the self, the letting be of the freedom evidenced therein, reemerge as multiple sites where the disclosedness of being unfolds. Freedom is not, then, a privileged capacity we possess due to our rationality, but instead is a power we acquire in partnership with being, by serving as a "place" for its disclosedness. Through this partnership and reciprocation, the self acquires freedom as the power to exercise choice. In his 1930 lectures on Kant, Heidegger summarizes his destructive-retrieval of the concept of freedom in this way. "Freedom ceases to be a property of human being," and instead "man becomes a possibility of freedom."[241] Put in other terms, the self becomes the "manager" or "administrator" of freedom, the vehicle for the distribution if its power.[242]

The self ceases to be the sole benefactor of freedom, insofar as Dasein receives freedom as belonging to a relationship (i. e., through its partnership with being). Because freedom arises in conjunction with being, the discharge of the power to be free occurs through the nexus of relationships, including Dasein's being with others, and implicitly even its affinity with animals, which comprises its worldly existence. Dasein receives the power of freedom by participating in the openness which being itself grants, by agreeing to safeguard freedom for the benefit of others as well as myself. By developing freedom in a

---

238  GA 3, p. 79; tr. 55–56.
239  GA 31, p. 168; tr. 118.
240  See Schalow, "The Topography of Heidegger's Concept of Conscience", pp. 255–273.
241  GA 31, p. 134; tr. 93.
242  GA 31, pp. 134–135; tr. 93.

way which dislocates its origin in the (moral) subject, Heidegger resurrects the concern for freedom on the other side of restriction to the discipline of ethics. In this way, the question of freedom re-emerges through the question of being. And, vice-a-versa, once restored to its radicality and original scope (i. e., in conjunction with truth as unconcealment), the question of being reappears as the question of human freedom. "The question concerning the ownmost dimension of human freedom is the most basic question of all, in which even the question of being is rooted."[243] But given the radicalization of the question of freedom, and its severance from the metaphysical assumptions of Kant's ethics, do we then say farewell to ethics altogether, specifically in its Kantian form? Nothing could be further from the truth. For in liberating the concern for freedom in this way, Heidegger instead heralds the rebirth of ethics by re-examining the origin of moral responsibility.

In developing ethics anew, Heidegger challenges the distinction which traditionally has given moral inquiry its focus, the division between theoretical and practical reason. Not only does Kant accept this distinction that originates as far back as Aristotle, but he reasserts it in order to reserve a place for moral volition apart from the rule of natural causality. By developing the problematic of world which is hidden in Kant's appeal to human finitude, Heidegger undercuts the theoretical/practical distinction as the flip-side of dismantling the remnants of Kant's archaic cosmology. This cosmology, as we have seen, pits the eternal realm of freedom against the transient realm of nature, while assuming a schism between the former as the haven of action and the latter as the haven of knowledge. In his 1930 lectures on Kant, however, Heidegger returns to the earliest Greek origins in order to recover freedom and nature in their interdependence with each other. Rather than simply constituting an aggregate of the inanimate objects, nature includes the diversity of whatever can become manifest, the dynamism of presencing itself (*physis*), like a flower that blooms and then withers away. Correlatively, freedom marks our participation in the opening of a world which we inhabit along with the diversity of everything else. Freedom does not separate us from nature, but instead inserts us into the tension of unconcealing/concealing as embodied in the self-emerging dynamic of nature itself. The emergence of this *"extra-human" origin of freedom provides the possibility of a "trans-human" ethic*, which extends its scope to include a concern for the welfare of our animal counterparts, as well as ourselves.

---

243 GA 31, p. 300; tr. 205 (translation modified).

**B**

If the question of human freedom directs us to our occupation of the *ethos*, and hence to the origin of ethics, how, conversely, does re-opening the question of ethics transplant us once again into what distinguishes (the heart of) philosophy, namely, the province of thinking? We might bring this question to light if we are to appreciate the larger repercussions of Heidegger's account of freedom, including its importance for demarcating the political realm or the domain of the *polis*. Though there has been a decided tendency to do so,[244] it remains problematic at best to address the controversy surrounding Heidegger's approach to politics without also delineating his concern for freedom and the manner of its finite "administration." Insofar as freedom is at the root of thinking as well acting, the possible connection between the two merits close consideration. In *What Is Called Thinking?*, Heidegger points to this unity: "The originary nature of freedom keeps itself concealed in the calling by which it is given to mortal man to think what is most thought-provoking. Freedom, therefore, is never something merely human, nor merely divine ..."[245]

In simplest terms, self's way of acting, either in exercising solicitude or circumspective concern, already presupposes its inhabitation of a world. When an explicit way of choosing my individuality accompanies the action, supplying for it its predicate, we can speak of self's acting "resolutely." Resoluteness of this form constitutes a mode of disclosure, that is, an instance of truth. By the same token, when we philosophize we may be involved in a venture that is traditionally characterized as thought. But insofar as thinking begins with our questioning being, we participate in truth when we think. We allow being to address us and thereby embody the freedom that permits us to participate in the dynamics of its unconcealment; freedom and truth are essentially conjoined ("*Wesensinnigkeit von Wahrheit und Freiheit*").[246] Thus, thinking is itself an activity, no less than resolute choosing is a mode of disclosure (truth), of "becoming free" for the possibilities of existence.[247] Thinking and doing are intertwined together, and each can complement the other because both are possibilities that transpose us into the openness of being-in-the-world. Each proceeds through the acceptance of an invitation, the heeding of a call, in which only as "answerable" can we be

---

244 See de Beistegui's work, *Heidegger and the Political*, pp. 155–165. Despite many of de Beistegui's insights, there is little effort to address Heidegger's concept of freedom, particularly as developed through his exchange with Kant.
245 Heidegger, *What Is Called Thinking?*, p. 153.
246 GA 69, p. 171.
247 GA 17, p. 111; tr. 81.

benefactors of the freedom, of thinking/deciding, we have granted to us. What, then, is the "element," which allows freedom to be appropriated in these diverse, but complementary ways? The "elemental," as Sallis suggests, is what maintains unity through the tension of inter-mediation, of setting in opposition.[248] And the dynamic which accomplishes this is nothing else than the relationship in which we already stand to language, deferring our power to speak in favor of listening, accepting our thrownness into it in order to participate in its disclosive power.

But if the tension of this twofold acclimates us to language — the differentiation of hearing and responding — then how is our participation in it also an instance of freedom? Are we free, most radically and dramatically of all, when our speech provides for us a space in which to think? The "freedom of thinking" would be what placing ourselves in position to heed what is most other, of allowing what we say to become an invitation to an opposite reply. Freedom becomes a way of "letting be," in which we participate in openness by predicating its possibility upon confronting the opposite prospect of concealment. The wrenching into unconcealment, of what tends to remain concealed, suggests the tension of the twofold which language upholds in providing an audience for what is most contrary. Freedom is crucial to thinking, and to our exercise of it, or philosophy, for it is only in the exchange that welcomes dissent that we become vessels in which to play out the tension of unconcealing/concealing. The "setting into opposition" of exchange or *Auseinandersetuzng* exemplifies this scenario of letting be, the freedom of/for dissent. Through this freeing/dissent, philosophy becomes an endeavor to which human beings are granted and whose mission, in questioning being, they are entrusted. Almost so elemental as to go unnoticed, philosophy becomes possible only through freedom. For only by safeguarding a forum for dissent, can thinking breech the status quo, and partner with the disruptive forces of what is unsaid and unthought.

In this context, "free speech" is not just a political aphorism, but is the safeguarding of speech in and through its allowance for dissent. As Heidegger suggests in his 1929/30 lectures, insofar as humans acquire the power to speak due to their "*open[ness] in their being with one another*," "individually" each can either "agree" or "fail to agree" about the appearance of the beings in whose midst each stands.[249] The permissiveness of assert/dissent is the "letting be" of freedom, albeit exercised as the spirit of philosophy, which is distinguished as much by the premium it places on questioning as by its creative venture with

---

248 Sallis, *Force of Imagination*, pp. 171–172.
249 GA 29/30, p. 447; tr. 309.

language. This letting be of free speech releases Dasein to pursue "philosophy as its free possibility."[250] Ironically, Kant had a presentiment of this relation between philosophy and freedom, when he stated in his lectures on *Logic*: "The true philosopher, as self-thinker, thus must make free ... the use of his reason."[251] In the *Critique of Pure Reason*, Kant makes this illuminating remark:

> Reason must in all its undertakings subject itself to criticism, should it limit freedom of criticism by an prohibiting, it must harm itself, drawing upon itself a damaging suspicion. Nothing is so important through its usefulness, not so sacred, that it may be exempted from this searching examination, which knows not respect for persons. Reason depends on this freedom for its very existence. For reason has not dictatorial authority; its verdict is always simply the agreement of free citizens, of whom each one must be permitted to express, without let or hindrance, his objections or even his veto.[252]

The inquiry into being can embody such "searching examination" only because of its permission of dissent in the freedom of speech. In this regard, scholars have underestimated the importance of the phenomenon of free speech as a philosophical problem, despite recognizing the importance of the correlation between freedom and language as it plays itself out in Kant's and Heidegger's thought.[253] In his essay "Perpetual Peace," Kant distinguishes the ethical and political implications of this freedom. "Kings or sovereign peoples (i. e., those governing themselves by egalitarian laws) should not, however, force the class of philosophers to disappear or to remain silent, but should allow them to speak publicly."[254] By exemplifying the trait which traditionally ethics has honored most, ontology paves the way for the *possibility* of what Heidegger in "Letter on 'Humanism'" first called an "original ethics."[255]

In what lies the *originality* of such an ethics? This is a obvious question to ask, but one that is all too frequently ignored. An original ethics begins by shifting the locus of action from its origin in a will or volition, to our own participation in freedom as letting be. Such an ethics, then, places itself in question in terms of a premise, of letting be, which admits no further grounding. In this response of questioning, as Charles Scott emphasizes, we must first experience how ethics is thrown into uncharted waters, absent of any manual that seeks direction from

---

**250** GA 24, p. 455; tr. 320.

**251** Kant, AA 9, p. 26; *Logic*, p. 30.

**252** Kant, *Critique of Pure Reason*, A 739/ B 767.

**253** See Schmidt, *Lyrical and Ethical Subjects*, p. 77.

**254** Kant, "Zum ewigen Frieden: Ein philosophischer Entwurf," AA 8, p. 369. "Perpetual Peace: A Philosophical Sketch", p. 115.

**255** GA 9, pp. 356–357; tr. 271. See Lewis, *Heidegger and the Place of Ethics*, pp. 7–18.

traditional guidelines and norms.[256] The undergoing of this hiatus, or, in Nietzsche's terms, of "going under" in order to "cross over," in order that the inertia in the prejudice infiltrating traditional ethics can be "overcome" through the momentum of the turning around of the question, of the question of being itself. Then ethics ceases to be defined by the imposition of values, and instead takes a more radical form through a change in our relation to language, in which our dwelling therein and our residence within the *ethos* become two sides of the same coin. Referencing the clue to our relation to language, we are granted freedom in proportion to the "stewardship" we exercise toward it, that is, by allocating it to the widest participants and the solicitude they can extend to the earth's diverse tenants — human and animal alike.

The key to an original ethics, then, lies in removing freedom from the interiority of the will to its emergence as the origin of our inhabitation of the world. An original ethics, then, hinges on this unique topography of freedom, insofar as the self inhabits a world through its companionship with others. As a power that can only be transmitted through an appropriative act, freedom catapults Dasein beyond itself through its affiliation with the other. The economy of freedom allows for a plurality of participants within the open expanse of being, in such a way that "I" can experience myself as free only through a reciprocal rejoinder linking me with the other. By heeding the other's welfare, for example, as a unique voice in a dialogue, the self is first "cleared" in its freedom to let the other be in the pursuit of his or her own possibilities. In *Being and Time*, Heidegger describes this way of responding to the welfare of the other, which acknowledges the singularity of his or her own way of being-free, a emancipatory solicitude.[257] Through solicitude, Dasein encourages the other to participate in the freedom that is essential to fostering the "owned" dimension of individuality. This owned dimension, however, is not a property of the self but, on the contrary, pervades the nexus of relationships by which the individual experiences his or her companionship with the other, the fabric of community. Insofar as the owned dimension of freedom always unfolds through an ever-widening circle of participants, Dasein comes to itself in the process of honoring its obligations. In this way, Heidegger brings to fruition his insight drawn early on from Kant's idea of a kingdom of ends and Schleiermacher's notion of "free sociality" that within a community — friendship, family, church, and state — provides the setting for the self to enact its freedom.[258]

---

256 Scott, *The Question of Ethics*, pp. 7–14.
257 See Birmingham, "*Logos* and the Place of the Other", pp. 51–55.
258 van Buren, *The Young Heidegger*, p. 346.

Through this emancipatory solicitude, Dasein champions the welfare of others in such a way that its interests, its administration of care, can extend to all corners of the world. Within an Enlightenment context, Kant had first characterized the self-legislative will as a kind of "hero" who rises above petty desires in order to act in behalf of all human beings, that is, become a "citizen of the world" (*Weltbürger*).[259] In his 1930 lectures on Kant, Heidegger develops this motif in the practical self whose steadfastness of commitment forms the predicate for upholding obligations to others.[260] Through the exercise of its ownmost responsibility, the practical self exercises the liberating or "emancipating" solicitude which invites each individual to participate in freedom and share its benefits with others. Through his emphasis on the essentially worldly human being, Heidegger suggests that the commitment of resolute self-choosing and the responsiveness of conscience help shape the *ethos* of Dasein's interaction with others. Through conscience Dasein not only heeds its appeal to be itself but, because this plea is always the voice (*Stimme*) of care, each of us also experience the attunement (*Stimmung*) that echoes the claim [*Anspruch*] of the other. In this regard, the voice of alterity transforms Dasein's responsibility into a mode of responsiveness.

Here we see the extent to which Heidegger's concept of resolve transplants on an existential footing the responsibility of the practical self. Conversely, when translated back into the context of the ethos of an original ethics, moral responsibility defines a way in which we comply to those concerns most in keeping with our finitude. While Kant describes freedom in abstract terms as the spontaneity of self-determination (autonomy), it turns out, quite paradoxically, that the fulfilling its obligations is a way in which the practical self "lets itself be" defined by those concerns most indicative of its nature as care. And this way of abiding in a commitment by "letting be" is the ownmost dimension of self-respect. As Heidegger states in the brief section in the Kant-book devoted to a destructive-retrieval of Kant's ethics: "The submitting, self-projecting onto the entire basis possibility of owned existence, which the law gives, is the ownmost dimension of the acting being-itself, i. e., of practical reason."[261] Respect can thereby also suggest the homage one pays to oneself by virtue of taking up those pursuits, including philosophy, that best exemplifies one's nature.[262] Precisely in this spirit Kant first spoke of our natural disposition to formulate philosophical

---

**259** GA 9, p. 153; tr. 119–120. See Kant, AA 5, KpV, pp. 87–88; tr. 90.
**260** GA 31, p. 264; tr. 181.
**261** GA 3, p. 159; tr. 111 (translation modified).
**262** See Crowe, "Philosophy, World-View, and the Possibility of Ethics in *The Basic Problems of Phenomenology*", pp. 184–202.

questions.[263] In his 1930 lectures on Kant, Heidegger underscores this point by maintaining that responsibility defines "the basic modality of being determining all human comportment."[264] What Kant described as the self-legislation of the moral or autonomy has it factical corollary in the self's way of responding to the claim of its own individuality (resoluteness). Resolve is the choosing of those finite possibilities, which brings the openness to fruition (rather than "decisionism"). As Heidegger states in his 1942/43 lectures on Parmenides, "'Resoluteness' in the modern sense is the fixed ordination of the will upon itself ... As understood by the Greeks, however, resoluteness, the self-disclosing opening up toward being, has another origin ... a different experience of being ..."[265]

Insofar the self assumes responsibility for its existence through this responsiveness, and this responsiveness allows the self to heed its obligations, the legislation of the moral law in Kant's sense equals self-responsibility. In one of his most pivotal passages from his 1930 lectures on Kant, Heidegger states: "Practical freedom as autonomy is self-responsibility (*Selbstverantwortlichkeit*), the personhood of the person ... the humanity of the human being."[266] Heidegger equates autonomy with self-responsibility, thereby anchoring Kant's atemporal concept of freedom within the temporalize enactment of exercising commitment toward resolve or resolute self-choosing. If this transposition is successful, we would be able to find a concrete example of autonomy, which accentuates the individualized locus of commitment and yet leaves the door open for acknowledging the rule of law (e. g., honoring authority), precisely as self-legislation. Of all sports, golf stands out as a game of honor. This is never more evident than with the fact that player is obliged to impose a penalty upon him/herself when he/she recognizes that a rule of the game has been violated. Indeed, there are instances, for example, when a player inadvertently causes his/her ball to move, where the player alone — even in the absence of any witnesses by fellow competitors and caddies alike — may be aware that an infraction has occurred, a rule broken. The rule of golf thereby translates into self-rule, an example of autonomy in which the canon of obedience is not external but is applied from within. The demands of honor, then, prevail over the personal interest in victory.

For Kant, autonomy allows one to heed the worth of his/her nature, over and beyond the fulfillment of self-interest. To draw the analogy, the honor of oneself

---

**263** Kant, Pr, AA 4 354. *Prolegomena to any Future Metaphysics*, p. 102. See Heidegger's discussion of the *Prolegomena*, and the complementary concern for "practical interest," GA 86, pp. 207, 210.

**264** GA 31, p. 262; tr. 180 (translation modified).

**265** GA 54, p. 111; tr. 75–76.

**266** GA 31, p. 296; tr. 200–201.

as guardian of the integrity of a sport supercedes the self-interest of personal success, even at the expense of losing a tournament (as the legendary golfer, Bobby Jones, did in calling a penalty upon himself for an infraction of inadvertently moving his ball that no one else witnessed). *Autonomy thereby translates into self-responsibility*, a way of acknowledging one's worth as a person, of allowing the uniqueness of who one is to flow forth independently of the external measures of success and achievement. Self-responsibility, then, becomes a way of delivering the individual over to that possibility of who the self can be, a mode of "letting be" in Meister Eckhart's sense. Freedom thereby resides in the stillness that gathers the self into its ownmost humility and poverty (*die Armut*).[267] In this way, Heidegger identifies a more radical origin of freedom in which freedom harbors within itself the root of necessity, and hence cannot be derived from it, including Kant's account of the necessity of heeding the moral law, *"der Zwang des Sollens."*[268]

By shifting the sense of freedom as the spontaneous determination of the will to the openness of letting be, Heidegger displaces the locus of the moral agent from subjectivity to the expanse of being-in-the-world. Given this new locus for human praxis, the initiative of choice as spontaneity hinges on an accompanying receptivity, whose inducement of openness relocates practical freedom in Dasein's finitude. In the Kant-book, Heidegger first argues that a receptive spontaneity and a spontaneous receptivity mark a more radical origin for both theoretical and practical reason in the transcendental imagination. In his 1930 lectures on Kant, Heidegger shows that the Kantian precept of moral autonomy presents the challenge for man's becoming an "administrator" of freedom. As administrators of freedom, we safeguard it as a power in which others can participate and towards whom we can exhibit solicitude.

Does not this reference to sanctioning the "other's participation" in freedom constitute the cornerstone of democratic practice? Ever so hesitantly, almost with bated breath, can we suggest that Heidegger, having joined the National Socialist party in the early 1930s, re-emerge as a closest proponent of democracy? Or, instead, is the situation a bit more complex, in which case this apparent anomaly becomes possible due to the path that Heidegger's thinking opens up as a result of his exchange with Kant? Indeed, it was Charles Sherover who *boldly* linked Heidegger's thought to democratic practice by accentuating their mutual interest in human freedom.[269] And while he recognizes Heidegger's and Kant's joint concern for

---

267  Heidegger, "Die Armut", p. 10; tr. 7–8.
268  Heidegger, "Die Armut," p. 9; tr. 7.
269  See Sherover, *Time, Freedom, and the Common Good*, pp. 7–22.

conscience,[270] Sherover does not proceed to the next level to address the exercise of conscience as the self's capacity to heed the claim of the other. As a result, the task remains of questioning back to the ground of the institutionalized protection of civil liberties, that is, the safeguarding of the power of *dissent*. Specifically, it is necessary to trace the possibility of dissent to its (ontological) origins in our participation in language, rather than exclusively as a "right" that a society grants to its members due to their inclusion within a *polis*. As Sherover states: "... the society needs, for its own health, to encourage a healthy diversity of interests and outlooks. The security of public liberty and the opportunities of freedom require a deliberate pluralization of factional interests, so that no one group may predominate and no coalition of factional interests may become so powerful as to overcome the diversity of interests upon which a consensual commitment to the public's freedom depends."[271] As compelling as this statement is, it *assumes* an important *difference* which sets Heidegger apart from Kant, and allows him to radicalize the latter's concept of freedom: that is, questioning language from *the roots of its gathering stillness prior to the creation of an open forum for our participation in it, i. e., through our ability to listen and become answerable.*

As Heidegger's thinking enters into the turning in a more pronounced way, as it bears the tension of "overcoming metaphysics," the concern for freedom becomes increasingly important. To employ Emad's unique coinage, Heidegger develops a "liberating ontology," which makes the concern for freedom, in conjunction with truth, the centerpiece of being-historical thinking.[272] Not only does freedom as "letting be" speak directly to our experience of being, the question of freedom also harbors the transformation of Heidegger's project of "being and time." Quoting a passage from Kant's *Foundation of the Metaphysics of Morals*, Heidegger (in his 1930 essay "*Vom Wesen der Wahrheit*") describes how experience of freedom as "letting be" transforms philosophy into the "'keeper of its laws'": that is, in a way that neither "clings to beings" nor submits to an "externally imposed decree."[273] He closes his 1930 lectures on Kant with this same quote from the *Metaphysics of Morals*: "Here philosophy is seen in fact to be placed in a precarious position which is supposed to be firm — although neither in heaven or earth is there anything on which it depends or on what it is based."[274]

As Heidegger will later respond to Father Richardson's query concerning the enigma of the "turning": while we begin by addressing man's relation to being,

---

**270** Sherover, *From Kant and Royce to Heidegger*, pp. 113–114.

**271** Sherover, *From Kant and Royce to Heidegger*, pp. 214–215.

**272** Emad, *On the Way to Heidegger's Contributions to Philosophy*, pp. 112–113.

**273** GA 9, p. 199; tr. 152.

**274** GA 31, p. 303; tr. 205–206. See AA 4, Gr, pp. 425–426; tr. 42–43.

we allow the turning to redirect us to "be-ing and its truth in relation to man."[275] In this quote, Heidegger appeals to a lecture-course from the Winter semester of 1937/38, which forms the backdrop for *Contributions to Philosophy*.[276] As von Herrmann points out: "... the study of this lecture text, which appeared in 1984 as volume 45 [of the *Gesamtausgabe*], is the most import and immediate preparation for understanding *Contributions to Philosophy*.[277] In *Contributions*, Heidegger emphasizes how his earlier inquiry into that the "there" already belongs to being and is defined through its participation in that openness. In a section entitled "The Relation of Da-sein and Be-ing," Heidegger points to the Kant-book as the foremost example of his initial attempt to address the interdependence of the two beyond the metaphysics of subjectivity:

> And that is attempted in the Kant-book; but that was only possible by using force against Kant, in the direction of a more originary grasping of precisely the *transcendental* projecting-open in its onefoldnesss, *by working out the transcendental power of imagination*. Certainly, this Kant-interpretation is "historically" [in history as a discipline] incorrect; but it is *historically [geschichtlich]* essential; i. e., considered as preparatory for future thinking ...
> And so the Kant-book is necessarily ambiguous, through and through — and is nevertheless not an accidental *communiqué* because Kant continues to be the only one since the Greeks who brings the interpretation of beingness into a certain relation to "time" and thus becomes a witness to the hidden reign of the connection between beingness and time.[278]

Of all of Heidegger's retrospective observations of the Kant-book, the preceding is among the most intriguing because it locates the destructive-retrieval of transcendental philosophy within the larger task of overcoming metaphysics. As we proceed to a further stage of Heidegger's destructive-retrieval of Kant, however, the issue of ethics does not recede. On the contrary, we will discover in the next chapter, the questions it continues to spark overshadow the most controversial, and yet, perhaps most ground-breaking period in the development of Heidegger's thinking. By following the path of *Contributions to Philosophy*, we will see that its enactment of being-historical thinking locates the place for the critical exchange between Heidegger and Kant. In the process, we will discover that the link between Dasein's lived-experience of space and the allocation of a place for thinking is more than accidental, having its roots in what Heidegger first describes in *Contributions* as time-space (*Zeit-Raum*).[279]

---

**275** GA 11, p. 151; tr. xx.

**276** GA 45, pp. 214–215; tr. 181.

**277** GA 65, p. 514; tr. 364.

**278** GA 65, p. 253; tr. 178–179.

**279** See Dahlstrom, "Heidegger's Transcendentalism", pp. 29–54.

# Chapter Five
# Translating the Political and the Rise of Technology

As we revisit the development of Heidegger's thinking during the 1930s, the question of his politics inevitably comes to the forefront. For example, various scholars have attempted to show that some of the most basic concepts which Heidegger developed in *Being and Time*, i. e., resolve, harbored "fascist" implications.[280] What goes almost undetected in this diatribe of incrimination/apologetic is how the question of freedom, from his 1930 lectures on Kant to his 1935/36 lectures on Schelling (with an almost identical title), occupies the center of almost every discussion he undertakes during this period.[281] Rather than re-open this diatribe, my aim in this chapter is to show, conversely, how Heidegger's dialogue with Kant harbors important clues to direct us beyond the impasse of this political controversy. In the process, I will show how the benefits that Heidegger reaps by radicalizing his concept of freedom as letting be also has drawbacks in thrusting his thought before an abyss devoid of any tactics to criticize the institutions which violate the individual's freedom. By addressing this multifaceted, even polyvalent phenomenon,[282] we will see how Heidegger's exchange with Kant propels us to the *threshold of freedom*, to its precarious emergence within the arena of historical conflict and modern humanity's encounter with technology.

My discussion proceeds in three parts. First, I will read back from Heidegger's embroilment in the turmoil of the 1930s, an unresolved ambiguity about the relation between philosophy and politics, which *skirts the periphery of his exchange with Kant*. While Heidegger's destructive-retrieval of Kant's practical philosophy does not necessarily spawn this ambiguity, its significance can still be heard in the echoes that reverberate in the exchange between these thinkers: for example, in extending the boundaries of the *ethos* to include "consideration" for our animal counterparts (as well as human beings). At this unlikely juncture where Heidegger's and Kant's thinking intersect, the possibility arises of "translating" the political: that is, of recasting social policies into directives which promote our capacity for "dwelling" on the earth. Ultimately, this translation will

---

**280** Wolin, *The Politics of Being*, p. 35.

**281** For a complete treatment of the concern raised by Heidegger's politics, see Radloff, *Heidegger and the Question of National Socialism: Disclosure and Gestalt*, pp. 310–342. Also see Radloff, "Machination and the Political in Heidegger's *Mindfulness*", pp. 145–165.

**282** See Schalow, *Language and Deed*, pp. 192–198.

pave the way for us to negotiate the controversial topic of the *polis* (πόλις), i. e., to traverse its "crossing."[283]

Despite the divergence between these two thinkers on the topic of politics, I will show, secondly, that a key area of discussion still remains via the emphasis which Heidegger and Kant both place on human freedom. For Heidegger, unlike for Kant, freedom is not a property of the self, but a capacity to which human beings are "owned over" (*übereignet*) and thereby disposed to safeguard in order to allow being become manifest. When Heidegger undertook the "thinking of enowning" (*Ereignisdenken*) as his chief venture, he implicitly called into question the assumptions on which various political institutions have traditionally rested — whatever ideology may define them.[284] When these institutions assume their own "agency," *apart from the freedom on whose appropriation they depend*, an increasingly precarious situation arises: the political institutions revert to the self-serving ends of preserving their own power (i. e., fascism), only to subjugate the individual to the authority of its leaders.

In pointing to the depths of his historical struggle, I will establish, thirdly, how Heidegger's *Ereignisdenken* appropriates Kant's philosophy in its greatest simplicity: that is, by conveying the message that only by answering to their ownmost *finitude* can human beings experience the singularity and uniqueness which freedom has to offer, i. e., letting be. By following this pathway, we may not only come to appreciate the nuances of what is expressed in Heidegger's dialogue with Kant, but perhaps, even more subtly, also heed what remains *unsaid*. We reach the crossroads, however, when the unsaid ceases to be an obstacle, and instead becomes the springboard for a new *departure* of questioning.

# 1 Anti-Humanism?

In the Part IV of the Kant-book, as we have seen, Heidegger refers to the "gigantomachy" to suggest how the ancients wrestled with the controversy concerning the relevance time has in determining the meaning of being. When Heidegger assumed the chair of philosophy in Freiburg in 1929, he found himself to be thrown into the crosscurrents of heated criticisms voiced from different philosophical camps: from variations of Neo-Kantianism a la Cassirer, to conflicting versions of phenomenology — one epistemically oriented, the other morally — a

---

**283** To appreciate Kant's view of the *polis*, and its grounding in the Enlightenment, *Cf.* his essay "Zum ewigen Frieden," AA 8, pp. 369–373. "Perpetual Peace", pp. 115–119.

**284** For an attempt to show how the ambiguity of Heidegger's political situation intersects with the question of freedom, see Schalow, *Language and Deed*, pp. 192–203.

la Husserl and Scheler, to an analytic form of positivism a la Carnap. After all, through the language of symbolic logic, specifically, the use of the negative operator, Rudolf Carnap mimicked Heidegger's graphic portrayal of anxiety as an experience in which *"Das Nichts selbst nichtet."*[285] Heidegger's rendition of hermeneutic phenomenology was in many ways so audacious, and so abrupt in its break from contemporary philosophical trends, as immediately to attract attention as a target of criticism. He epitomizes this quandary through his exchange with Kant. And the reason why is that Kant stands at the watershed of all modern philosophy.

Because of the focal point that Kant's thought occupies, any interpretation of it underscores the originality of one's own philosophy. Perhaps even more so than in the case of German Idealism, Kierkegaard and Nietzsche, the audience of one's own philosophy increases to the extent that one can amplify it by drawing parallels to Kant's thinking, by "returning" to the Kantian roots of philosophy. Heidegger was fully aware of the controversy surrounding the re-interpretation of Kant's thought. In reflecting on the importance of the Kant-book in a lecture course from 1929/30, Heidegger states: "In that book I was not concerned with providing a better interpretation of Kant. What the Neo-Kantians and the old Kantians like to think about Kant is a matter of complete indifference to me."[286] Six years later, Heidegger adds: "This return to Kant was called Neo-Kantianism, in contrast to the disciples of Kant's lifetime, the former Kantians. When from our present position we survey this return to Kant, it must become immediately questionable whether it could have been regained, or could even *find* at all, Kant's basic position, which German Idealism had also simply skirted or leapt over."[287]

The confluence of all these historical factors never becomes more prominent than when Cassirer, as a spokesperson of the "back to Kant" movement, confronts Heidegger for recasting Kant's thought in phenomenological terms. Debating whether there is a pure strain of Kantianism in one thing; but advancing a "heterodoxical" version of Kantian thought, which uproots its own foundation in reason, is quite another. What in the end spearheads the Heidegger-Cassirer controversy becomes evident only in retrospect, both professionally as Heidegger adds fuel to the fire by radicalizing his concept of freedom and personally as he lands in a hotbed of political turmoil, is the stance either stakes toward the basic assumptions of Kantian ethics. Paul Tillich provides an interesting reflection on this very topic:

---

285 GA 9, pp. 113–114; tr. 90.
286 GA 29/30, p. 306; tr. 209.
287 GA 41, p. 59; tr. 60.

Two years prior to Hitler's coming to power there was a very interesting discussion in Switzerland between Cassirer and Heidegger. This discussion probably reveals as much about the situation as can be shown, namely, the conflict between one, who like Cassirer came from Kantian moral philosophy with rational criteria for thinking and acting, and one who, like Heidegger, defended himself on the notion that there are no such criteria. Two years later Cassirer was in exile and Heidegger was rector of Freiburg.[288]

In this regard, a comment which Heidegger makes to Cassirer in their conversation proves to be prophetic.[289] Among the students at the seminar, one interjects a concern about the gap in terminology separating these great thinkers. Heidegger acknowledges this concern by suggesting that what separates his thought from Cassirer's is not simply his concept of Dasein, but instead his account of how Dasein exercises its freedom.

The difference is clearest in the concept of freedom. I spoke of a freeing in the sense that the freeing of the inner transcendence of Dasein is the fundamental character of philosophizing itself. In so doing, the ownmost sense of this freeing is not to be bound in becoming free to a certain extent for the forming images of consciousness and for the realm of form. Rather, it is to be found in becoming free for the finitude of Dasein. Just to come into the thrownness of Dasein is to come into the conflict which lies within the essence of freedom. I did not give freedom to myself, although it is through being-free that I can first be I myself.[290]

Here Heidegger gives a clue to what makes his concept of freedom so enigmatic, while offering an example to illustrate its novelty. On the one hand, his identification of freedom with openness (truth) appears foreign to most philosophers. On the other hand, philosophy embodies freedom by making the endeavor of questioning more important than any arriving at specific answers, that is, through the openness of investigation. Philosophy, then, formally indicates freedom through its spirit of open inquiry.

But if freedom is openness, this does not mean that its exercise is indiscriminate and devoid of guidance. On the contrary, Heidegger suggests that the disposition toward openness exacts of Dasein the greatest of all changes, insofar as its places it before its own finitude and thrust it into the historical crucible of "conflict." But to what Cassirer's exchange with Heidegger initially points, and which Tillich's remarks above make explicit, is how amorphous Heidegger's concept of freedom appears to be. Indeed, amorphous might be the best description of how the openness of freedom seems to occur independently, as Tillich

---

**288** Tillich, "Heidegger and Jaspers", p. 25.

**289** Cristaudo, "Heidegger and Cassirer: Being, Knowing, and Politics", pp. 473–483.

**290** GA 3, p. 298; tr. 203 (translation modified).

suggests, of any criteria to give definition and direction to its exercise. Tillich's criticism, however, only becomes relevant when we transplant it into an historical context. Specifically, Heidegger circumvents the Enlightenment view of freedom, insofar as it is expressed through such ideals as equality and justice, in order to arrive at an alternative whose mode of expression, in lieu of these ideals, becomes much more problematic. Within the Enlightenment, freedom finds expression through the administering of justice, as well by honoring the individual's equality and dignity, so as to spawn an entire discourse to define these cornerstones of a "free society." But in developing freedom as openness, Heidegger allows the immediacy of the phenomenon itself to speak in place of its mediation through Enlightenment ideals. But without the mediation of this social-political setting, the freedom to which Heidegger appeals lacks a precedent, for its expression, other than how it is formally indicated through the act of philosophizing.

And it is precisely at this point in his dialogue with Kant that Heidegger detaches the concept of freedom from its Enlightenment setting in the social-political order, and thereby enters into uncharted waters. When expressed through the element of philosophy, freedom is implicated through that very activity. In lieu of direction offered from political and social quarters, the question then arises as to whether forms of leadership can emerge that profess the kind of freedom which philosophy embodies. Such "profession" needs to be taken in a double sense in which the "words" to express freedom — in lieu of Enlightenment ideals — can find their concrete example through actions within the world. Put in the simplest terms, at stake is how a singular experience of freedom enables the constituents of society to engage in dialogue with each other. What the Enlightenment had advocated through the ideals of dignity and equality, Heidegger retrieves through the counter movement of phenomenological destruction. For him, the protection of the individual's uniqueness, if not diversity, occurs by maximizing each person's opportunity to participate within a dialogue and welcoming the voice of dissent that the other embodies.

An ambiguity permeates Heidegger's concept of freedom as far as the political goes. Something like a *via negativa* emerges in which every time a moment arises to turn the political in the direction of custom and convention, it quickly recedes. The accumulative wisdom that we might draw upon to address the political, to develop a "theory of justice," as John Rawls does by honoring Kant's and Rousseau's legacy, and Sherover does by reinstating a contemporary rendition of a "social contract"[291] to set parameters to administer freedom, withdraws from Heidegger's reach. As Heidegger reflects in *An Introduction to Metaphysics*

---

291 Sherover, *From Kant and Royce to Heidegger*, pp. 193–202.

(1935), he finds the Western democracies, the United States in particular, and the communist system of Russia, both to be unpalatable. Not only do his historical circumstances pose an historical gulf. But more importantly, history itself appears as a riddle, in a way unlike for Kant and Hegel, in which the presumption of progress no longer holds.[292] Indeed, as little as Kant addresses history, he sees it as offering a *telos*, if not an actual time-line, toward which we advance in our moral development. And Hegel's philosophy epitomizes this penchant for progress by distinguishing not only the *telos* directing history's advance, but also by outlining the pattern for its development through the dialectical mediation of conflict.[293] But when historical progress ceases to be a given, and, indeed, may become problematic by masking the imminence of a "danger" shaking the roots of civilization, what we may mean by the political recedes into darkness.

It will be a few years before Heidegger, in *Contributions* (1938) begins to describe this danger as machination, and, ultimately, as "technology."[294] Yet his ability to address it *as* a danger already emerges in his 1930 lectures on Kant. This danger appears as such in light of paradigm of shift, which brings the possibility of politics itself into question. Politics hangs in the balance when the policies by which it organizes its citizens become compromised by the unfettered drive of "market forces," i. e., of pursuing, wealth and power, comfort and convenience, as ultimate ends. As we will see, technology gives shape to these excesses by implementing various schemes of manufacture, manipulation, and domination, which reduce human beings to their achievements as producer and consumer. But, in the process, we become captive to an illusion, namely, that by benefiting from the advances of technology we are also in position to control whatever risks it poses. This illusion, as it were, conceals to us the danger of technology, insofar as the comforts it extends insulate us from its destructive potential, for example, the convenience of travel on air planes in the face of the terrorists who hijack a plane or detonate bombs on them. In contrast to one power among others we have at our disposal, freedom is the temporalized dynamic which directs us to act and thereby offset the tendency to control and manipulate.

Ironically, to confront technology in this way, and to raise a question concerning its ownmost nature, humanity must have, as it were, an extra-human origin. So too must be the freedom by which human beings are distinguished. In his 1930 lectures on Kant, Heidegger remarks: "... *freedom must itself...be more primordial than man.*"[295] A year earlier in the Kant-book, Heidegger advances one

---

**292** Sherover, *From Kant and Royce to Heidegger*, pp. 50–52.
**293** See Schalow, *Language and Deed*, pp. 12–21.
**294** GA 65, pp. 125–134; tr. 88–93.
**295** GA 31, p. 134; tr. 93.

of his most provocative, as quoted in the previous chapter: "More original than man is the finitude of the Dasein in him."[296] Almost thirty years later, while addressing repercussions of modern technology, Heidegger cites this key passage: "But the abiding (*Wesen* in the verbal sense) of the human being, 'the Dasein in the human being' (Cf. *Kant and the Problem of Metaphysics*, section #43) is not something human."[297] The fact that only through its reciprocity with being does the self acquire the power to be free means, correlatively, it is by appropriating this capacity that "man" is rooted in the extra-human origin of its finitude. But what does this have to do with the political? Does this mean that the political can only serve the organization of exclusively human ends, the "city of man?" Or, on the contrary, does the ownmost of freedom reserve a divine origin for the political, the "city of God?" Neither would seem to be the case, for both versions of the political share a common "anthropocentric"or even "theocentric" premise about the origin of freedom that Heidegger displaces. But if the political can no longer serve the organization of human ends, even if they are those in concert with what God sets for us, then what can its scope be?

In retrospect, this question raises a concern about the need for a methodological shift or correction in Heidegger's approach to the *polis*, which reintroduces finitude as a curb on the administration of freedom explicitly on a social as on an individual plane. The discernment of a further constraint or check, on what we might call a leader's natural impulse toward self-aggrandizement, stems from a provision whose deployment Kant first reserved to (transcendental) *dialectic*. For Kant, the dialectic restores the distinctions that stems from our finitude, in order that we can curb the impetus to identify with a totality, the presumption of a "totalizing impulse," in either knowledge or action. The presumption is such that the totality can be achieved only by championing one perspective to the *exclusion* of another. In this political realm, this will to exclusivity constitutes the most destructive mutation of a will to power, in which an elite, in the name of society *as a whole*, justifies its own supremacy at the expense of, and even elimination of, an opposing social faction. To be sure, the worst case scenario of this tyrannical will to power would be genocide, or the extermination of a specific group of people or ethnicity. As Hans Sluga remarks: "Politics is therefore always a process of self-legitimation in which particular priorities of action and particular social structures must be justified."[298] By discharging the power to choose within the widest expanse of possibilities, ontological freedom may also have a problematic

---

**296** GA 3, p. 229; tr. 160.
**297** GA 9, p. 397; tr. 300.
**298** Sluga, *Heidegger's Crisis*, p. 22.

drawback. For the expanse of openness does not explicitly preclude the proliferation of individual wills that serve the whims of their indulgences and special interests, in an analogous way to the unownedness of those acting in behalf of the "they-self."[299] Perhaps Heidegger himself has the best presentiment of the need for this dialectic, when he remarked in his debate with Cassirer at Davos:

> Truth itself is unified with the structure of transcendence on the most intimate level in order for Dasein to be open to others and to itself. We are a being who holds itself within the unconcealedness of beings. To hold oneself in this way within the openness of beings is what I describe as being-in-the-truth, and I go further and say: On the ground of the finitude of being-in-the-truth of human beings, there exists at the same time a being-in-the-untruth.[300]

By monitoring the human propensity toward dissimulation, such a dialectic would prompt an additional legislative act in order to check the aberrations of the individual will, which result in hegemonic political practices, e. g., totalitarianism. By stifling the forum of "free exchange" and dissent in which the political finds its original place (*Ort*), totalitarianism necessarily supports acts of violence against those individuals who oppose its autocratic rule.[301]

While not explicit in his writings on Kant, the importance of this dialectic emerges in Heidegger's subsequent appropriation of the Kantian concept of freedom in his 1936 lectures on Schelling. In a lecture course that bears a title reminiscent of his 1930 lectures on Kant, Heidegger wrestles with the further dynamic of freedom as it intersects with the constellation of a political realm and brings the cutting edge of the conflict between *good and evil* to the foreground.

> But in the moment of the decisive experience of human being we are, as in no other experience of the self, protected from the vanity of self-overestimation and the self-righteousness of self-depreciation. For in the decidedness of our own being, we experience the fact that no one attains the height of what is his best as little as he attains the abyss of what is his evil, but that he is placed in this between (*Zwischen*) in order to wrest his truth from it which is in itself necessary, but precisely for this reason historical.[302]

Within the political realm, the dialectic legislative in behalf of diversity, providing a further zone of demarcation against the rule of tyranny, in order that another

---

**299** See Haar, *Heidegger and the Essence of Man*, p. 126. Also see Schalow, "Beyond Decisionism and Anarchy: The Task of Re-thinking Resolve", pp. 359–376.
**300** GA 3, p. 281; tr. 176.
**301** See Schmidt, *Lyrical and Ethical Subjects*, pp. 82–86.
**302** GA 42, p. 269. For an earlier English translation, not based on the *Gesamtausgabe* edition, see Heidegger, *Schelling's Treatise On the Essence of Human Freedom*, p. 155.

mode of governance can prevail: preserving the uniqueness of the individual against the will of the collective. Freedom thereby has as one avenue for its administration accommodating the otherness of the other, the letting be that welcomes diversity. In this way, the liberating spirit of love, as Schelling emphasizes, can prevail over the will of subjugation and tyranny.[303] In *Mindfulness* (1938/39), Heidegger explicitly denounces the "exploitation of the 'youth'" by "dictators" who, in the name of machination, advocate conformity over individuality.[304]

The diversity that comes to fruition through love, however, may not be confined to those beings of human origin. Insofar the freedom we are privileged to "manage" has an extra-human origin, our capacity to love can be extended to include other forms of sentience beside rationality. The transitoriness of our sojourn on the earth qualifies us to serve as stewards over its diverse habitats, introducing as a further clause of self-legislation a mandate to dwell in harmony with nature as well as to exercise compassion toward others. A politics that coincides with human interests plays into the hand of technology, as it regulates the cycle of production and consumption. Within this cycle human beings stand side by side with what they exploit, natural resources, to the point that the boundary separating them becomes increasingly blurred. The more the self depends upon what it produces, the more it becomes a cog in the relentless drive of production, in the impetus to increase productivity, and reciprocally, in increasing the desire to consume. By contrast, to displace anthropocentricism is, paradoxically to direct the response of freedom to what is non-human, in countering its reduction to human interests, allowing nature to unfold in its weightedness apart from its subordination to human ends. The proper response, then, is "letting be." Correlatively, within this historical orbit, human beings participate in freedom insofar as they provide a place for being's manifestness. Because thought depends on the relationship to which it enters with being, the activity of thinking requires the allocation of a place. And it is by inhabiting this place that we participate in openness, and, as free, allow the diversity of what is to manifest itself. In contrast to the manipulative hold of technology, we are free insofar as we cultivate diverse possibilities of manifestation, in homage of nature in the ancient sense as self-emerging presence. In contrast to the Enlightenment split between freedom and nature, freedom in Heidegger's sense transposes us into the midst of nature. Would it not be strange, then, if politics begins not from the premise of our preoccupation with human ends, as the Enlightenment does,[305] but, on the

---

**303** GA 42, p. 277; tr. 160.
**304** GA 66, p. 19; tr. 14. See Emad and Kalary, "Translators' Foreword," p. xl.
**305** See Sherover, *From Kant and Royce to Heidegger*, pp. 55–56.

contrary, by fostering what we have in common with nature, the occupation of a habitat? Thus, it is in the verbal expression thereof, or by "inhabiting," that the parameters of the *polis* reemerge from its coincidence with exclusively human ends. When we cross over to rediscover ourselves through what we hold in common with nature, we engage in what Heidegger calls "dwelling."

Heidegger's advantage in overcoming the metaphysical split between freedom and nature occurs at the expense of (his) jettisoning the world-view surrounding the liberal tradition of the Enlightenment. Is Heidegger then a "reactionary" in the sense that he resists, on the one hand, the advances of technology, and, on the other, denounces liberalism altogether?[306] Perhaps that might explain why the politics of National Socialism appeared so seductive to him — to the extent that such an explanation is even possible — but perhaps that is not the most important point. On the contrary, against the backdrop of politics of Heidegger's era, we bring to the forefront what really hangs in the balance in his debate with Cassirer at Davos: that *humanism is itself under attack.*

Insofar as its assumptions, including those consistent with Christianity, shape the politics of modernity, to overthrow humanism is to redefine ourselves by what is both "farthest" and "closest" to us. The crossing with nature, then, interjects Dasein into an area in which it belongs in the company with others in part through its occupation of a habitat that it also shares in common with non-human creatures. In this regard, for example, the compassion we show toward our animal counterparts might provide a better indication of the "humanity" that we claim qualifies us as equal members of a community.

But what does Kant say on the topic of whether we have responsibility to protect the welfare of our animal counterparts? Surprisingly, he says more than we might expect, and this fact has motivated scholars to extrapolate on what would constitute an updated Kantian vision of animal welfare. Even though animals do not rise to the status of persons, as humans do, our higher status mandates that we avoid any unnecessary exploitation of animals. Indeed, Kant argues that we lose respect in our own eyes when we mistreat animals or inflict pain upon them. Thus, we do not have a direct duty on an explicit obligation to protect animals on the basis of their inherent worth. Rather, it is because we can ascend to the highest level of the sublimity of our natures that we can go the extra mile of exercising compassion toward those supposedly inferior to us. Julian Franklin has gone a step further to argue that it is consistent for Kant to include all sentient beings, not just rational ones, in the requirement of the categorical imperative to treat those possessing awareness as "ends" and not merely as

---

**306** Zimmerman, *Heidegger's Confrontation with Modernity*, p. 13.

"means."[307] Franklin claims that the umbrella of the categorical imperative can be extended to include moral patients, or those sentient beings who cannot legislate the moral law, as well as moral patients, or those rational beings capable of such self-legislation. "The obligation of the categorical imperative, although it is imposed on humans and other rational beings only, must apply to all sentients."[308] As admirable as Franklin's argument is, he assumes a more radical ontological perspective than Kant himself could develop; but, which on the contrary, Heidegger can illuminate given the thrust of his being-historical thinking: namely, the overturning of the anthropocentric prejudice of the Enlightenment. Kant develops the categorical imperative in terms of a "kingdom of ends," extending its application to include a community of self-legislative beings. Even if one argues (as Franklin does) that moral patients are worthy of equal consideration of treatment as moral agents are, we still need to explain, beyond Kant, the underpinnings for the organization of such a community prior to the ontological disjunction between persons and things.

Heidegger allows for the possibility that natural beings may be interwoven into the fabric of the human community; for he (unlike Kant) circumvents the bifurcation between freedom and nature, and the parallel one between rational and non-rational beings. In principle, animals can merit equal consideration to animals, not because (as moral patients) they merit consideration analogous to persons, but because the freedom of letting be originates in reciprocity with, rather than in opposition to nature. Hence, this "extra-human" freedom can serve non-human as well as human interests, weaving both humanity and animal kind together into one and the same community.[309] A trans-human ethic thereby becomes possible which, while it endorses the Kantian platform of the categorical imperative, extends the membership of its community to animals as well as human beings. If we can turn a phrase from Nietzsche, a "community of the future" would extend its borders to include the habitat we share with the diversity of life, most notably our animal counterparts.

If there is a discourse distinctive of the political, apart from that couched in liberal terms, it would involve shifting the emphasis toward the grammar of middle-voice, of how to undertake the task of dwelling. Does the grammar of middle-voice then provide the key for *translating* social policies into ecological ones? Rather, by reading back the concern for our manner of dwelling back onto the question of the political, we reclaim the original meaning of ecology as a

---

307 Franklin, *Animal Rights and Moral Philosophy*, pp. 32–35.
308 Franklin, *Animals Rights and Moral Philosophy*, p. 48.
309 Schalow, *The Incarnality of Being*, pp. 121–125.

speaking in behalf (*logos*) of the residence (*eco*). This speaking in behalf of points to that attunement which occurs concurrently with our attempt at dwelling, that is, in a way that harmonizes with the diversity of life. That attunement, as we will see, points back to the community we belong, not simply as the rational agents of Enlightenment liberalism, but as incarnated individuals who exist in the company of animals.

The reference to incarnality becomes important if we are to understand the change which transpires in the actual composition of the political, to the "organicity" of its development. In this regard, the term "political body," which we might take only "figuratively" to suggest the organization of its constituents, takes on a more literal meaning to indicate how our "exposure to the flesh" places us in proximity to, and perhaps disposes us to care for, our animal counterparts. Our exposure to the flesh has the double importance not only of placing us in a position to appreciate their potential for suffering, but, in the trajectory of our transcendence, we experience the distance through our proximity to them, which can provoke initiatives to safeguard the habitat we share with animals in a way that they cannot directly envision. Within the fleshly texture of the political body, the animal's alleged inferiority to us may not serve as an excuse to show indifference toward them, but, on the contrary, may serve as a rallying cry to come to their defense in the face of the onslaught of technological mechanisms of exploitation, e. g, the use of animals for medical research.

We can defend those who are not in a position to speak on their own behalf, to exercise their own defense. Could this be a motto within the language of the political, within its declension, which would mark a new demarcation of the body-politic? Such a political body would be interwoven into a context of interrelationships which would "distribute the good," if not exercise compassion, through a balance of the earth's (and animals') welfare along with human beings' — "terrestrially" as well as "socially." At the very least we can say that Heidegger does not exclude this possibility. If freedom is inherently finite, as Sherover properly emphasizes this key Heideggerian precept,[310] and in addition, if its origin is extra-human, then, by extension, the distribution of its power is not to be confined to the benefit of human beings alone. On the contrary, as our way of entering into the open expanse of possibility, freedom serves our stewardship of being's manifestation, implying an exercise of care (*Sorge*) in behalf of the diversity of life itself. In other words, the *economy of freedom* requires not only the inclusion of the widest constituency of participation on a social level, but, on a terrestrial level, the crossover into the realm of animal sentience as well.

---

**310** Sherover, *From Kant and Royce to Heidegger*, pp. 193–198.

In this regard, the allusion to animals is not a chimera because, not only is it implied within the lexicon of dwelling, but is also lies at the root of our being-in-the-world. Indeed, in order to address the relationships which animals stand to humans and vice-a-versa, Heidegger devotes his entire 1929/30 lectures course to its discussion. On the one hand, because of their deprivation as "world-poor," animals point to the periphery of the community that human beings occupy.[311] On the other hand, by standing at this periphery, animals point back to the natural element which goes unspoken in our membership within a human community, the character of our "inhabitation" and "rootedness." Indeed, the analogy we can draw with animals, by appealing to *physis* as self-emerging presence, gives us a clue to the idioms by which we can express the dynamics of our inhabitation of the world. Heidegger sandwiches his provocative discussion of animals between his 1928 lectures on Kant and his writings devoted to renewing that exchange in the 1930s'. Surprisingly or not, in marking Kant's neglect for the *problem* of world, Heidegger alludes to animals at the outset of his *Phenomenological Interpretation*. "Animals are not extant like rocks, but they also do not exist in the manner of comporting themselves to a world. Nevertheless in plants and animals we find a kind of orientation toward other beings which in a certain way surround them. As distinguished from the extantness of material things and from the existence of humans, we call the mode of being of plants and animals: life."[312]

In light of his exchange with Kant, Heidegger shows a more nuanced concern for animals than does his contemporary, Max Scheler. In a parallel manner to Scheler, Heidegger points to the "world-openness" in which human beings participate, the capacity that animals lack. Scheler, however, reinstates the Enlightenment concept of the person as the center of the conscious-experience of both world-openness, and empathetic intentions toward others. By implication, animals are relegated to the camp of non-persons, and they are described in negative terms as a comparative marker as lacking what human beings possess. In abandoning the Enlightenment concept of the person, Heidegger denounces the humanistic premises that Scheler holds in common with Kant, despite criticizing the "formalist" bent of the latter's ethics.[313] Given the different orientation of his phenomenology, Heidegger resists the modern prejudice, as epitomized by Descartes,[314] of dismissing the importance of animals because they lack the rational trait of self-consciousness (intentionality, personhood) — the hallmark of humanism.

---

**311** GA 29/30, pp. 263–264; tr. 177–178.
**312** GA 29/30, p. 20; tr. 16.
**313** Schalow, *Renewal of the Heidegger-Kant Dialogue*, pp. 270–271. See GA 63, p. 26; tr. 22.
**314** Descartes, *Discourse on Method*, p. 79. Descartes refers to the "fantasy which can change" or mutate ideas. See Sallis, *Force of Imagination*, pp. 85–89.

The problem with humanism is that it begins from certain preconceptions that extol the human at the expense of everything that is not human. Characteristics like soul, consciousness, rationality, spirit are those which we believe are inherently distinctive of us, and thereby place us at the pinnacle of nature in comparison to which all other creatures appears disproportionately inferior. In Scheler's modified anthropocentricism, for example, the characteristics of the person, which elevate us above animals, are precisely those that extend our spirituality in the direction of the divine. The actualization of the person occurs in this movement of religious transcendence, in which the self overcomes its finitude by realizing its ancestry in the infinite. Yet as early as his lectures 1923 lectures on the hermeneutics of facticity, Heidegger challenges Scheler's concept of personhood by underscoring the latter's misunderstanding of Kant's concept thereof. "Scheler so little understands Kant's basic approach to the idea of person that in characterizing his notion of the idea of respect merely as an 'odd exception' in his position he is unwilling to see that his own idea of person is distinguished from Kant's only insofar as it is more dogmatic and allows the borders between philosophical and theology to become even more blurred ..."[315] Because Heidegger does not buy into their preconceptions, he can circumvent the traditional dichotomies in which the views of the self — from Plato to Scheler — play themselves out: soul versus body, rationality versus instinct, spirit versus flesh. As Derrida emphasizes, any attempt like Scheler's to distinguish characteristics intrinsic to human versus animals provides an opening for anthropocentricism according to a hierarchy in which humans beings have "dominion" over their animal counterparts.[316] Insofar as Heidegger does not assign nature a position of inferiority versus the supernatural, our differences from animals do not necessarily elevate us above them. We are different from animals primarily due to our ability to forecast the eventuality of our own death, an advantage of fore-sight, ironically, that binds us to our finitude, our "earth boundedness," rather than severs us from it.

In *Basic Problems*, Heidegger argues that Scheler misunderstands Kant's notion of respect (for persons).[317] In *Being and Time*, Heidegger suggests that if Kant's view of the person rests on unexamined premises, Scheler adds to the confusion with his *Wertphilosophie*. "Even the theory of values, whether it is regarded formally or materially, has as its unexpressed ontological presupposition a 'metaphysics of morals' — that is, an ontology of Dasein and existence."[318]

---

315  GA 63, p. 26; tr. 22.
316  Derrida, *Of Spirit*, pp. 51–53.
317  GA 24, p. 193; tr. 136.
318  GA 2, pp. 388–389; tr. 339.

As Heidegger suggests, Kant came closest to providing such an ontology; but as the cornerstone of the categorical imperative, he still subscribed to a disjunction between persons and things.[319] Persons have absolute value, or are ends in themselves; things, on the other hand, have relative or instrumental value, or are means to the realization of some other end. In accordance with the acknowledgment of our essential humanity, we are required to treat persons as ends in themselves, and never merely as means, that is, in a way which prohibits us from exploiting people or reducing them to their use-value. But while Kant predicated the categorical imperative on this distinction between persons and things, he does so at the risk of leaving animals in somewhat of a grey area as to what are obligations toward them are.

In its Kantian formulation, the difficulty with the categorical imperative is that it upholds the inherent worth of person *without* the ontological underpinning which can reserve a place for "equal consideration" of animals. Because Heidegger opposes the metaphysical premises of the Enlightenment, his non-anthropocentric concept of humanity, while it does not go as far as to grant "intrinsic value" to animals,[320] curbs the Enlightenment tendency to reduce our animal counterparts to the status of mere instruments of exploitation. Animal rights activists have debated whether Kant's categorical imperative, despite privileging persons, must necessarily exclude animals from meriting consideration as ends in themselves. As mentioned above, Franklin argues that the second formulation of Kant's categorical imperative could be restated to replace "humanity" with "sentient beings," such that we acts always to treat sentient beings as ends in themselves.[321] Even though animals are not moral agents, they can still be "moral patients," insofar as their sentience exacts of us a level of concern concomitant with that we maintain constitutes an obligation in the case of our fellow human beings. The only problem with this argument is that it presumes the kind of criticism that Heidegger advanced against Scheler, which de-centers human personhood in order that animal sentience can merit equal consideration.

For Heidegger the differences between animals and humans are instructive because we have a common interest by the fact that we are, as it were, co-inhabitants of nature. Regardless of the ecological implications of Heidegger's hermeneutic phenomenology, his concern for animals brings to the foreground an aspect of space which remains concealed in Descartes's mathematical portrait of nature, that is, the exercise of dwelling or as a way of inhabitation. As

---

**319** GA 24, p. 198; tr. 139.
**320** Zimmerman, "Heidegger's Phenomenology and Contemporary Environmentalism", pp. 73–74.
**321** Franklin, *Animal Rights and Moral Philosophy*, pp. 32, 44.

Heidegger emphasizes in his essay on "Building Dwelling Thinking," originally space has to do with place, in the primitive sense, in which a gopher seeks residence through a hole in the ground and a bird does so through a nest in a tree.[322] Insofar as space pertains to our manner of residing, like animals, we are spatial due to how our way of occupying it transforms spatiality into the uniqueness of a "place" in which to reside. A place, then, refers not only to a "wherein," but also to the enowning by which we transplant ourselves into a residence. Not only do we make the abode our own, but we also enown ourselves through the exercise of dwelling, or taking up roots. Given his emphasis on rootedness, critics often provide a caricature of Heidegger as a "primitivist" who reacted against modernity and sought refuge in a pristine form of Germanic provincialism.[323] But we can also depict Heidegger as a proto-ecologist who sought to re-infuse space with its own dynamics, such that we own ourselves by allocating it as a "place" to inhabit. As Heidegger emphasizes, space is the "freeing" of something to "settle" where it *belongs*, or is the delineating of boundaries in which various locations can arise where a living being can reside. "Accordingly, spaces receive their being from locations, and not from 'space.'[324]

The space we allocate in dwelling is also in a certain sense "cleared," that is, distributed within an expanse of openness whose boundaries coincide with the world itself. As Heidegger suggests in this 1936 lectures on Kant, *Die Frage nach dem Ding*, animals "spatialize" in the sense that their orientation to the environment allows them to engage in such activities, for example, as "playing" with each other.[325] Human beings, however, can occupy space in a unique way of harboring the negative, that is, as a removal from proximity, "dis-placing" of what is (environmentally) given in favor of an influx of possibility which adds the dimensionality of depth and breadth to space. As Heidegger states, perhaps as a rejoinder to Scheler, no animal can proclaim the otherness of the "I," that is, participate in the counter-movement of "clearing" in which things recedes in favor of the expanse of openness that allows them to appear, the no-thing of openness.[326] In discussing Kant's formulation of the synthetic a priori principles of nature, Heidegger makes a comment that would seem almost out of place were it not for the fact that he developed his second major reinterpretation of the

---

**322** GA 7, p. 161. For an English translation, not based on the *Gesamtausgabe* edition, see Heidegger, *Poetry, Language, Thought*, pp. 156–157.

**323** Wolin, *The Politics of Being*, pp. 35–38.

**324** GA 7, pp. 158–159; tr. 154–155.

**325** GA 41, p. 223; tr. 221.

**326** GA 41, p. 223; tr. 221.

*Critique of Pure Reason* (the Kant book comprising the first) on the heels of drafting his monumental essay, "The Origin of the Work of Art":

> In this showing of what is in its openness, that doing has a special task which shows things by creating them in a certain sense, the creation of a work of art. Work makes world. World within itself first reveals things. The possibility and necessity of the work of art is only *one* proof that we come to know what is, only when it is specifically [presented] to us.[327]

In addressing art, Heidegger brings the discussion of spatiality to the forefront, as yielding the dimensionality by which we participate in the openness.

Nature and animals, spatiality and art, freedom and openness: all of these are topics which not only seem foreign to Kant, and at best seem to occupy the periphery of Heidegger's radical reinterpretation of transcendental philosophy. Nevertheless, the discourse which allows us to address the interdependence of time and space becomes crucial, if we are to extend the reciprocal rejoinder of these two thinkers, and proceed with the translation of the political, i. e., the task of translating social policies into ecological ones. Let us consider the further development of this rejoinder, as Heidegger takes it up in *Contributions*.

## 2 Thing and World

Heidegger's effort to address the origin of the work of art does not seem to be particularly relevant to his attempt to retrieve the ontological underpinnings of Kant's critical enterprise. But despite the radicality of the Kant-book, echoes still resound (beginning with Cassirer's critique of it) as to the one-sidedness of Heidegger's appropriation of transcendental philosophy. And these are concerns which Heidegger might broach if they are to be incorporated into the form of a self-criticism about expanding the radius of his philosophical inquiry. If a concern for temporality directs the inquiry into the meaning of being, then a discussion of spatiality cannot be too far behind. For spatial connotations are already implied in the way that we express being's disclosure through time as variations, for instance, of the "open" (*Offene*) and clearing (*Lichtung*). Kant himself also emphasized the conjunction of space and time as pure forms of sensory intuition, although he prioritized time as the precondition of all human awareness, of our self-perceptions (e. g. introspections) as well as of objects (given "externally" or in relation to space). Despite all the attention Heidegger devotes in the Kant-book to recovering the origin of primordial time, are there any textual instances where

---

327 GA 41, pp. 209–210; tr. 207–208.

he acknowledges the reciprocal importance of space (within the overall problematic of fundamental ontology)?

In a pivotal passage toward the conclusion of the Part III of the Kant-book, Heidegger makes a very provocative statement:

> But, one could object, if transcendence is not to be grounded in time alone, Kant is just [being] consistent if, with the delimitation of the priority of time, he eliminates the pure power of imagination. Yet, with this reflection we forget that as pure intuition, pure space is no less rooted transcendentally in the transcendental power of imagination than "time," insofar as this is understood merely as what is formed in pure intuition as the pure intuited, the pure succession of the sequence of nows. In fact space in a certain sense is always and necessarily equivalent to time so understood.[328]

Could it be, that after having given inordinate attention to time, spatiality must re-emerge as a problem in its own right, and that it is the need to include this further permutation of inquiry which prompts his abrupt discussion of the origin of the art-work in the mid 1930s? From Heidegger's own testimonials, there are indications that *Die Frage nach dem Ding* speaks to a "one-sidedness" in the Kant-book, and discusses, for example, the Kantian "principles of the understanding," which he omitted in his earlier interpretations of transcendental philosophy. Indeed, in a parenthetical remark in his 1935/36 lectures on Kant, Heidegger suggests that his discussion of the universal laws of nature compensates for his earlier omission. "The following interpretation makes up for what the writing *Kant and the Problem of Metaphysics* 1929 lacked."[329] Where in the Kant-book Heidegger equates the problem of schematism (temporality) with the crux of transcendental philosophy, in his 1935/36 lectures in Freiburg he allows the principles of understanding to serve as the centerpiece of the first *Critique*.[330] Could it be that the "second" Kant-book speaks not just to omissions in the first, or to Neo-Kantian criticisms voiced by Cassirer, but instead fits into an overall mosaic of interpretation that addresses the importance which space has in the dynamic of being's disclosure?

Indeed, at the beginning of this book, Heidegger prefaces the question concerning the thing with this query:

> Our question "What is a thing?" includes, therefore, the questions "What is space?" and "What is time?" It is customary for us to speak of them both together. But how and why are space and time conjoined? Are they conjoined at all, as though externally thrust onto one

---

**328** GA 3, p. 203; tr. 141–142.
**329** GA 41, p. 127; tr. 125.
**330** GA 41, pp. 132–133; tr. 130–131. See Dahlstrom, "Heidegger's Kant-Courses at Marburg," p. 294.

another and into one another, or are they primordially at one. Do they stem from a common root, from some third, or better, some first which is neither space nor time because more primordially it is both? These and other related questions will occupy us ...[331]

With an eye to Kant, Heidegger points to a "span of time" (*Zeitraum*) to indicate the interplay of time and space through which the appearance of the thing becomes possible. "That we name time first, that we say *Zeitraum* and not *Raumzeit*, should indicate that time plays a special role in this question. But that should not mean at all that space can be deduced from time or that it is something secondary to it."[332] Yet in developing the preceding questions (quoted immediately above), Heidegger allows the thinking of the ontological difference, implicit throughout Kant's account of human finitude, to redirect us to the unity of time and space. That is, time and space not just exclusively (transcendental) preconditions of the appearances of beings, as Kant suggested. Rather, the conjunction of time and space pertains to the dynamic of being's self-manifestation, to the experience of the "there is" in which the openness itself emerges in contrast solely to the appearance of beings. As such, being-historical thinking addresses "*time as the time-space of the clearing*" (*Zeit als der Zeit-Raum des Lichtung*).[333]

Heidegger employs the term *Zwischen* or "between" to characterize this thought's emergence into this clearing, which unfolds through the tension of *Zeit-Raum* (versus *Zeitraum*). As Parvis Emad and Kenneth Maly point out in their "Foreword" to *Contributions*: "In order to say what is being-historically ownmost to time and space, Heidegger uses the word *Zeit-Raum*. We translated *Zeit-Raum* with *time-space*. Note that this hyphenated word is quite different from *Zeitraum* (written without a hyphen), which we have translated as 'span of time.' The phenomenological context of *Zeit-Raum* includes the word *Zwischen* and its variants ..."[334] Being-historical thinking allows us to address the thing, not just in its generic characteristics as an object of natural science, but, in a manner parallel with art, in the singularity of its manifestation. Things that reside in their unique place are not defined as objects that stand over against a representing subject. Rather, a thing appears from the depths of its manifestation, insofar as it returns to the "abiding of the expanse" and makes way for its own occupancy, its play-space.[335]

---

**331** GA 41, p. 16; tr. 16.

**332** GA 41, p. 16; tr. 16–17.

**333** GA 69, p. 98. For a further discussion of the issue of "time-space," see Schalow, "The Twofold Image of Space: Heidegger's Unwinding of the Kantian Premise", pp. 359–371.

**334** Emad and Maly, "Translators' Foreword" to *Contributions*, p. xxxv.

**335** Heidegger, *Discourse on Thinking*, p. 67. See Schalow, "Thought and Spatiality: The Later Heidegger's Quandary", pp. 157–170.

When Heidegger addresses art, he specifically directs attention to what other-wise goes unnoticed, the element of spatiality to which art gives expression, that is, as a "work." We tend to look at art either in terms of the creativity that it embodies or the beauty it evokes. But what we tend to neglect is how a work of art is an experiment or venture with limits, the setting of which gives border or definition to the indeterminacy from which disclosedness prevails over its opposite. The work is in fact a deed, but one whose flights of fancy, like imagina-tion, connects us with the roots of our inhabitation, with the fabric of our being-in-the-world. We speak of the materiality of the work of art, including the literal elements of paint and canvas, clay and wood, but what they imply, according to Heidegger, is that dimension of rootedness in which the tendency counter to unconcealment resides, namely, the earth. The earth points not only to the periphery of our inhabitation, but also counterposes the dynamic of concealment in tension with its opposite, or concealment. If world is that by virtue of which a community of human beings experience this unconcealment, then earth embo-dies the counter movement of concealment. Gadamer summarizes this key devel-opment in Heidegger's thinking:

> It was not merely that Heidegger now brought art into the basic hermeneutical approach of the self-understanding of humans in their historicality, nor even that these addresses [on the origin of the work of art] understood art to be the act that founds whole historical worlds (as it is understood in the poetic faith of Hölderlin and George). Rather, the real sensation caused by Heidegger's new experiment had to do with the startling new conceptuality that boldly emerged in the connection with this topic. For here, the task was of the "world" and the "earth." From the very beginning, the concept of the world had been one of Heidegger's major hermeneutical concepts. As the referential totality of Dasein's projecting-opening, "world" constituted the horizon that was preliminary to all projecting of Dasein's concern ... The new and startling thing was that this concept of the world now found a counterconcept in the "*earth* ..." "Earth" is a counterconcept to world insofar as it exemplifies self-sheltering and closing-off as opposed to self-opening.[336]

Thus, world and earth unfold through this tension of strife, and is the vessel for playing out this resonance/counter resonance and, most of all, for providing us with an "outlet" to participate in this strife. The outlet is the unique cultural permutation or pursuit that allows us to re-enact the drama of that strife, to stand at the brink where unconcealment momentarily prevails over its opposite. As Vallega-Neu states: "the original strife of truth must be transformed into the strife between world and earth ... Heidegger designates the world as the 'reigning of vastness' (*waltende Weite*) where connections and paths open and where histor-

---

**336** Gadamer, *Heidegger's Ways*, pp. 99, 103.

ical decisions of humanity take shape (Heidegger mentions birth and death, disaster and blessing, victory and disgrace, endurance and decline)."[337]

The emphasis on re-enacting a drama reverberates with a sense of tragedy with all its implications for life. The appeal to art refers to the incursion of the instance, or the singular, in the way we experience the dynamic of unconcealment. We will return to discuss the importance of tragedy later in regards to *Contributions*, but, at the very least tragedy suggests a lexicon to address the unique interweaving of the cosmic and human dimensions of the "strife"; while art points to the singularity of that experience, the offering of an instance, by which an individual is granted access to this unconcealing event. Art, then, is the granting of this accessibility that does not simply define unconcealment, but extend an entryway to it, indeed, precisely at the point where its closure also obtrudes. And our way of being born into strife, and carried along by it, constitutes its tragic character. Heidegger thereby establishes the concreteness of our experience of truth, as a conflict into which Dasein is transported in such a way that each of us is a potential protagonist in a tragedy. As such a protagonist, the self ex-ists in the element that art extends to us, the incarnality of the conflict, the allocation of a space/place through which being appears through the opposing of difference in the coming into presence and withdrawing into absence. But what motif in Heidegger's dialogue with Kant marks the confluence of all of these issues, harboring an implicit allusion to the singularity of the work of art as well as a reference to the temporal play of presence/absence? The answer is obvious: imagination, but as soon as we say as much, we discover the paradox that in his second major work on Kant, unlike the first, Heidegger avoids any mention of imagination and of its unique "economy."[338]

In simplest terms, Heidegger shifts the focus of his analysis to the results of schematism, the canon of rules which determine any object as an object in conformity with (the conditions of human finitude). But even if the axis of his interpretation of Kant shifts, this does not preclude the possibility that what Heidegger thinks through the imagination can emerge, although in a transformed way. What comes to light in the problematic of human finitude is not the possibility of understanding being, but how our own ex-istence is granted within the area of the difference between being and beings. Heidegger calls this area, in which our being is defined through its capacity to carry out the tension of this differentiation, the "between" (*Zwischen*). If the ontological difference first be-

---

**337** Vallega-Neu, *The Bodily Dimension in Thinking*, p. 92.

**338** As Sallis points out, after the "Origin of the Work of Art", Heidegger rarely speaks of the imagination. See Sallis, *Echoes*, p. 134.

comes concrete or factical through Dasein's transcendence, then the flip side is also the case: Dasein is defined by its service in allowing this tension of differentiation to prevail. In the second instance, the inquiry shifts to addressing the dual way in which Dasein's occupies the "between," as the witness both to the holding in abeyance of being's power to become manifest and to the beings that testify to this manifestation. Dasein, as it were, vouches for the asymmetry of this relationship, in which being recedes into the economy of its own potential for manifestation, and beings attest to, but can never exhaust, this potential.

In his lectures on Nietzsche, Heidegger asks a provocative, if not leading question: "Is Dasein the ground of the ontological difference, or is the ontological difference the ground of Dasein?"[339] If the Kant-book addresses the first side of this question by addressing finite transcendence, then *Die Frage nach dem Ding* considers the second side of this question by considering the "between." Put in simple terms, the "between" is the dynamic whereby the openness emerges in tension with its opposite, such that the "stretch" of its boundaries is simultaneously "restricted" by what appears therein. As a being, Dasein occupies both "fronts" of this openness simultaneously. The openness, however, is not something to which our understanding/knowledge contributes; but, as is already implied in the Kant-book, is already circumscribed by and delivered over to this openness. Whatever determinateness and insight understanding can arrive at ultimately depend on re-allocating the boundaries of its openness, which is turn have their origin out and beyond what we pre-understand. Openness, then, is always born within this circle of possibility, to which Kant himself gives testimony in suggesting that the "transcendental" alternates between projecting-open the preconditions of experience and showing how what we experience exhibits precisely those determinations. The principles which give expression to the transcendental are always a departure from and return to this circle of possibility, a moving back and forth across the expanse of this openness. "Experience is in itself a circular happening through which what lies within the circle opens up (*eröffnet*). This open (*Offene*), however, is nothing other than the between (*Zwischen*) — between us and the thing."[340]

In *Die Frage nach dem Ding*, Heidegger appeals to Kant's declaration of the reciprocity between "the possibility of experience" and the "objects of experience" — the message of the highest principle of synthetic judgments — to distinguish how openness is always an emergence from, and an challenging of, its own boundaries. The boundaries are always to be prepared to be stretched,

**339** Heidegger, *Nietzsche, Zweiter Band*, p. 243. Heidegger, *Nietzsche, Vol. 4: Nihilism*, p. 185.
**340** GA 41, pp. 244–245; tr. 242–243.

and hence exhibit a kind of elasticity in which what is admitted within the openness can provide further impetus for its expansion.

> Kant's questioning about the thing asks about intuition and thought, about experience and its principles, i. e., it asks about man. The question"What is a thing?" is the question "Who is man?" That does not mean that things become a human product (*Gemächte*), but, on the contrary, it means that man is to be understood as he who always already leaps beyond things, but in such a way that this leaping-beyond is possible only while things encounter and so precisely remain themselves — while they send us back behind ourselves our surface. A dimension is opened up in Kant's question about the thing which lies between the thing and man, which reaches out beyond things back behind man.[341]

Though Heidegger does not put it in quite this way, the incarnality of ex-istence is such that we are perpetually challenged to place ourselves into question by whatever our openness brings us into close proximity. In this way, the so-called thing, or, more precisely, the novelty of manifestness that it embodies, can become the harbinger of a *logos* which reciprocally addresses me, and, in its very manner of presencing, pose a question about my own way of belonging to, and participating in the openness. Thus we hear the echoes of Heidegger's reformulation of Kant's question about the possibility of synthetic a priori judgments: "The question 'What is a thing?' is the question 'Who is man?.'"[342]

In this way, Heidegger arrives at the threshold of Kant's problematic, because he is able to take the latter's question and counter pose it in a new and radical way. Kant himself maintained that all philosophical questions reduce to one, the possibility of synthetic a priori judgments. Heidegger confirms the radicality of his destructive-retrieval of Kant, not simply through the innovativeness of his analyses, but, indeed, by restoring the ultimate economy of Kant's question, by counterposing it within a different context where its significance can ring again, albeit with an even deeper and simpler resonance behind all the complexity of the critical enterprise: the economy of all economies. In arriving at his economic reformulation of Kant's question, Heidegger makes an interesting remark about Kant's highest principle of synthetic judgments, that the "conditions of the possibility of experience are likewise the conditions of the possibility of the objects of experience":

> Whoever understands this principle understands Kant's *Critique of Pure Reason*. Whoever understands this does not only know one book among the writings of philosophy, but masters a fundamental posture of the history of man, which we can neither avoid, leap over,

---

341 GA 41, p. 246; tr. 244.
342 GA 41, p. 246; tr. 244.

nor deny in any way. But we have to bring this by an appropriate transformation to fulfillment in the future.[343]

Any mere explanation of the meaning of Kant's principle, no matter how illuminating, does not do it justice. For what matters is not how we can explain it; but,
as Heidegger suggests in the final sentence of the above passage, how that
principle directs us back to the *question* of human finitude and has its impetus
therein.

By taking up Kant's questions anew, Heidegger allows them to speak again in
terms of the relevance they have for today. Kant's questions becomes relevant
insofar as they cultivate those possibilities from the future which reconnect us
with the origins of the tradition. Through his *retrieval* of transcendental philosophy, Heidegger can seek in the Kant's questions the posing of a further question,
which addresses an ambiguity that only becomes apparent given the advantage
of an historical perspective foreclosed to the latter. As Heidegger emphasizes at
the beginning of *Die Frage dem Ding*, the question concerning the thing is as old
as philosophy itself.[344] But the need to re-ask the question become increasingly
urgent, however, when the concern of modernity, including the truncated ways in
which the thing appears according to the law of Newtonian science, began to
overshadow philosophy. The modern quest to determine the thing according to its
conformity to a preset mathematical model of calculation — by which technology
begins to gain its foothold — restricts its appearance to precisely those generic
features governing its determination as an object universally knowable to a
subject.[345] The historical perspective of retrieval allows Kant's thinking to span a
key ambiguity. On the one hand, the modern interest in the subject provides Kant
with clue to re-open the problematic of finitude, and implicitly, its relevance for
establishing temporality's role in outlining the horizon to understand being. On
the other hand, the development of this finitude in the understanding by which
modern science "mathematically projects" the thing rests on its truncation in
terms of generic characteristics. The term "mathematical project" is employed "to
refer to that which is taken by an epoch to be axiomatically or self-evidently true,
and thus is known in advance," about nature's conformity to quantitative principles.[346] The ambiguity that thereby emerges speaks not only to our way of
questioning the thing, but also to Kant's place within modern philosophy. Per-

---

343 GA 41, p. 186; tr. 183. See Schalow, "Reinscribing the *Logos* of Transcendental Logic,"
pp. 195–205.
344 GA 41, pp. 1–3; tr. 1–3.
345 See Ballard, *Philosophy at the Crossroads*, pp. 230–233.
346 Ballard, *Philosophy at the Crossroads*, p. 233.

haps the way that Kant conceives of the twofold boundaries of pure reason contributes to this ambiguity. For not only do these boundaries curb metaphysical speculation about supersensible objects. The other side of our concession to finitude is to avoid the reductionist, even fascist tendency to deny any kind of discourse about human nature and being than can be represented in terms of empirical data. If the concept of noumenon be taken in a merely problematic sense, it is not only admissible, but as setting limits to the sensible is likewise indispensable."[347] Today's *cognitive science*, which reduces the openness of our imaginative powers to neurological functions, is another stage in this spirit of modern positivism.

Heidegger's recognition of Kant's ambiguous place in modern philosophy gives rise to a strikingly different orientation, indeed, tonality, that emanates from the pages of *What Is a Thing?*, in contrast to the Kant-book. As we have already seen, Heidegger claims that his discussion of the principles of understanding, and their implication for the development of modern science, compensates for a certain one-sidedness endemic to his earlier over-emphasis on schematism. In this regard, his 1935/6 lectures on Kant serve an ancillary role of "out- flanking" the Neo-Kantian's appeal to the priority of understanding and reason at the expense of intuition. In the Kant-book, Heidegger emphasizes the priority of pure sensibility as a hallmark of human finitude. But it is as if now he comes full circle to rip the sword of criticism from the Neo-Kantians by providing a more radical and compelling account of the role of understanding than they themselves do. His counter response to the Neo-Kantians and his fuller rendering of the first *Critique* notwithstanding, is there perhaps another factor to be explored in Heidegger's "second" interpretation of Kant? Could it be that this "second" interpretation is a response to the doubling of the question of being, the turning around of the question in which its very point of departure (including the appeal to transcendental philosophy) undergoes transformation?

Indeed, Heidegger does not simply abandon Kant, anymore than he abandons the project of "being and time." But as the landscape of that project changes, so does context in which he reinterprets transcendental philosophy. And leading that reinterpretation, as brought to light in *Contributions*, is the need to include the problematic of space as well as time, or *Zeit-Raum*. Perhaps the most pointed criticism that can be made of Heidegger is not that he cleaves to a brand of "transcendental-horizonal" thinking in Kantian fashion; but rather, he empha-

---

**347** Kant, *Critique of Pure Reason*, A 256 / B 311. See Körner, *Kant*, pp. 158–159. "The reason for the prevalence analytical philosophy may lie in the prevalence of the post-Kantian philosophers who paid no need to the Transcendental Dialectic" (p. 158).

sizes the priority of time (with the importance of space's importance occupying a distant second) in a way that mirrors Kant's emphasizing schematizing power of time wherein the role of space becomes secondary. Scholars like Blattner have then criticized Heidegger for harboring a latent "idealism" in which being, and the appearance of beings, reduces back to an occurrence of Dasein's subjective temporalizing.[348] In *Being and Time*, Heidegger seems almost to anticipate this criticism when he states:

> If what the term "idealism" says, amounts to the understanding that being can never be explained by beings but is already that which is 'transcendental' for every being, then idealism affords the only correct possibility for a philosophical problematic. If so, Aristotle was no less an idealist than Kant. But if "idealism" signifies tracing back every being to a subject or consciousness whose sole distinguishing features are that it remains indefinite in its *being* and is best characterized negatively as 'un-thing-like,' then this idealism is no less naive in its method than the most gross militant realism.[349]

Yet, even if we grant the importance of the ontological difference, its unfolding itself undergoes a kind of change corresponding to Heidegger's attempt to balance the importance of time with space. Specifically, the concrete unfolding of the difference takes shape as the allocation of the interval "between," as articulated in the passages from the conclusion of *Die Frage nach dem Ding?* quoted above. The thing, as Heidegger describes it, is not exclusively correlated with its appearance through Dasein's transcendence, but itself harbors the counter claim of (the) otherness (of manifestation) which "sends us back behind ourselves and our surface." Much like Scheler's notion of "vital resistance," things "remain themselves" and point back to an origin of manifestation over which we never have mastery.

Kant's thinking, then, falls within the double meaning of the thing, as an object of natural science and as a hidden locus of singularity of manifestness. Modern philosophy (including Kant's and even Husserl's transcendental thinking), with science emerging as its counterpart, wrestles with the truncation of the thing, the thing in its generality. By contrast, Heidegger's questioning of the thing, as its reaches back into the origins of philosophy, recalls what remains withdrawn in the truncation of the thing, the singularity of its manifestation. The thing in its singularity emerges in contrast to its generality; but where can we turn in order to offset the prejudice of modern philosophy in favor of the latter, in order to consider the dynamics of the thing's manifestation as such? We cannot develop

---

348 Blattner, *Heidegger's Temporal Idealism*, pp. 42–53.
349 GA 2, pp. 275–276; tr. 251–252.

this question, however, without also confronting the limitations of Kant's transcendental philosophy, and, conversely, the distance that both separates it from Heidegger's thought and creates a space for the exchange between them.[350] The allocation of this space becomes crucial, insofar as it emerges at the historical crossing where the success of modern science begins to usurp the sovereignty of philosophical inquiry and its unique manner of speech.[351] Philosophy reaches the heights of its crisis, then, when its renewal depends upon partnering with an altogether different enterprise in order to recover the roots of its most primeval idioms of expression. This enterprise, namely, poetry, epitomizes a special guardianship of the word. Thus, it is in partnership with *poeisis* that philosophy can recover the originality of its own manner of expression, by its tendency toward innovation which can circumvent the linear models of conceptual representation. Heidegger, then, turns to poetry in order to find the clue to how philosophy can recover its intimacy with language and thereby reside in the freedom of its element. And thus, it is in its singular attunement to the distinctive tonality of the word that philosophy can seek in its ally, within the arena of art and poetry, an example of the self-showing of the thing, of the singularity of its manifestation. In the work of art, the thing as thing emerges through the radiance of its own manifestation.

Through his dialogue with Kant, Heidegger allows the question concerning the thing to indicate the crisis of philosophy, and, conversely, allowing the confrontation with that crisis to point us in the direction — of art and poetry — of recovering the thing as thing. In *Die Frach dem Ding*, Heidegger poignantly addresses the imminent transformation emerging when we hover at the cusps of the limits of Kant's thought:

> If [the transformation of the grounding of his own project on logic] also did not lie within Kant's capacity, it was because such a task exceeds even the capacity of a great thinker. It demands nothing less than to jump over one's own shadow. No one can do this. However, the greatest effort in attempting this impossibility — is the decisive ground-movement of the action of thought. We experience something of this fundamental movement in quite different ways in Plato, Leibniz, and, above all, in Kant and later in Schelling and Nietzsche. Hegel alone apparently succeeded in jumping over this shadow, but only in such a way that he eliminated the shadow, i. e., the finiteness of man, and jumped into the sun itself ... The longer the shadow, the wider the jump.[352]

---

350 See Schalow, *Renewal of the Heidegger-Kant Dialogue*, p. 128.

351 We see an example of how natural science, in the guise of evolutionary theory, becomes underwritten by recent forms of positivism. See Schalow, "Essence and Ape: Heidegger and the Question of Evolutionary Theory", pp. 445–462.

352 GA 41, pp. 153–154; tr. 150–151 (translation modified).

By pointing to Kant's limits, Heidegger anticipates a change in the landscape of philosophical inquiry that occurs on the heels of the transformation of logic itself. Because the appearance of the thing within the pre-established parameters of modern science occurs in tandem with the generality of the concepts that logic employs, philosophy can recover its intimacy with language (λόγος) only by severing its ties with logic. But by divorcing itself from logic, philosophy does not simply revert and dissolve into a mindless chaos devoid of guidance. In the absence of any canon of reason or logic, we must seek guidance from a new "authority." This authority, however, is granted not only through philosophy's executing the plan of destructive-retrieval, but also through a play of semantics that colors the mode of expression with connotations which harmonize with the newly uncovered originality. Thus, the authority does not reside in an eternal norm (like a rational canon), but rather, by being transposed and incarnated through the moment of temporalization, re-emerges instead as a way of *honoring* our beginnings. What Heidegger will ultimately characterize as thinking (*Denken*), in place of logic, must exact the profoundest guidance of all, that is, through an apprenticeship with language that steadfastly stands in service of the word. When philosophy assumes this role of safeguarding the word, in an analogous manner to the task practiced in art, thinking evolves into a form of "craftsmanship." "We are trying to learn thinking. Perhaps thinking, too, is just something like building a cabinet. At any rate, it is a craft, a 'handicraft.'"[353]

To practice the craft of thinking, however, is to become proficient at what in *Contributions* Heidegger calls "being-historical thinking." By enacting such thinking, Heidegger arrives at the key idioms to "translate" the complexities of Kant's Critical philosophy into the wider context of the problematic of "being and time," insofar as the *attempt to say the unsaid is itself an exercise in translation.*[354] Through this "returnership," the task of retrieving transcendental philosophy crosses a more circuitous path, along which thinking travels in route to the other beginning. As Heidegger states most provocatively in the Appendix of *Mindfulness*: "The actual dynamics of thinking itself as the striving for the basic positioning of the other beginning lies behind the educational will to develop and strengthen the power of questioning, and the unrestrained mastery of the craft of philosophizing."[355] Let us briefly consider the development of thinking in this way, and consider how it extends the frontiers of Heidegger's dialogue with Kant.

---

353  Heidegger, *What Is Called Thinking?*, p. 16.
354  GA 55, p. 63.
355  GA 66, p. 424; tr. 301.

## 3 Being-Historical Thinking and the Space of Dialogue

According to Gadamer, as Heidegger advances his radical critique of the history of metaphysics, his criticism of Kant becomes increasingly pointed.[356] But what Gadamer neglects to mention is *that the turning around of the question itself creates the historical distance by which Heidegger can approach Kant more critically; and, conversely, his own confrontation with Kant helps to shape the contours of this turning.* If we are not merely embellishing the importance of Heidegger's exchange with Kant, is there any specific evidence to suggest its unique role in radicalizing the question of being, of reshaping the topography for re-asking that question? The turning creates the momentum for the doubling of the question, of allowing for its re-inception at the nadir of its neglect, which historically means at the point where beings are one-dimensionally revealed in terms of their prospects of manipulation and exploitation, production and consumption. The curvature of the turning allows the question of being to revert into the question concerning technology, by which we have in mind not only the technicity of using beings but also the "(natural) science" that bends knowledge to serve these macro schemes of organization. In *Contributions to Philosophy* (1938), Heidegger forecasts his later formulation of the question of technology by describing the modern preoccupation with "machination" (*Machenschaft*).[357] On this note, however, we cannot discount what so many scholars have, namely, that *three years earlier*, in the 1935–36 lectures comprising *Die Frage nach dem Ding*, Heidegger first addresses the "mathematical projecting-open" of science, i. e., how beings-in-a-whole admit their disclosure in terms of quantitative models, which bring to light the *calculative will* driving modern technology.

We can hardly find a zero point in Heidegger's *Gesamtausgabe* where his concern for technology originates. Rather, the turning yields *many different paths*, of which revisiting his interest in Kant is one, to address the transformation of the question of being into the question of technology. Because Kant explored the emergence of modern science from its deepest metaphysical roots with unmatched precision, he once again enters the limelight of Heidegger's destructive-retrieval of the philosophical tradition. As a result, we should not view his increasing criticism of Kant negatively; we should instead see it as measuring the space in which that exchange can first occur and provide the historical setting to re-ask the question of being by confronting its neglect throughout the history of metaphy-

---

**356** Gadamer, *Heidegger's Ways*, p. 162. See GA 66, pp. 399–400; tr. 283.
**357** GA 65, p. 130–131; tr. 91.

sics. Though I suggest as much elsewhere,[358] the unfolding of this distance to criticize metaphysics ultimately takes its lead from Heidegger's enactment of being-historical thinking in *Contributions to Philosophy*. We must still consider how *this thinking creates the separation, as it were, within which Heidegger can first experience his proximity to Kant's thought*, that is, weave together the tapestry of parallels of the kind we find in *Basic Problems* and the Kant-book.

The term "being-historical thinking" already implies that the question of being is inherently historical, but, more radically, that various point counter point between thinkers is our way of experiencing the differences in being's diversity of manifestations. When placed in its historical setting, Heidegger's dialogue with Kant brings us to the threshold where we experience being not in its unambiguous luminosity, but rather in the *ambiguity marking the transition from forgottenness to recollection*. We consider the giving of being, and, reciprocally, the role time plays in this dynamic: "there is being" only insofar as "there is time." What remains unthought in the turning of time and being, however, is the *refusing within the giving*. This counter-movement of refusing is not merely negative and deficient, but is also positive because it envelops the giving in its own abeyance and dormancy. How do we think this negativity, as it were, in its positive dimension; how do we address the concealment that pervades being potential for unconcealment? In *Contributions to Philosophy*, Heidegger raises these questions, insofar as an enigma in how concealment not only prevents the truth of being from emerging, but, in the process, provides a haven or shelter for being in which its own elusiveness can portend a mystery. Insofar as it potential for unconcealment is always couched in its opposite, being harbors an aura of mystery within its own dynamic. Heidegger suggests as much when he emphasizes that concealment carries the connotation of "sheltering" or "protecting." He also emphasizes that the history of metaphysics, even though it stands as a monument to untruth, creates crevices in which to house being's potential to breakthrough into unconcealment. To be sure, there may be mystical incantations in the difficult language of *Contributions*. But the overall message is nevertheless clear of how the history of metaphysics transmits itself through various periods, each of which holds in check or in abeyance dormant possibilities for addressing being. The retrieval of these possibilities, through their arrival from the future, in turn re-enacts the giving of being that at the inception of metaphysics has been refused but nevertheless pervades its history.

As the Heidegger-Kant dialogue first illustrates, history allows us to experience being in a way that directs us into the partnership that its unconcealment

---

358 Schalow, *Renewal of the Heidegger-Kant Dialogue*, p. 146.

has with language. The giving of be-ing (*Seyn*) invites our participation, because through our inhabitation of language we acquire the potential to become the place (*Ort*) for its unconcealment, i. e., through such activities as thinking. Thinking then becomes a way of responding to the claim (*Anspruch*) of being, the reverberations of which hark back to the historical origin of philosophy itself. In *What Is Called Thinking?*, Heidegger refers to Socrates as the "purest thinker of the West," because he never wrote anything but instead stood ready to heed the invitation from being that resonates through the most basic words of the tradition.[359] Insofar as being has already directed its claim toward thought, even in the refusing of its giving, the modalities in the permutations of receiving and responding to this claim, have as their amphitheater the entire history of philosophy. Because philosophy begins as a response to being, and possibilities are as diverse as being's potential for manifestations, philosophy is necessarily predicated on multivocality, the welcoming of diverse and dissenting voices in their reciprocal rejoinder with each other. In the historical enactment of this multivocality, to which *Contributions* first supplies the clue, lies the intrinsic possibility of Heidegger's *Auseinandersetzung* with Kant. Given that this is the case, we may then find in *Contributions* an example which summarizes the import of Heidegger's exchange with Kant, insofar as it continues to reverberate across the amphitheater of history.

Among the scattered references to Kant in *Contributions*, does any single passage stand out which unifies the thread of Heidegger's exchange with Kant? Recalling that the transcendental imagination provides the fulcrum for this exchange, Heidegger's way of thinking changes with the landscape for re-asking the question of being. As Heidegger initially attempted to do in the Kant-book, we think the origin of imagination when we allow it to direct us to the dynamic of being's unconcealment, to the clearing as such. Rather than think being through what becomes manifest through it, or beings — the beingness of beings — we seek to think being in and of itself, without beings, as Heidegger suggests in his Nietzsche lectures.[360] When we think in this way, as Heidegger suggests in *Contributions*, we engage in being-historical thinking. The commissioning of history as the site for the breakthrough of being's appearance, our historical thrownness as the way by which, in our finitude, we respond to this claim, prepares us to think with this originality. In recalling imagination's centrality in the Kant book, Heidegger's own project of being and time moves explicitly into

---

359 Heidegger, *What Is Called Thinking?*, p. 26.
360 Heidegger, *Nietzsche, II*, pp. 239–244; tr. 182–186.

the orbit of being-historical thinking: "'Imagination'" as occurrence of the *clearing* itself."[361]

In finding the exception to Sallis's remark, we discover that imagination, and the rejoinder with Kant that amplifies its importance, continues to attract renewed attention. And at the same time, among the scattered references to Kant in *Contributions*, we also find indications of Heidegger's attempt to accent the radicality of his own point of departure and to mark its divergence from modern philosophy. In referring to his own confrontation with the history of metaphysics, with the "first beginning," Heidegger writes: "to re-enact *Kant's* main steps but overcome the 'transcendental' point of departure through Da-sein."[362] Here Heidegger succinctly distinguishes the double movement of destructive-retrieval, of dismantling the rationalist elements of Kant's thought in order to retrieve the implications that its problematic of finitude has for re-asking the question of being. Heidegger then follows this remark by adopting the same strategy to retrieve the problematic of freedom from Schelling's thought: "to question thoroughly Schelling's question of freedom and nevertheless to place the question of 'modalities' on another ground."[363] Being-historical thinking employs a discourse of a double gesture that allows the omissions of what is negative to become a signpost to a mystery that being calls us to address. In the doubling of the question, we undergo the transition, from one to another, which Heidegger characterizes as the inception of the "other beginning" in contrast to the "first beginning."

In the subsequent section of *Contributions*, Heidegger describes this transition as a "crossing to the other beginning."[364] The crossing, however, does not simply abandon the one for the other, but, on the contrary, allows the tension between them to bring possibilities held in dormancy in the one to re-emerge in its play through the other. If transcendental-horizonal thinking characterizes the approach to being reminiscent of the first beginning, then being-historical distinguishes the otherness by which being addresses us. The other beginning yields a *new departure* for thinking toward which we cross, not simply through our initiative, but, on the contrary, through a prior invitation from being itself. The reciprocity between being and thinking provides the historical expanse within which the perennial questions of philosophy remain "open-ended" and thereby preserve their relevance, that is, through the opportunity for their renewed appropriation under the heading "*Ereignisdenken.*" The variations in the ways of posing

---

**361** GA 65, p. 312; tr. 219.
**362** GA 65, p. 176; tr. 123.
**363** GA 65, p. 176; tr. 123.
**364** GA 65, p. 177; tr. 124.

these questions, whether transcendentally/finitely or hermeneutic/historically, are only provisional, or even fallible attempts, of "projecting-open" the question of being from out the historicality of the claim by which be-ing first addresses thought. The crossing to the other beginning does not mean that we simply relinquish transcendental-horizonal thinking; on the contrary, we can appreciate the inherently historical character of the question of being by coming to terms with the variations of posing that question.

Heidegger begins *Being and Time* by addressing the everydayness of Dasein's indifference toward the question of being. A tendency which at first appears as accidental re-emerges as a necessary development in the history of metaphysics. The obviousness that feeds Dasein's indifference to being stems from an essential dimension of truth, in which the holding in reserve of concealment simultaneously preserves the mystery of being. Just as everydayness harbors Dasein's experience of untruth, the dynamic of truth as concealment has its historical corollary in the way Dasein falls prey to tragedy. In this regard, the experience of tragedy provides a cultural way by which human beings experience the twist of fate and destiny in which the journey of understanding inevitably takes a detour along the path of destruction. In this regard, tragedy is more than just a metaphor to describe the dynamic of being's retreat into the depths of concealment and the abruptness of its re-emergence into unconcealment. Quoting Schelling, Heidegger calls our participation in this occurrence as the "the deepest abground" and the "highest heaven."[365] Indeed, the enactment of strife, between world and earth, unconcealment and concealment, or the "thing itself," dictates the element in which to couch the language of philosophy: that is, that gives right to the singularity of manifestation, as poetry does, in contrast to generality of conceptual representation. In the figure of the poet's poet, or Hölderlin, *poeisis* becomes the vanguard of thinking, insofar as it cuts to the simplest, to the most primordial level, to give voice to the complex permutations of being's strife. As Hölderlin's states, our time typifies a neediness "'in the no longer of the gods who have fled and in the not-yet of the god who is coming.'"[366]

In the closing part of *Contributions*, Heidegger brings Hölderlin's remarks back into his discussion of enowning by considering the "last god." The last god does not refer to anything explicitly religious, but instead points to the refusal in the giving of an epiphany and hence to the preservation of the mystery in the Divine apart from any form of sectarian belief (or "disbelief," for that matter).

---

**365** GA 42, p. 281; tr. 167–168.
**366** GA 4, p. 47; tr. 64.

We move into the time-space of decision of the flight and arrival of gods. But how does that happen? ...
What if that domain of decision as a whole, flight or arrival of gods, were itself the end? What if, beyond that, be-ing in its truth would have to be grasped for the first time as enownment, as that which enowns what we call *refusal?*
That is neither flight nor arrival, and also not flight *and* arrival, but rather something originary, the fullness of granting be-ing in refusal. Here is grounded the origin of the future style, i. e., of reservedness in the truth of be-ing.[367]

In this way, the last god epitomizes the refusing in the granting of being, as historically coming to pass in the way that beings are abandoned to the manipulation of technology and humanity falls prey to this relentless drive of production and consumption. Insofar as *Seinsvergessenheit (forgottenness of being)* resides in *Seinsverlassenheit* (abandonment of being),[368] the abandonment of being displays a twofold dimension: 1). the extreme concealing of the truth of being at the completion of metaphysics and 2). the one-dimensional manifestation of beings (including nature in its wealth of resources) in terms of usefulness, consumption, and exploitation. Even in this refusing there must be a grain of experience that human beings have of it in order that, conversely, they can experience the promise of the re-inception of the granting. Without the darkness of the descent into being's abandonment,[369] no haven can be reserved for a mystery from whose depths unconcealment first arises — the turn back (*einkehren*) to beings as they re-appear in light of the clearing.

In different places, Heidegger suggests that the period of the incubation of the potential for the breakthrough of this mystery may be longer than the entire history of metaphysics. In "Overcoming Metaphysics," Heidegger states: "Experienced in virtue of the dawning of the origin, metaphysics is, however, at the same time past in the sense that it has entered its ending. The ending lasts longer than the previous history of metaphysics."[370] In the opening line to his discussion of the last god, Heidegger gives the positive flip side to this longevity: "The last is that which not only needs the longest fore-runnership but also itself *is*: not the ceasing, but the deepest beginning, which reaches out the furthest and catches up with itself with the greatest of difficulty."[371] Given the necessity of this interlude, in what can we take haven and still engage in the strife of the world and earth? And this question is why, even in *Contributions*, Heidegger still appeals to

---

**367** GA 65, p. 405; tr. 285.
**368** GA 65, p. 114; tr. 80.
**369** GA 69, p. 38; tr. 169–171. Also see Heidegger, "Seinsvergessenheit", pp. 9–16.
**370** GA 9, p. 69; tr. 85.
**371** GA 65, p. 404; tr. 285.

imagination. For imagination is that inherently temporal power which allows us to reside within that interlude, not passively, but through the play of possibility. If it is through our historical thrownness that we experience being's granting-refusal, then, as a companion to our incarnality, imagination places us at the portal of the birth of new possibilities.

The deployment of imagination is one of the greatest legacies of Kantian thought, because it can duplicate as a vanguard for the renewal of philosophy in the absence of any specific guidelines and directives. In this regard, imagination serves as a make-shift bridge in the crossing over to the other beginning, the creative impetus in overcoming metaphysics. Accordingly, it is in light of being-historical thinking that Heidegger reinterprets the contribution made by his reinterpretation of Kant, as this parenthetical remark from *Mindfulness* (1938–39) illustrates:

> The Kant-book is meant to show that *in a certain way* Kant is thrust into the sphere of the truth of be-ing, but shrinks back from it and does not know the question that belongs to the truth of be-ing and cannot know that question within the basic stance of metaphysics as such.
> The interpretation of Kant's transcendental philosophy with a view to "schematism" and "the power of imagination" *exaggerates* deliberately in order to show that already *within* the history of metaphysics itself there is the necessity of a rigorous transformation of the question of metaphysics. That attempt is least interested in supplying the "historical" Kant, "as he has been." Therefore, one can imperturbably go on to prove the inaccuracy of that attempt. But in this way one proves only one's inability to think-through rigorously the question of *being*.)[372] In "Overcoming Metaphysics" (1954), Heidegger aptly summarizes the challenges posed through a destructive-retrieval of Kant's thought:
> At first the overcoming of metaphysics can only be presented in terms of metaphysics itself, so to speak, in the manner of a heightening of itself through itself. In this case the talk about the metaphysics of metaphysics, which is touched upon in the book *Kant and the Problem of Metaphysics*, is justified in that it attempts to interpret the Kantian idea from this perspective, which still stems from the mere critique of rationalist metaphysics. However, more is thus attributed to Kant's thinking than he himself was able to think within the limits of his philosophy.[373]

In the figure of imagination, what still remains to be addressed, if not at the center of the Heidegger-Kant dialogue, at least at its periphery? Could it be through the directive of being-historical thinking that Heidegger, following Hölderlin's example, courts the deepest recesses of poetic language? Could it be that through a detour, provided by Kant's *Critique of Judgment*, we have circled back to the

---

372 GA 66, p. 377; tr. 265.
373 GA 7, p. 77; tr. 92.

beginning of the Heidegger-Kant dialogue, only to *arrive at what still remains unsaid*? Could this beginning signal a new *departure* in its own right at the crossroads between these two thinkers?" Could this departure guide us, not only in seeking to translate the "measure" governing the political, but also in advancing our journey along the path of thinking?

# Chapter Six
# Echoing the "Unsaid": Opening the Question of Language

Even while rebuking Kant for his "recoil" from imagination, Heidegger only skirted the edges of the tapestry of issues pervading the third *Critique*. Despite making the first and second *Critique* the focus of his destructive-retrieval of transcendental philosophy, he appears curiously indifferent toward the work where Kant devotes the greatest attention to the imagination. Did Heidegger fall victim to a similar recoil, or did his reticence allow that work to pose a still greater challenge by inviting thought to undertake a "leap" (*Sprung*), much like that enacted in *Contributions to Philosophy*? Presumably, such a leap would gather its momentum through a new awakening to language, which in its poetic guise solicits from an opposite spectrum our unique participation in a saying (*Sage*) appropriate to thought. If this were the case, we would discover that at the juncture where the third *Critique* recedes as a work of aesthetics, it reappears not only as a nascent concern in Kant's transcendental philosophy, but also as a possibility which Heidegger never fully developed in his radical retrieval thereof. In developing this possibility, we would be *opening* another chapter in Heidegger's exchange with Kant, which *attunes us to the "echo" of what is "unsaid" in his philosophy concerning the limits of language and its power for figurative, as well as conceptual expression.* Given the importance that this exchange with Kant has in the transformation of Heidegger's own philosophy, we would be taking a further step along the path of thinking. Such a path turns from the tendency of thought to become entangled in representationalism, and returns to the artist's example of exulting in the ecstasy of play.

On the surface, the third *Critique* raises issues about artistic beauty and aesthetic pleasure that seem to be only loosely connected to Heidegger's quest to outline being's projecting-opening upon time and its disclosure through language. If there is any way of surmounting the gulf between Heidegger's thought and the concerns raised by the third *Critique*, it can only arise through the dynamic of imagination. As Tamar Japaridze emphasizes: "The 'recoiled path' of Kant's thought [about imagination] hinted, as Heidegger remarked, at Kant's awareness of the proximity of sensibility and understanding and was just a glimpse into the 'labyrinthine' path later taken by critical thought in his aesthetics."[374] As far as his rejoinder with Kant goes, Heidegger refrains from pursu-

---

374 Japaridze, *The Kantian Subject*, pp. 13–14.

ing this path, perhaps leaving it to one of his foremost students, Hannah Arendt, to do so. Indeed, this path may not simply lie in pursuing what, from the retrospective glance of *Contributions* appears obvious, the link between the creative power of imagination and the origin of the work of art. Rather, we might be better served to address those dimensions of experience that Heidegger took as peripheral to Kant's overall project, but which, upon second glance, merit attention by marking the limits of Heidegger's destructive-retrieval of transcendental philosophy: the concern for nature as well as art, the emphasis on the awe of the sublime as well as the appreciation of beauty, and, as Hannah Arendt demonstrated, the formation of the body-politic through the free exchange of its members. Would we not be bringing Heidegger's own interpretation within the same historical orbit as he did with Kant, namely, by considering what remains "unsaid" in the former's quest to establish imagination as the linchpin of the entire Critical enterprise?

If this were the case, then would we not simply be "criticizing" Heidegger's Kant-interpretation. For any such critique, if it is to advance us along the path of thinking, must allow another voice to be heard. Criticism of this sort is an exercise of multivocality, in which we also extend the audience who can heed the subtleties of the exchange between these two great thinkers. Correlatively, we must develop the questions raised about Kant's third *Critique* to elicit, the tonality of attunement (*Stimmung*), which first disposes us to listen to the hidden stirring of the λόγος. To address the spectrum of these issues, I will develop this chapter in three parts.

First, I will consider how the third *Critique*, with all its emphasis on human subjectivity, makes its greatest inroad by pointing to the phenomenon of language as a topic of inquiry. Though Kant may have viewed the *third* Critique as unifying the Critical project as a whole,[375] we will also see that its primary message lies in unraveling the *presupposition* of his enterprise. *By unfolding this presupposition, we will discover the hermeneutic thread which leads from the third Critique back to the first Critique, the "ellipsis" in which Heidegger's radical reinterpretation of transcendental philosophy turns.* Secondly, I will re-examine the importance of imagination, not only as a power we retrieve by dismantling the rationalist premises of transcendental philosophy, but, also as the springboard for undertaking that quest, *the unthought presupposition of the Kant-book as such.* Thirdly, I will show how, beyond merely a doctrine of "aesthetics," the third *Critique* suggests a novel way of saying, and therefore "thinking" being

---

375 For a recent discussion of this, see Hiltscher, *Die Vollendung der Transzendentalphilosophie in Kants "Kritik der Urteilskraft"*, pp. 7–18.

beyond the constraints of subjectivity and its Cartesian emphasis on representationalism.

## 1 Sensus Communis and Language

Just as the English-speaking world has witnessed an explosion in Heidegger scholarship, there has also been a resurgence of interest in the *Critique of Judgment* above perhaps all of Kant's writings. These two developments may be more than coincidental. Certainly, Heidegger created an opening for the hermeneutic tradition to explore this facet of Kant's thought. In a prophetic remark in Part Three of the Kant-book, Heidegger states: "We cannot discuss here the sense in which the pure power of imagination recurs in the *Critique of Judgment* and above all whether it still recurs in express relationship to the laying of the ground for metaphysics."[376] In "Notes on the Kantbook," which appears in the *Gesamtausgabe* edition (GA 3) of *Kant und das Problem der Metaphysik*, Heidegger expands upon this remark. "Critique of Judgment/Aesthetics: Only considered far enough to be able to see that it is not contradicted ... whereupon taste (reflection-imagination) looks out (into itself)."[377] Indeed, from the standpoint of contemporary hermeneutics, the third *Critique* appears as virgin territory. For it stands at the crossroads of the Critical enterprise itself. Here the emphasis lies in how language comes to expression as such, how it communicates through our participation in it, rather than proclaiming the laws that legislate over the realms of science or morality, respectively. In the aforementioned "Notes," Heidegger cryptically points to imagination as the field of figurative expression. He cites section 59 of the third *Critique* where Kant identifies imagination as filling in the gap of what cannot be given to intuition, the engenderment of analogy and symbol in order to depict graphically a meaning for which there is no corresponding concept.[378]

Though easily overlooked, Heidegger points out at the opening of the *Basic Problems* that Kant coins the term *Weltanschauung*, literally, "world-intuition," in the third *Critique*.[379] With Kant, the term "world-view" carries an important ambiguity. On the one hand, it points to the need to develop a concept of philosophy which is sufficiently universal or, in the lexicon of the Enlightenment, "cosmopolitan." On the other hand, world-view also points to the "sensuous" expression of that concept, the "*mundus sensibilis*." It is ambiguous whether the

---

376 GA 3, p. 161; tr. 110
377 GA 3, p. 250; tr. 175–176.
378 GA 3, p. 250; tr. 175–176. See Schmidt, *Lyrical and Ethical Subjects*, p. 86.
379 GA 24, p. 4; tr. 6.

sensuous presentation of the world is also determined by an orientation to the subject's personal experiences. In this regard, world-view is a term that has come to distinguish an individual's personal, even pre-philosophical grasp of how he/she looks upon his/her position in life or place in society. Thus, a world-view can either prefigure a concept of philosophy that strives after universality or can presuppose the formality of that philosophical understanding. To be sure, Heidegger dismisses the idea of a "world-view" as tainted too much with the historicism and relativism of Dilthey's life-philosophy. Yet Heidegger also appreciates the challenge with which Kant originally struggles to reconcile the universal spirit of philosophy with the personal conviction of the individual's life-experiences. Thus, in appealing to the third *Critique*, Heidegger points to an *unspoken* link between hermeneutics and Kant's transcendental philosophy.

There is still another angle by which we can discover this link to hermeneutics, insofar as we seek its origin through the development of the concept of facticity, of factic life-experience. Indeed, Heidegger points to a passage in the third *Critique* as textual evidence (one of his only references to the "Critique of Teleological Judgment") of Kant's nascent attempt to root his supertemporal concept of practical freedom in human facticity. There is, as Heidegger suggests, a distinctive "fact" of freedom that we experience, as it were, retrospectively through the example provided by the occurrence of moral praxis. "Only one negative point is initially clear, namely that practical freedom, according to Kant's own unambiguous statement, is not an empirical concept. However, this statement runs up against Kant's contrary claim, in the *Critique of Judgment*, that practical freedom is a 'fact'. To be sure, the latter statement comes five years (1790) after the first (1785)."[380] According to Heidegger, we can "reconcile" the apparent contradiction by emphasizing that facticity is nascent in Kant's account of world, a transcendental concept which lies at the midpoint between Humean empiricism and Leibnizian rationalism. Insofar as world arises at the periphery of the boundaries of pure reason, and thereby circumscribes the scope of human finitude, to define freedom as factical is another way of distinguishing its finite origin. Freedom is thereby a "fact" in light of the situational way in which we experience it, that is, as a power that the self exercises in relation to one possibility (and course of action) in exclusion of another. Moral praxis, through which the self bears the weight of this exclusivity, i. e., finitude, is thereby the factical root of freedom. Even though Kant's thinking spawned a constellation of

---

**380** GA 31, p. 267; tr. 183. Heidegger cites section 91 of the third *Critique*. See AA 5, KU, p. 468; tr. 321. "This is the idea of *freedom*, whose reality ... may be exhibited by means of practical laws of pure reason ... in actual actions, and, consequently, in experience. This is the only one of all the ideas of pure reason whose object is a thing of fact ..."

hermeneutic concepts like world, freedom, and finitude, overall he fell short of developing a hermeneutics of facticity. And perhaps in the end what eluded his grasp was the self-signifying dynamic of that nexus of concepts, prior to all predication, which springs from the hidden depths of language.

In standing at the threshold of both German Idealism and hermeneutics, Kant's apparent indifference toward language is especially ironic in light of the considerable attention devoted to that topic by his successors.[381] And yet if there is any place in Kant's writings where a trace of interest can be found, it surely lies in the enigmatic pages of the third *Critique*. As Dennis Schmidt emphasizes, while Kant did not "thematize the question of language," in the *Critique of Judgment*, he nevertheless pointed to the "problematic relation between aesthetic experience and language in general."[382] This may not be particularly surprising. For in this work Kant addresses concerns that are otherwise relegated to the extreme margins of his other writings, but which in their inconspicuousness may still orient the attempt to delimit pure reason. As Jean-François Lyotard suggests: "Thinking must observe a 'pause,' where it suspends the adhesion to what it believes it thinks. It listens for that which orients its critical examination."[383] The transcendental analyses of cognitive experience and moral conduct shifts the parameters of discourse away from the discursivity of thought as outlined by formal logic. How does reason's self-examination, as the inescapable trademark of Kant's project, suggest a unique detour within a discourse which is designed to enunciate the laws of nature and morality? Could Kant have entered into the nebulous region of the third *Critique*, in order to follow this detour, perhaps partially in response to criticism voiced by Herder that the former has inadequately addressed the place that language occupied in his Critical philosophy?[384] Often a thinker leaves behind the trace of style that may not be completely reconciled with the actual execution of his/her task.[385]

Having already reserved significance to what can be defined conceptually as a transcendental condition, Kant considers how responses wholly singular and unique can achieve expression. One's encounter with the beautiful must be able to convey a "universal communicability."[386] But that experience cannot be regulated in advance by a conformity to a universal principle (a determinate judgment). Through the unique pleasure aroused by it, a beautiful artwork must

---

381 See Caputo, *The Mystical Element in Heidegger's Thought*, p. 260.
382 Schmidt, *Lyrical and Ethical Subjects*, p. 8.
383 Lyotard, "Reflection in Kant's Aesthetics", 375–411.
384 See Zammito, *The Genesis of Kant's Critique of Judgment*, pp. 7–15.
385 AA 5, KU, pp. 295–296; tr. 138.
386 AA 5, KU, pp. 295–296; tr. 138.

instead implicate a wider context in which assent of others becomes possible (a reflective judgment of taste). For Kant, taste is then the faculty of judging the communicability of feelings without relying upon a prior concept. In his words, "... since the freedom of the imagination consists precisely in the fact that it schematizes without a concept, the judgment of taste must be found upon a mere sensation of the mutually quickening of the imagination in its freedom and of the understanding with its conformity to law."[387] In discussing aesthetic experience, Kant retains his transcendental vocabulary, but with one decided twist. The demand to extract truth through an objective principle must now take a detour through a field of ambivalence, and locate new limits which can counterbalance the indeterminacy of subjective viewpoints. Given this transcendental focus, the possibility of aesthetic experience hinges on a "shared" state of mind, which is turn presupposes a form of articulation common to all (a *sensus communis*), and perhaps, in Heidegger's terms, an even deeper ground in an attunement (*Stimmung*) by which each of us inhabits a world.[388]

These limits can prevail despite soliciting a minimal agreement among diverse individuals. *Truth thereby emerges in a new form: not as the basis of an objective judgment, but as the self-gathering of logos (λóyoς) in the guise of the sensus communis.* The agreement that thereby becomes possible — through the assent of individuals (in a "reflective" judgment) rather than the universality of a concept (a "determinate" judgment)retains an affinity with an ideal, and yet calls upon the individual's discretion to give assent vis-à vis the concrete situation of the person having the experience. Thus, the field we can share in common as participants, disposing each person to respond in a way potentially concurrent with the other, introduces a universal communicability for the experience. In this spirit, we can concur as to the beauty of art by deferring our isolated view of the "formal purposiveness" of an object, in favor of responses which are universally communicable. Since such propensity toward concurrence cannot be captured by any pre-existing principle, but must instead call upon a minimal degree of discursivity available to us all, Kant refers to a *"sensus communis,"* a common sense.[389]

While suggesting the manner of our participation in it, the *sensus communis* does not reveal language as a phenomenon. To use the connotation Heidegger employs to distinguish nuances within a phenomenon, we can say that language at best "announces itself" in the third *Critique*, that is, as arising from a judgment

---

**387**  AA 5, KU, pp. 300–301; tr. 143.
**388**  See GA 65, p. 502; tr. 353–354.
**389**  AA 5, KU, pp. 293–296; tr. 135–138.

exempt from universal concepts.[390] The allusion to Heidegger's phenomenology proves particularly important. For his method already includes a link between language as the letting-be-seen of *logos* and the dynamics of manifestation, so as to suggest a relation of correspondence that we must experience in order to become speakers. In this way, Heidegger transfers the emphasis on *logos*, from the modern sense of combining various meanings into identity relations within a judgment, back to the Greek sense of "gathering together." That Greek meaning can also include the joining of members of a community, which is echoed in Kant's appeal to the communicability of the *sensus communis*. As Heidegger states in his 1929/30 lectures: "Words emerge from that *essential agreement* of human beings with one another, in accordance with which they *are open in their being with one another for the beings around them* ..."[391] In this way, the intersubjectivity of *sensus communis* becomes possible. "Only on the grounds of this originary, essential agreement is discourse possible in its essential function ... giving that which is understandable to be understood."[392]

As Arendt emphasizes, perhaps Heidegger underestimates the importance of the *sensus communis*, particularly its importance in organizing the *polis* through the establishment of a forum for exchange among its members. Yet even without this political wrinkle, Arendt's development of the *sensus communis* raises questions whether Heidegger sufficiently addresses the social dimension of language. Ironically, he includes dialogue as an enactment of language, which provides the basis for social interaction. But here Heidegger's distinction between discourse as the way in which we engage in speech, or a social practice, and language as the disclosedness which makes possible that practice, may be helpful. Discourse, however, is not restricted to the utterance of words; since the gestures of our embodiment, for example, a wink of an eye, can convey my intimacy with the other better than the most elegant of speeches. In this regard, Heidegger diverges from the Frankfurt school of Habermas that places a premium on linguistic practice.[393] Accordingly, the disclosedness of language precedes such linguistic practice, and, in the guise of dialogue, is that to which each participant remains subordinate. Indeed, by giving priority to hearing over speaking, and thereby deferring to the disclosive power of language, the participants of a dialogue can allow their differences to widen the expanse of openness. By pointing back to the pre-articulated origin of language, the *sensus communis* of linguistic practice

---

**390** GA 2, pp. 42–43; tr. 53.

**391** GA 29/30, p. 448; tr. 309.

**392** GA 29/30, p. 448; tr. 309.

**393** See Habermas, *The Theory of Communicative Action: Reason and Rationalization of Society*, pp. 45–55. Also see Schrag, *Communicative Praxis and the Space of Subjectivity*, pp. 195–198.

becomes an important entry point for addressing the complex tapestry of issues of the third *Critique*.

Upon retracing the initial steps in the development of Heidegger's phenomenological approach to language, we gain a clearer indication of why he may not have found it incumbent to address the third *Critique* in his major writings on Kant. For in this work, Kant examines the roots of discourse in terms of judgment, albeit by seeking an alternative to the customary operation of synthesizing and combining a manifold by concepts. His attempt to emphasize the jurisdiction of neither reason nor understanding leads into an indeterminate zone of judgment where the patterns of conceptualization exhibited in the former case gives way to a diffuse power to judge without conceptual guidance. A gulf thereby opens up between the philosophical practice of circumscribing meaning through concepts, and a more provocative attempt to elicit meanings through an indirect appeal to (figurative) responses aroused in aesthetic experience. Kant defines the experience of beauty as "disinterested pleasure," that is, which heeds the formal purposiveness of the art work without any further premise of use or instrumentality.[394] For example, the kind of arousal that occurs in sexual desire taints the experience of beauty by subordinating the formal purposiveness to an impulse of (the beautiful object's potential for) gratification. Far from being passive, the disinterested pleasure is a comportment toward beauty that keeps it open as a possibility, deferring its interest as an object of desire. To use the terminology that Heidegger coins in the Kant-book, the *comportment toward beauty is a form of receptive-spontaneity and spontaneous-receptivity.*[395] In this balance between receptivity and spontaneity, the mediating function of judgment is deferred in favor of its deeper constellation as a power, or judging as such. The simplicity of this insight, which Hannah Arendt emphasized, seems to get lost in the complexity of Heidegger's hermeneutic situation.[396] For in his hermeneutics, Heidegger had already developed interpretation and understanding as a disclosure apart from propositional claims. Hence, Kant's appeal to an arcane form of (reflective) judgment to uncover a new axis of meaning appears rather redundant from the perspective of Heidegger's phenomenology.

As Makkreel argues, the attempt by a reflective judgment to implicate the context which sustains it, to elicit the whole pervading each of the parts, suggests a hermeneutic venture in its own right.[397] Hermeneutics arises as an attempt to interpret the diversity of human experience in its concrete enactment. While in

---

**394** AA 5, KU, pp. 204–205; tr. 38–39.

**395** GA 43, p. 143.

**396** Arendt, *Lectures on Kant's Political Philosophy*, p. 4.

**397** Makkreel, *Imagination and Interpretation in Kant*, p. 5.

Kant's case such historical awareness does not lead to taking up the question of being, the measure of that question's originality still lies in acclimating philosophical language to its resonance with history. If we look at the issues which remain peripheral throughout the third *Critique* and yet delimit all the hermeneutic questions of aesthetics and teleology subsequently raised, we find that, in fact, the proper counterpart to the issue of language can be nothing other than history. The historical sense that begins to emerge from the discussion of teleological judgment indicates that the new foil of meanings is to be distributed across a field of possibilities, rather than in relation to discrete objects and things. In turn, language finds its abode as interwoven inconspicuously into this field and marks the transition in the way we can understand ourselves from period to period. As Dennis Schmidt suggests, history unfolds "as the events of mortals in their brief appearance, that is, those events must be thought as passing away and leaving no trace behind save what is translated into the memory of the idiom of the word and the happening of the work of art."[398]

When traced to its historical element, Kant's *sensus communis* points to a deeper sense of a common ancestry, which links us together as participants in culture and elicits an exchange within the context of history. Such an historically prompted exchange takes the form of a dialogue, which (as Arendt recognizes) is the necessary precondition for opening a political space that can join freedom with governance.[399] As Arendt states: "With *word and deed* we insert ourselves into a world, and this insertion is like a second birth ..."[400] But without dwelling on the political implications of such an exchange, we can at least recognize that for Kant language can enter the forefront of questioning where the need arises for philosophical questions to become broadly historical.

While from the outset the third *Critique* appears to center on the topic of aesthetics, a nascent concern for language ultimately directs this inquiry. A *figurative* mode of linguistic practice, as enacted through an *exchange* between members of a community, grounds the discourse which Kant presupposes in embarking upon a "critical" self-examination of pure reason. Ultimately, the ground of Kant's project lies suspended in this ambiguity about the language (an "ab-ground"), insofar as the reciprocity between being and Dasein remains unthought.

> Kant's *Critique of Pure Reason*, in which after the Greeks another essential step is taken, has to presuppose this context without being able to grasp it as such and to ground it fully (the

---

398 Schmidt, "Changing the Subject: Heidegger, 'the' National and Epochal", p. 452.
399 Arendt, *Lectures on Kant's Political Philosophy*, pp. 26–30.
400 Arendt, *The Human Condition*, pp. 176–177. For a further discussion of this "second birth," see Schalow, *Language and Deed*, pp. 16–161.

turning relation of Dasein and being). And because this ground was not grounded, the *Critique* remained without a ground ...[401]

By unfolding this presupposition about language, we find a tacit hermeneutics interwoven into Kant's thought, a hermeneutic thread, which forms an "ellipsis" circling back from his discussion of aesthetics in the third *Critique* to his account of schematism in the first *Critique*. In the end, *Heidegger's radical reinterpretation of Kant moves within this ellipsis.*

## 2 Imagination vs. Representationalism

By disrupting the perfect identity between reason and language, the third *Critique* spawns ripples which we still experience today whenever we undertake experiments in thinking. To a large extent, Heidegger's destructive-retrieval of Kant rides the crest of these waves, insofar as imagination usurps the priority of reason. If truth were simply the transparency of reason, and language reflected this perfect self-coincidence, we could be more or less content to construe our relation to language instrumentally, as a means to an end. But the growing sense, beginning with Heidegger, that truth retains a mysterious element and conveys its appearance only in tandem with its opposite, yields a much more complex scenario. As the pre-Socratics realized, an unfathomable affinity with darkness accompanies truth, leaving in its wake a void and a "nothing," and interspersing asymmetries in the process. These asymmetries break the seams in most attempts to render experience uniform and whole. The abrupt overthrow of conventional patterns of organizing experience can occur only by accentuating tensions implicit within language, by unpredictable and subtle twists of meaning. Such linguistic dexterity, which approaches language more as the rhapsody of a dance than as a calculative instrument, invites a new sensitivity toward style. Traditionally, such attentiveness has been more the forte of the poet than the philosopher.

And yet, having lingered dormant throughout the tradition, a peculiar reminder resurfaces as to the affiliation between these two tasks in the inscrutable guise of imagination. As Heidegger himself illustrated through his analysis of schematism, Kant's account of imagination, in reconciling concept and intuition, preserves a trace of its deeper affinity with the asymmetrical, creative facets of experience. For it is only by drawing upon a more figurative, innovative, and stylistic power that imagination can point out the symmetries which produce a

---

**401** GA 65, p. 315; tr. 221.

unified vision of an object, the sensible pattern for its schematic presentation. The emphasis on symmetry via cognitive rules within a determinate judgment cannot rule out a deeper alliance with the asymmetries essential to the creativity of a reflective judgment. In his initial reading of Kant in the late 1920s, Heidegger overlooks the way in which reflective judgment transposes our understanding of *technē*, that is, by allowing the novelty of what appears to shape our experience of truth.[402] The possibility that truth can unfold on adjacent axes, of *technē* and *physis*, remains a nascent concern for him. For in the 1920s Heidegger is still underway to the assignment of a place for truth, a *topos*, which is ultimately consecrated through the glory of art. At this site we can then reconsider the play of imagination, in allowing differentiation to unfold, to direct us to that power by which language brings itself in concert with truth. A return to imagination would then reveal philosophy's need for a more profound orientation to the power of language, which harbors a level of "figurative" expression. Kant's treatment of art and aesthetics intersects with a deeper concern for the "pre-predicative" roots of language. As Japaridze aptly states:

> Kant attempted to show in the analytic of the beautiful that sensation becomes a form of language prior to the production of signification. In the identification with the other, in the transference that takes place during the aesthetic communication that Kant calls silent, sensibility endows a precognitive experience with form and signification. This experience, moreover, becomes the condition of the possibility of all linguistic communication, as it defines the unity of the speaking subject as such.[403]

In the poet, in the artist, Heidegger appeals to their pursuits as examples of how to practice its would be craft. The thinker becomes an apprentice, insofar as it is a craft that invites humility by acknowledging its dependence on language. "Resolve always to be beginner," is a suggestion that Rilke offers to the poet that Heidegger would reiterate as applying equally to the thinker, albeit in a more radical way.[404] As Heidegger states in *Mindfulness*: "Everything depends on there being again a beginning of philosophy wherein philosophy is itself this beginning so that be-ing itself sways as origin."[405] Because we are thrown into language, language can become the element of thought only as we exercise a reciprocal guardianship towards it. Thus thought can become introduced to its matter (*Sache*) only by disavowing itself of its simple possession and deferring instead to the mystery of being's occurrence. In this self-deferral, an area of differentiation

---

**402** Derrida, *The Truth in Painting*, pp. 85–90.
**403** Japaridze, *The Kantian Subject*, p. 126.
**404** Rilke, *On Love and Other Difficulties*, p. 25.
**405** GA 66, p. 53; tr. 44.

opens up as yielding the corollary site of finitude on which all inquiry depends. The difference does not abide in tranquil solitude, but instead calls for or invites our active engagement with it. Through such engagement, we as thinkers draw upon the innovation of alterity to break the bonds of representationlism. This innovativeness first surfaces through the ineluctable play of imagination. In the Kant-book, Heidegger sought to undo the antiquated character of Kant's architectonic by deposing the authority of reason in favor of imagination. Hence there emerged an abyss from which Kant recoiled. Yet, if Kant did recoil from the deeper implications of his own doctrine of schematism outlined in the first *Critique*, it is because his task must still encounter an even more unsettling slippage, a vertigo which relinquishes the stability of any philosophical footing in favor of a not-yet initiated leap. That crucial juncture occurs by offering a new site for philosophical questioning that arises through its partnership with *poiesis*. Hence, the new mandate for philosophy is not systematic completeness but the innovativeness of style. As Heidegger points out as early as 1923, a hermeneutics of facticity is incompatible with Hegel's dialectical attempt to construct a system of reason.[406]

We need to consider this more radical unfolding of imagination in order to appreciate why Heidegger only skirted the edges of the third *Critique*. For this work begins a movement to shift the orientation of philosophy toward the emphasis that is granted rather ambiguously by art, and without the benefit of an hierarchical order of philosophical concepts. The architectonic that had governed Kant's own thought on reason, understanding, and judgment relinquishes its stability at the point where the elusive linchpin, or judgment, unravels through an imaginative venture divorced from concepts, a free play of imagination.[407] As Kant indicates in the "Introduction" to the third *Critique*:

> But there is still further in family of the supreme cognitive faculties a middle term between the understanding and the reason. This is the *judgment*, of which we have a cause for supposing according to analogy that it may contain in itself, if not a special legislation, yet a special principle of its own to be sought according to laws, though merely subjective *a priori*.[408]

At this point, imagination no longer outlines the temporal movement in which the contours of the ontological difference becomes apparent. The difference between being and beings is a corollary to the trajectory of finite understanding (transcendence), providing the presupposition for the situated occurrences of our worldly

---

406 GA 63, p. 43; tr. 34–35.
407 See Nuyen, "On Interpreting Kant's Architectonic in Terms of the Hermeneutical Model", pp. 154–166.
408 AA, 5, KU, p. 177; tr. 15.

comportment. By contrast, the concern for the tension of differentiation to which imagination enigmatically points does not privilege any single potentiality (transcendence), but instead locates itself within the open expanse of possibility. Within this open expanse, we can experience the reciprocity of being and time, as well as the deferring movement of language through which the middle-voiced advent of world first happens. Thus, imagination ceases to be a unique way to sculpture the finite horizon of transcendence, and instead configures what already distinguishes the primary concern of thought, the ontological difference, as it reappears through art. For Heidegger, the difference which appears through the disclosive power of art, and its unique capacity for play, is the tension between world and thing.

The play which Heidegger emphasizes brings to the forefront what we might call the innovative side of freedom or the impetus to "let be." By letting be, we attend to an improvisation exemplified by the particular; we marvel at its nuances of disclosure as the blossoming of a rose, and thereby safeguard its uniqueness. By contrast, the difficulty with metaphysics is that it relinquishes the eclecticism of the singular in favor of envisioning an homogeneous set of characteristics that are already present. From the standpoint of Heidegger's destructive-retrieval of Kant, the third *Critique* embodies the tension of this ambiguity of rescuing the eclecticism of the singular from the clutches of representational models of the generic. As Heidegger turned his attention to addressing the "origin of the work of art" and the "question of the thing" in his lectures on Kant — in the mid 1930s — he recognizes that an otherness of manifestation must still precede the thing's restricted appearance to scientific-mathematical models of representationalism. The prevalence of this otherness reserves a place for the thing within the open expanse, despite the narrowness of its representation for us. By addressing the uniqueness of art on the one hand, and by employing cognitive models of representation to do so on the other, Kant gives expression to this ambiguity at the heart of the thing's manifestation.

Perhaps this ambiguity provides the best clue as to why Heidegger circumvented the third *Critique*, at least as offering a book on aesthetics. Not only does Heidegger reject aesthetics as distorting the ontological import of the work of art. But, perhaps more subtly, he resists the Kantian version thereof because it becomes a repository to idealistic assumptions about the formal composition of the subject who can be affected by the experience of beauty. On the one hand, the prospect of retrieving imagination in the third *Critique* offers a further opportunity to carry out a critique of the subjectivity of the subject. In *Contributions*, Heidegger suggests as much in an oblique reference to his *Seminare: Leibniz–Kant* in the summer semester of 1936 (GA 84): "The 'historical' lectures belong to the sphere of this task ... to re-enact *Kant's* main steps but to overcome the 'transcendental' point of departure through Da-sein."[409] On the other hand, a recursion of the problem of materiality in the origin of the work of art transposes the concern for beauty away from the narrow confines of aesthetics, as well as from the idealistic assumptions of Kant's treatment of art in the third *Critique*. Materiality does not denote the merely physical, but, in terms of aesthetic judgment, serves as a "boundary concept" for "transcendentally reflecting" on singularity through the tension of relational pairs like identity and difference.[410] Transcendental reflection is Kant's rather obscure way of explaining of how we can demarcate the margins of experience, e. g., through such distinctions as a priori and empirical, form and content, from which patterns of determinancy begin to emerge from the void of indeterminacy. In the "Appendix" of the Kant-book, Heidegger makes an oblique reference to Kant's interest in transcendental reflection, particularly as enacted in the third *Critique*, and thereby points to the *origin* of the work of art that withdraws at the threshold of Kant's aesthetics.[411]

The work of art gives voice to the strife between world and earth, in such a way as to relocate the experience of beauty on a completely new axis which, to employ's Michael Zimmerman's phrase, "eclipses" subjectivity.[412] In "The Origin of the Work of Art," Heidegger redefines beauty (*Schönheit*) as *"one way in which truth essentially occurs as unconcealment."*[413] Where Kant, for example, placed considerable emphasis on the role of "genius" as the progenitor of art, Heidegger displaced the locus of creativity from the interplay of our cognitive powers to the openness unfolding through the strife of world and earth. As Gadamer states:

> The characterization of the work of art as standing-in-itself and opening up a world with which Heidegger begins his study consciously avoids going back to the concept of genius that is found in classical aesthetics. In this effort to understand the ontological structure of the work independently of the subjectivity of the creator beholder, Heidegger now uses 'earth' as a counter concept alongside the concept of the 'world,' to which the work belongs and which it erects and opens up.[414]

Insofar as subjectivity encapsulates the modern view of imagination, Heidegger takes the first step toward overcoming the metaphysics of subjectivity by radicalizing the Kantian version of imagination. In *Contributions to Philosophy*, Heidegger summarizes this movement when he equates imagination, not with a mental

---

**409** GA 65, p. 176; tr. 123.
**410** Bell, "Relations and Reversals: Deleuze, Hume, and Kant", pp. 191–193.
**411** GA 3, pp. 249–255; tr. 175–179.
**412** Zimmerman, *Eclipse of the Self*, pp. 8–14.
**413** GA 5, p. 43; tr. 56.
**414** Gadamer, *Heidegger's Ways*, p. 103.

faculty, but with the clearing itself. Heidegger's appeal to the work of art, to the materiality of the earth, provides the impetus for this movement. Imagination can then appear, not exclusively in its Kantian form, but in a more radicalized way to graph the dual vectors of the (movement of) this displacement. In its temporal enactment, then, imagination embodies that counter valence of absence from which presence emerges. The tension of presence/absence that imagination plays out yields us access to the strife between world and earth which the work of art sets in motion. In this regard, the work of art brings to fruition the wellspring of creativity in which imagination resides. The imagination will then address the *singularity* in which creativity exults, of which the work of art, by enacting the play of the fourfold — of earth, mortals, sky and gods — provides the foremost expression.

In "The Origin of the Work of Art," Heidegger then comes full circle from his reading of Kant to the implications that a study of the third *Critique* would have upon that interpretation. For the work of art embodies the singularity of the thing's manifestation, insofar as the thing gathers together, and provides a site for, the manifestation of world. The thing's singularity stands in stark contrast to its generic appearance as an object of scientific representation, the Newtonian presupposition for the manifestation of being which Kant adopts in the first *Critique*. While discussing Kant's formulation of the principles of nature in *Die Frage nach dem Ding?*, Heidegger counterposes these two distinct determinations of the thing: "Like the tradition before him and after him, [Kant] skips that sphere of things in which we know ourselves immediately at home, i. e., things as the artist depicts them for us, such as Van Gogh's simple chair with the tobacco pipe which was just put down or forgotten there."[415] As Gadamer summarizes the permutations of this development: the remorse of losing the thingness of the thing within the scientific model of representation is counterbalanced by the rejoice at its preservation in the work of art. "Preservation, however, presupposes that what is preserved still truly exists. Hence the very truth of the thing is implied if this truth is still capable of coming forth in the work of art. Heidegger's essay [on Kant], *Die Frage nach dem Ding* thus represents a necessary advance on the path of this thought."[416] We would be mistaken, then, to view Heidegger's discussion of the work of art as a belated attempt to come to terms with Kant's third *Critique*. *Rather, the "Origin of the Work of Art" brings thinking into the orbit of the turning whose mission to overcome the metaphysics of subjectivity begins with, and gives direction to, Heidegger's exchange with Kant.*

---

**415**  GA 41, p. 214; tr. 211.
**416**  Gadamer, *Philosophical Hermeneutics*, p. 227.

This turning engenders a tension between thought and *poeisis*, in which the impetus to engage in each feeds off each other. For Heidegger, *poiesis* draws forth the radiance of what can show itself with a majesty that can be found even in something most mundane. Witness the way in which the work of art brings the world itself to bear, in the play of the fourfold — of earth, mortals, sky and gods — in Van Gogh's painting of the peasant's shoes. World is not only the meaning-giving horizon of human activity, but is also the jutting forth of the openness whereby being addresses those whose journey crisscrosses the paths of birth and death. "World is ... that to which we are subject as long as the paths of birth and death, blessing and curse, keep us transported into being."[417] In its interplay with the thing, world exhibit a special tension of a dif-fering; this tension demarcates not only what can be present but also implies absence, serving as the haven for a mystery, as its shelter (*Bergung*). The mystery that evokes awe in us is not necessarily of supernatural descent, but rather can appear in what seemingly is most inconspicuous and set in its "earthliness," for example, the peasant shoes.[418]

The *Critique of Judgment* finds its entry point at the juncture between world and thing, in the space reserved for the double genitive "of." In this space, language first comes into its own as the "ringing of stillness" (*das Geläut der Stille*).[419] Yet we would be mistaken to maintain that Heidegger's thought provides a simple formula for the complexity interwoven into many of the distinctions which typify this work. On the contrary, it is equally the case that within the hidden depths of the third *Critique* Kant holds open a poetic measure for philosophy, which tilts its balance as much toward style as system. Indeed, Kant's insight proves to be so decisive, that even while the ontological difference silently shapes his transcendental philosophy, an entirely new nomenclature of difference is required in order to appreciate this emphasis on style. Correlatively, from the perspective of his own being-historical perspective, Heidegger recognizes that the "varying attempts ... to master the 'ontological difference,'" of which "*Vom Wesen des Grundes* and the Kant-book" are the two foremost examples, yield to a more original response to the dynamic of differentiation as such.[420] By extending Heidegger's appropriation of Kant's thought to include the third *Critique, we further demarcate the crossroads between these two thinkers whereby language yields the place for thinking (Denken) to come into its own.*

---

417 GA 5, pp. 30–31; tr. 44. See Heidegger, *Sojourns*, p. 49.
418 GA 5, p. 32; tr. 46.
419 See GA 12, p. 204. For an English translation, which is not based on the *Gesamtausgabe* edition, see Heidegger, *On the Way to Language*, p. 108.
420 GA 65, p. 250; tr. 176.

As Heidegger recognized through his close connection with Hölderlin, philosophy comes into its own, into its proper limits, when it recognizes that the clue to its proper stewardship does not arise directly from itself, but from its counterpart in the poetic arena, from art and *poiesis*. Thus the turn to style suggests a poetic measure which subverts, as if by mockery and play, the constraints of representationalism and bids thought to undergo a leap.[421] In this leap, the twofold of differentiation emerges as that which both determines, and comes to expression, in the saying of the double genitive. The tension of this twofold relation, being and beings, invites thought or first summons from it a response that takes shape through language. Thus, thinking necessarily unfolds as a mode of responsiveness, as answering the call, which abides according to the lawfulness abiding within the twofold. Due to this lawfulness, thinking can then become the recipient of its matter and acclimate itself to the precise tonality required to speak the twofold as the relation between being and beings. As Heidegger summarizes this movement in translating a pivotal statement of Parmenides from the Greek, "It is useful to let-lie-before-us- and so the taking to heart also: beings in being."[422] The twofold appears as the new nomenclature of the difference, because its concern can no longer be circumscribed exclusively by ontology. Beginning in *Zur Seinsfrage* (1957), Heidegger crosses out the word *Sein*, in order to indicate the deferral of its meaning (*Sinn*) in favor of the twofold of difference.[423]

In the late 1920s, Heidegger has emphasized the importance of nourishing the intelligibility of being by virtue of a distinction which had permitted its utterance in conceptual terms. Dasein's understanding of being has for its encompassing horizon the world, which in turn forms the counter focus for what can be explicitly encountered therein in regards to beings. But the new emphasis on the twofold begins instead with the differentiation itself through which such a counter focus can arise.[424] The nomenclature of difference calls forth world as correlative with and gathered into the thing, rather than as a transcendental horizon to which an ensemble of beings remains subordinate. In this way, language can appear more directly as the opening forth of the world, for its unique cadence creates the rhythm in which world and thing mutually reveal each other, a rhythmic event whose possibilities reside in *poiesis*. "Language is, as world-moving saying, the relation of all relations. It relates, maintains, proffers, and

---

**421** GA 65, pp. 303–304; tr. 214–215.

**422** Heidegger, *What Is Called Thinking?*, p. 223.

**423** GA 9, p. 411; tr. 310–311.

**424** GA 11, pp. 68–69. For an earlier English translation, not based on the *Gesamtausgabe* edition, see Heidegger, *Identity and Difference*, pp. 61–62.

enriches the face-to-face-encounter of the world's regions, holds and keeps them, in that it holds itself — saying — in reserve."[425] The search for this new nomenclature of difference brings language to the forefront in way which confirms Heidegger's earlier suggestion that discourse preunifies the modes of disclosedness which are embodied in either understanding or dispositions. As a continuation of Heidegger's retrieval of transcendental philosophy, this search transposes the locus of Kant's enterprise back to the concern for art which the third *Critique* provides. On the one hand, Heidegger's concern for the "origin of the work of art" emerges at a key breach in his *Auseinandersetzung* with Kant. On the other hand, Heidegger's muted interest in the third *Critique* harbors a possibility not only of extending his dialogue with Kant, but also deepening its implications. For the risk of not exercising every opportunity to address the twofold lies not simply in granting inordinate importance to beings but to the homogeneity of their appearance, so as to accommodate our representational models of technicity.

Does Heidegger's plan to address the third *Critique* meander throughout the labyrinth of his writings and lectures like an unfulfilled promise? Viewed from one perspective, "The Origin of the Work of Art" fulfills a larger promise of rediscovering the singularity of the thing, its uniqueness of manifestation, in the disclosive power of *poeisis*. Indeed, *poeisis* provides an avenue by which we can experience the difference between world and thing, and find in it a nomenclature to speak the tension of the differentiation between being and beings. But an explicit encounter with the Kantian text remains at the periphery of this discussion (i. e., the clues offered by Heidegger's "Seminar on Leibniz-Kant" lecture-course). But why should Leibniz's philosophy preface Heidegger's attempt to confront the intricacies of Kant's aesthetics? As is the case in Heidegger's 1928 lectures on logic, Leibniz's concern for the uniqueness of each monad speaks to the problem of the singular character of aesthetic experience. For Kant, knowledge and action privilege the universal, leaving the singular to how we respond to beauty in aesthetic experience. The work of art, even as Kant begins to address it, becomes an index for the uniqueness of all beings. As Sherover suggests, in one way or another Kant's transcendental philosophy begins and ends with the Leibnizian problem of how to grasp the unity of human experience throughout its diversity.[426] Without invoking the viewpoint of the infinite (monad), art brings forth what is missing in Leibniz's scheme, that is, the weight of diversity in which *beauty magnifies what is distinctive* in each instance of manifestation throughout

---

**425** GA 12, p. 203; tr. 107.
**426** Sherover, *From Kant and Royce to Heidegger*, p. 42.

beings in a whole.[427] Just as for Heidegger anxiety provides the "placeholder" for the "nothing," so art offers an outlet to experience the plurality of being's manifestations.

While reserving a greater opportunity for manifestation afforded to the thing within Kantian thought, Heidegger refrains from addressing the converse concern as to how Kant's aesthetics can alleviate the tendency toward representational-ism.[428] A possible exception lies in Heidegger's Nietzsche-lectures, which he composed shortly after *Die Frage nach dem Ding*. In these lectures, Heidegger acknowledges the often overlooked subtleties in Kant's account of aesthetic judgment. According to Heidegger, the "disinterested" character of a judgment of taste still involves a comportment, which holds forth the unique manifestation of an artwork as provoking a sense of harmony in us.[429] Yet the possible interface between the disclosedness proper to art and imagination as the disclosive power within cognitive and moral experience, sparks no further inquiry into Kant's thought except to suggests a way of "surpassing [hitherto] impoverished concepts of imagination."[430]

Subsequent thinkers like Arendt and Lyotard have taken Heidegger's inatten-tiveness toward the third *Critique* as a springboard to developing concerns that recede at the periphery of the question of being, for example, the pathos of the other and those disenfranchised within the mainstream of society. If ever there were a work that invited a multivocality of responses, it is the *Critique of Judgment*. By intermediating between the theoretical and the practical, the work gives reign to a heterogeneity of imagination, of improvisation and governance of freedom and law, the claim of the singular and the rule of the universal, the beautiful and sublime. For Kant, imagination nurtures different alternatives in which something can become manifest according to limits not set in advance by concepts. We should remember, however, that such appearance is not totally gratuitous. Whether it be a purposiveness without a purpose in the case of the beautiful, or the circumventing of purpose in the case of the sublime, aesthetic experience still harbors a disposi-tion toward governance. Such governance invites our participation, precisely insofar as the measure of lawfulness is always coordinated with an equal opportu-nity for improvisation. Thus, Kant refers to the free play of imagination. Freedom elicits the dynamics of manifestness in a way that defers to the possibilities harbored therein. Correlatively, the law does not involve regulating a state of affairs, but instead arises as the space for imagination to exult in the abundance of

---

427 The publication of GA 84, *Seminare: Leibniz–Kant*, will be of interest here.
428 Taminiaux, *Poetics and Speculation*, pp. 37–39.
429 GA 43, pp. 131, 143.
430 Sallis, *Echoes*, p. 185.

possibility, to embody the improvisation of play. "Now, if in the judgment of taste the imagination must be considered in its freedom, it is in the first place not regarded as reproductive, as it is subject to the laws of association, but as productive and spontaneous (as the author of arbitrary forms of possible intuition ...)."[431]

In this manner, the power of imagination unfolds on two fronts at once. On the one hand, its play provides a new demarcation of freedom and lawfulness which exults in the particular, and, on the other, circumvents the univocity of representation which adheres to preset rules. As Kant states: "Hence it is a conformity to law without a law; and a subjective agreement of the imagination and understanding ... can subsist along with the free conformity to law of the understanding (which is also called purposiveness without purpose) and with the peculiar feature of a judgment of taste."[432] In drawing upon the eminence of the possible, such playfulness invites the diversity of manifestation. Just as a determinate judgment preserves the status quo of order for cognition and morality, so a reflective judgment welcomes the emergence of novelty. The emphasis on creativity attends to the nuances of manifestation (to be found in either art or nature), an attentiveness to difference as the hallmark of letting be.

In his analysis of the sublime, Kant recognized that imagination can engage in a dialogue with reason that exults in the disproportional appearance of nature's expanse in comparison to us, while eliciting at the same time the contrast which awakens us to our higher destination. "Thus that very violence which is done to the subject through the imagination is judged as purpose in reference to the whole determination of the mind."[433] The sublime constitutes imagination's sojourn into the singularity of nature's manifestation, that is, outside a representational framework.

> The transcendent ... is for the imagination like an abyss in which it fears to lose itself; but for the rational idea of the supersensible it is not transcendent, but in conformity with law to bring about such an effort of the imagination, and consequently here there is the same amount of attraction as there was of repulsion for the mere sensibility. For just as imagination and understanding, in judging of the beautiful, generate a subjective purposiveness of the mental powers by means of their harmony, so imagination and reason do so by means of their conflict.[434]

Through the prism of this showing, a light can appears whose incandescence exceeds all attempts by representation to render transparent a reality which has

---

**431** AA 5, KU, p. 240; tr. 77.
**432** AA 5, KU, p. 241; tr. 78.
**433** AA 5, KU, p. 259; tr. 98.
**434** AA 5, KU, p. 254; tr. 92.

only one facet and hence only one dimension. As Lyotard recognized, the many-faceted character of the sublime offsets the technological attempt to make all reality conform to the control sought by our one-dimensional models.[435] In experiencing the sublime, imagination oscillates between "repulsion" and "attraction," the suspension of the expedient concerns of inner worldly time which regulates the frantic pace of technology.[436]

The more we combat the constraints of representationalism, the more we are summoned by the ominous pages of the third *Critique*. That venture has as its way a new experience of language which prepares for the saying of the twofold. In his destructive-retrieval of Kant, Heidegger began by considering the import of the ontological difference as marking the historical origin of the philosophical task. He leaves it to us to unfold the full implications of confronting the third of Kant's critiques, insofar as it provides the inspiration for an altogether new nomenclature of difference, the saying of the twofold through the interplay of world and thing. In retrospect, the momentum for a destructive-retrieval of Kant's thought stems from a leap into the tension of this "between." Such a leap becomes possible, however, only when we begin to experience the playful innocence of poetry.[437] Through this playfulness, the freedom of imagination outmaneuvers all representatationalism, so that the showing of philosophy can abide in the stillness of simple saying

The doubling of imagination, as an emissary of freedom, as well as the root of temporal synthesis, is the *Abgrund* from which Heidegger not only reinterprets transcendental philosophy, but transposes his own inquiry (of "being and time") into the wider orbit of being-historical thinking. As such, the phenomenological inquiry into imagination reverts into the enactment of thinking, as undertaken through the freedom by which words first acquire the power to speak. "Freedom is not 'condition of the possibility' of the word, but it is ... the *silence* of be-ing [*des Seyns*] itself, is 'word.'"[438] In this way, the freedom of the word, as Heidegger emphasizes in *Die Geschichte des Seyns*, yields the clearing for the stillness of being (*Lichtung der Stille des Seyns*).[439] Conversely, making silent, or "sigetic" (*Sigetik*), re-emerges as a new "logic" of thinking which, as Pöggeler suggests, re-asks the question of being from out of the other beginning.[440]

---

**435** Lyotard, *Heidegger and "the jews,"* pp. 31–32.
**436** AA 5, KU, p. 258; tr. 97.
**437** See Gosetti-Ferencei, *Heidegger, Hölderlin, and the Subject of Poetic Language*, pp. 22–27.
**438** GA 85, p. 76; tr. 66.
**439** GA 69, p. 126.
**440** Pöggeler, *Martin Heidegger's Path of Thinking*, p. 223.

The new logic is not based on the rationality of reason that Kant inherited, but on a recovery of the language as *logos*, an attunement (*Stimmung*) to the word. When executing within the province of the third *Critique*, the destructive-retrieval of Kant returns us to "thinking" in a more original form, that is, not its division against being, or even in its dialectical mediation in the guise of the Hegelian Absolute, but, instead to way in which being and thinking belong together. Heidegger's pointed refrain in *Was heißst Denken?* that was the most "thought-provoking" thought given to us to think is that we are still not thinking, takes on a new meaning. For the question of being must be addressed on the side of its withdrawal from thought, and simultaneously, in terms of the initial invitation to thinking, the "innovation" of thought (e. g., in its belonging together to being). Yet, to negotiate this difficult, and nebulous path of inquiry, a new road map is required. The detour of the destructive-retrieval of Kant around the periphery of the third *Critique* suggests such a map: namely, by showing how the cultivation and safeguarding of the word defines the primary mission of thinking, not through its abstraction into a separate discipline (e. g., traditional logic), but through its reciprocity with being itself.

Heidegger's initial attempt in the Kant-book to overcome the supremacy of reason through the power of imagination enters a new phase or chapter. For the negative thesis of dismantling reason has as its counter balance the transformation in which thinking defers to the (power) of the word, and conversely, comes into its own by reciprocating and responding to a prior claim, i. e., of being itself. This radical transformation of thinking into a response *thrusts language itself into the forefront of the inquiry into being*. But, where, then, does language leads us in this inquiry into being, if not into the familiar terrain of the spinning of conceptual formulas, then presumably into a new "frontier"?

## 3 "... Without a Concept"

In those rare cases where we arrive at the limits of language, the focus shifts away from what we are trying to express to the mode or manner of expression itself. Though Kant does not exactly formulate the problem this way, the third *Critique* struggles precisely with this corundum: however idiosyncratic it may on the face appear to be, the uniqueness of the *experience* of beauty must still be "communicable"in some way. In the case of reflective judgments of taste, as we have seen, the modes of signification are not restricted by preset predicates, but rather are open to spawning new distinctions and nuances. The intriguing scenario, then, of "schematizing" minus predicates, or "without a concept," harbors an alternative pathway for philosophy, namely, that thinking no longer needs to assume a subordinate position to language, but *instead the words themselves, and their power of signification, are intrinsic to the creative thrust and task of thinking.* From Heidegger's perspective, the irony is quite evident: that in a text what appears not in the least to be relevant to ontology, a clue emerges to the transformation he envisioned at the deepest root of language which would allow it to direct thought in *responding* to, rather than "representing" being. Once these shackles of representation have been broken, the *idiom of the word* can itself emerge, in philosophy as well as in poetry.

Gadamer makes a profound, yet perhaps overly presumptuous statement, when he states that "Hölderlin loosened Heidegger's tongue" in order that he could overcome metaphysics."[441] Whatever (or whoever) may have promoted Heidegger's original insight into the saying of language, the corundum Kant struggles with in the third *Critique* serves, as it were, as an unread "signpost" to this crossing. The crossing harbors a new relation between being and thinking, where the former arises from unconcealment and the latter echoes the depths of silence. Through the attunement which first acclimates thinking to this silence, allowing it to heed the claims (*Anspruch*) of being, thinking first becomes behold to the idiom of the word. But what is the source of the idiom, where does it originate? It does not merely spring from a vacuum. Rather, the word arises from, and transports us into, the crucible of being-historical thinking.

If thought is to be aligned more with art (*poeisis*) than science, as the unread signpost of the third *Critique* suggests, how can it fulfill the traditional mandate of truth and admit a form of governance? The path leading beyond *Being and Time* entails a further breakthrough which Heidegger began to make in *Contributions to Philosophy*; there he shows the need for a further differentiation that diffuses the sense of withholding as a negative effect and instead prepares for its positive transformation as sheltering (*Bergung*) what it withholds. This more radical mode of negativity reserves for truth a kind of initiative even in its omission and absence, the withholding of presence which departs from the hermeneutic meaning of the "not" from the Hegelian. In this way, it becomes possible to introduce in the movement of philosophical inquiry a radical shift in momentum. As a dimension of the "turning," the ambivalence shrouded in the "not" induces a transposition in which philosophy abandonment to the historical travails of concealment offers a complementary pathway of return under the guardianship of unconcealment. For Heidegger, thought comes under this claim of *returnership* by heeding the finitude of which it is already a part and to which it remains enowned, namely, its character as thrown into a historical arena.

---

441 Gadamer, *Heidegger's Ways*, p. 190.

The movement of this "returnership" both anticipates and prepares for the arrival of the "other beginning" beyond the limited horizon of metaphysics. The philosophical tradition thereby shelters what remains "unsaid" through this lengthy history, which in turn keeps in abeyance or "incubation" (*Incubationzeit*) the plurality of ways to express being and transcribe its meaning into words. In commissioning history as its own amphitheater of expression, language bears the grounding words which allows what is unsaid in the thought of previous philosophers to become the wellspring to spawn what still remains open to thought in the future. The manner in which the possibility of unconcealment arrives from the future yields the "tone" or pitch of attunement; this intonement enables words to resonate in their ancestral import, thereby establishing the place (*Ort*) in which etymologies, through the intralingual translations of the grounding words, first become possible. The idiom of the word in its unique power over us incites both a reverence and awe, as well as a sense of proportion, which renounces the mastery of representation in favor of the impromptu character of play. In cultivating the impromptu character of the idiom, like the "free play" of imagination in Kant's sense, a radical break must be ventured, in order that a representational idea cannot bloc our entrance into the open expanse of being. It is within this ecstatic domain that the eccentricities of speaking (for example, the etymological link between "thinking" and "thanking"), the reverberations of its play, induce new guidance for thought beyond such traditional cannons of clarity and distinctness.

Thinking is always underway through its movement of recollection and "returnership." By locating itself more decisively in history, thought discovers that it is only by yielding before what merits its attention that it can first attend to the activity essential its own, its "ownmost" possibility. The urge to capture itself in a moment of "reflexivity" thereby dissipates, in such a way that the empowerment of thought resides elsewhere in its most acute vulnerability to the intimations of language. If there is a kind of comportment (*Verhalten*) to thought which parallels its wordliness, it can only lie in its holding itself within an attunement, whose very tension catapults us (as if by a leap) into the open expanse of being. As Parvis Emad aptly states: "The attuning that grounds thinking is one in which the echo of *Ereignis* is held back and kept in reserve ..."[442] In this counter point of "reservedness" arises the counter tension which tears asunder the constraints of representationalism and its grounding in the reflexivity of the *cogito*. In place of this simple reflectivity, thinking instead embarks upon a sojourn which is governed by the *sway of a mystery*, the dual holding in reserve and preserving of what still remains worthy of thought or the sheltering of the truth of being.

---

442 Emad, "The Echo of Being in *Beiträge zur Philosophie*", p. 33.

When the grounding words direct the course of philosophical inquirer, rather than a determinate ideational content, thought unfolds as "being-historical thinking." This venturesome leap catapults the inquirer into the orbit of being-historical thinking, whereby he/she as "thinker" responds to the *challenge of transcribing the grounding words*, or their intralingual translation, by simultaneously engaging previous thinkers in "conversation." By disposing itself to the intralingual translation (and deeper etymology) of the grounding words, thought answers the finite plea which delivers each thinker over to a conversation with his/her predecessors. Accordingly the enactment of being-historical thinking occurs in and through this "face-to-face" relationship, "*das Gegen-einander-über.*" In this exchange or conversation resides the "otherness of the matter of thought" (*Verschiedenheit der Sache des Denkens*).[443] We cannot overlook that, among all of this exchanges with previous thinkers, perhaps Heidegger's *Auseinandersetzung* with Kant sets the tone for this historical endeavor. Such is the case even in *extending this conversation* by revisiting the most enigmatic of Kant's texts, the *Critique of Judgment*.

Can our detour into the third *Critique* help us to project-open this frontier? Can its theme, if not as the formal study of beauty or aesthetics, then in an alternative way, i. e., through the "figurative" power of speaking reserved to art (*poiesis*), direct us to this new landscape of inquiry? The discussions in this chapter provide affirmative answers to both of these questions. Ultimately, our way of "doubling back" upon one of the most enigmatic of Kant's texts catapults us to an important "crossing," that is, where the crafting-building-poetizing power emerges as the ground-razing and clearing of the "house of being." The ground plan and design of this new residence ceases to be "architectonic," and instead becomes the *craft* of thinking.

---

443 GA 11, p. 56; tr. 46. See Schalow, "Language and the Etymological Turn of Thought", p. 201.

# Chapter Seven
# The Ellipsis of the Third *Critique*: From Art to Nature

On whichever trail we approach Kant's philosophy, the "front" way via the first *Critique*, or the "back" way through the third *Critique*, the destination still remains the same: re-opening the question of being. In the former case, the understanding of being provides the direction and its expression in language was secondary. In the latter case, the depth, fecundity, and power of the word itself, along with its potential enrichment and preservation through innumerable varieties of historical idioms, gives the inflection, intonement, as well as the import of any articulation of being. We come to question being, then, in concert with the possibilities for expressing its *meaning*, i. e., in terms of the "opening" of the play-space which grants the occasion for the inaugural saying of the word through the hermeneutic medium of "translation." Just as imagination emerged into the forefront of the initial phase of Heidegger's dialogue with Kant, so the "play" of the word itself becomes the new vanguard for a "leap" toward a future possibility of thinking.

In this regard, the third *Critique* bears a special importance as a text that harbors hidden pathways of thinking, where the traditional lines dividing beauty and truth, style and logic, art and philosophy, instead reconnect at different points along the curvature of a circle. If this is the case, could a detour into the realm of the poet, otherwise foreclosed to the thinker, invite a new subtlety of response prefiguring all philosophy? By the same token, could a lecture-course during this period, included in one of the last volumes to be published in Heidegger's *Gesamtausgabe*, help us in undertaking this detour?[444] In raising these pertinent questions, we arrive at the crossroads of Heidegger's exchange with Kant.

In this regard, the aforementioned "crossing" harnesses the creative tension between these two thinkers, in order to open new avenues for addressing the most pressing concerns of our day. Heidegger already had an intimation of such when in *Contributions to Philosophy* he spoke of the "ones to come" who herald the arrival of be-ing (*Seyn*) and prepare the way for human beings to inhabit the earth in their mission of "dwelling."[445] Accordingly, I will consider, first, how imagina-

---

444 See GA 84. In this context, we find important intimations of Heidegger's continued interest in Kant's *Critique of Judgment*, particularly in regard to the enigmatic relation between nature and freedom through the exercise of teleological judgment, in a newly published volume of the *Gesamtausgabe*. See GA 86, p. 200. Also see GA 66, p. 424; tr. 374 (Cf. note #24).

445 GA 65, pp. 395–401; tr. 277–281.

tion provides a unique springboard into the abode of language, which we inhabit not as rational agents, but as creatures of the earth who are awe struck by the beauty of art, the sublimity of nature, and the appearance of the sacred. The outcome of this leap, however, is not simply negative, since the monolithic character of reason is dislodged in favor of discovering the diversity of our ancestry as "earth-bound" creatures, as incarnated within the domain of nature.

Secondly, I will consider the "underplayed" importance that "spatiality" has in Heidegger's exchange with Kant, and thereby underscore the differences as well the similarities that shape the dialogue between these two thinkers. We will thereby show Heidegger revisits the topic of imagination in such pivotal texts as *Contributions to Philosophy* and *Mindfulness*, leaving us with the faint, but important suggestion that the "free play of time-space" provides the new springboard for "being-historical thinking," much as the "transcendental" power of imagination had served as a catalyst to radicalize phenomenology. Given this more expansive, "being-historical perspective," "*riches*" of what is "*unsaid*" in Kant's philosophy can then re-emerge at the juncture where thinking abides within the silent depths of the word.

By virtue of this historically enriched orientation, I will then, thirdly, consider what still remains "unthought" in the most enigmatic of Kant's texts, the *Critique of Judgment*. We will discover that a more concrete idiom of the word is required to give voice to Kant's intimations concerning the "grandeur" of nature and the possibility of our experience thereof within the wider expanse of human dwelling. This idiom holds the memory of both tragedy and transitoriness, as well as the anticipation and hope, which characterizes Dasein's temporal sojourn on the earth. The so-called "Conclusion" or "Postscript" of our study is also the acknowledgment of the "beginning" of our arrival at the "crossroads" which perpetuate the dialogue between these two thinkers. In sheltering the unsaid, being-historical thinking gathers forth the possibilities of the Heidegger-Kant dialogue, in order to preserve what still remains worthy of question.

## 1 Of Things Heavenly and Earthly

The system builders of German Idealism viewed the third *Critique* as Kant's effort to bridge the disparate parts of his system, the theoretical and practical realms of philosophy.[446] The first and second *Critique* establish two different realms of jurisdiction, the former devoted to the principles of nature (understanding), the

---

446 See Hegel, *Logic*, pp. 65–94.

second to the laws of freedom/morality (reason).[447] Given Kant's architectonic, judgment emerges as the linchpin to mediate between the separate realms of understanding and reason. In the "First Introduction to the *Critique of Judgment*," which has published separately from that text due to its length, Kant remarks:

> The critique of taste, however, which otherwise is useful only for the improvement of strengthening of taste itself, fills a gap in the system of our cognitive faculties if one considers it form the transcendental standpoint; it disclosed a striking and, I believe, highly encouraging prospect of a complete system of all the powers of the mind in their relationship not only to things of sense but also to the suprasensuous, without removing the limitations of their use in the latter respect laid down by a strict critique.[448]

Imagination epitomizes the creativity of this mediating power. In one way or another, either as the schema of the pure concepts of understanding, or the "typic" of practical reason, the first and second *Critique* implicate the importance of imagination.[449]

Yet the priority that the third *Critique* grants to imagination, and its position in Kant's architectonic as a median, also gives a hermeneutic spin to the importance of this work.[450] For the imagination emerges as a gathering point for a discourse which can express the reflexivity of reason's self-examination, that articulates the activity which is provided by the example of reason's self-criticism. In the figure of imagination, the third *Critique* adds another level of depth to what Heidegger first characterized as the unspoken element in the insights about human finitude, temporality, and the possibility of experience that the Critical enterprise brings to light. In this regard, the third *Critique* emerges as a hermeneutic oracle in allowing the singular to invite responses through which, as it were, the participants of a dialogue can occupy a common universe of discourse. The third *Critique*, then, is hermeneutical in the most primeval manner of all, in the sense that it returns us to the inception of language as the dynamic of intermediation, as the relation of all relations. In his dialogue with a Japanese philosopher in *On the Way of Language*, Heidegger recalls the simplicity of this origin of hermeneutics: the interposing of difference, the eliciting of a relationship, through which thinking assumes the position of a respondent to being.[451]

---

447 AA 5, KU, pp. 171–176; tr. 7–15.
448 Kant, "*Erste Fassung der Einleitung die Kritik der Urteilskraft*," AA 20, pp. 244–245. "First Introduction to the *Critique of Judgment*", p. 48.
449 See Freydberg, *Imagination in Kant's Critique of Practical Reason*, pp. 124–129. Also see Schalow, *Imagination and Existence*, pp. 162–167.
450 Makkreel, *Imagination and Interpretation in the Third Critique*, pp. 172–177.
451 GA 12, p. 91; tr. 9–10.

In undertaking his destructive-retrieval of Kant, Heidegger implicitly follows the hermeneutic pathway which the third *Critique* provides. That is, the language that governs reason's self-examination extends a common reference point or "index" of exchange, a *sensus communis*, to its various participants, namely "finitude." According to Heidegger, "ontology is an index of finitude";[452] this index allows individuals of the most diverse backgrounds to be drawn into a conversation about the most perennial philosophical questions. The possibility of death, and the temporality enacted through it, extends a kind of analogical thread by which different individuals can be delivered over to, and be claimed by, a *logos*, in order to play out the permutations of philosophical exchange (*Auseinandersetzung*). The thread of this language even allows the exchange between Heidegger and Kant to get underway. For finitude is the common element that allows Heidegger to draw a parallel between the way temporality is investigated through a hermeneutic of human existence and a critique of pure reason, respectively.

Insofar as the concern for language hovers at the periphery of Heidegger's hermeneutics in the 1920s, so, within the context of retrieving transcendental philosophy, he assumes its relevance as far as retrieving the importance of the third *Critique* goes. In his "Seminar on Leibniz and Kant" from the summer semester of 1935/36 and his discussion of Herder's essay on language in the summer semester of 1938,[453] Heidegger provides some tantalizing suggestions about a primitive referential dimension within the aesthetic experience of beauty. The "disinterested" pleasure of experiencing beauty disengages us from our immediate identification with our desires, interjecting a second level in which how the experience *affects us*, can allow *this* experience to say *something about* its importance to us. At work is a double intentionality, rather than singularly directed intentionality that, Husserl, for example addresses in describing the act of perception. The doubling of the intending gives birth to the communicability of the experience, in order that the speaker can convey its relevance and situate what he/she experiences within the larger compass of nature, the world, and perhaps, even history.

In a decidedly unique way, Hans-Georg Gadamer appeals to the third *Critique* as both a new springboard for developing the hermeneutic method, and for illustrating a crucial development in the history of aesthetics. In an essay from 1960, Gadamer summarizes the historical impact of the *Critique of Judgment*:

---

**452** GA 3, p. 281; tr. 197.
**453** See Heidegger's discussion of Herder's view of language, GA 85, pp. 34–44. For an outstanding discussion of this topic, see Kovacs, "Heidegger in Dialogue with Herder: Crossing the Language of Metaphysics toward Be-ing-historical Language", pp. 45–63.

... [I]n his third *Critique* – the *Critique of Aesthetic Judgment* – Kant established the problem of aesthetics in its systematic significance. In the subjective universality of the aesthetic judgment of taste, he discovered the powerful and legitimate claim to independence that the aesthetic judgment can make over against the claims of the understanding and morality. The taste of the observer can no more be comprehended as the application of concepts, norms, or rules than the genius of the artist can. What sets the beautiful apart cannot be exhibited as a determinate, knowable property of an object; rather it manifests itself as a subjective factor: the intensification of the *Lebensgefühl* [life feeling] through the harmonious correspondence of imagination and understanding. What we experience in beauty – in nature as well as in art – is the total animation and free interplay of all our spiritual powers.[454]

In his famous work *Truth and Method*, Gadamer marks the overlap between hermeneutics and aesthetics.[455] Like his mentor, who also gave priority to art, Gadamer focuses his attention on the singularity of the aesthetic experience that first comes to light in Kant's account of beauty. For the singularity of the experience of beauty, and its expression of art, can only be understood by unfolding different horizons of interpretation. No solitary interpretive horizon can necessarily exhaust the manifestation of beauty, and thereby a disposition of openness becomes crucial to the interpretive process. Yet like his contemporary, Hannah Arendt, Gadamer develops his own reading of Kant and approach to hermeneutics, which does not explicitly aim to re-open the question of being and pursue its radicalization in terms of the parallel question of language.

In suggesting an alternative pathway leading directly from Heidegger's thinking (and his destructive-retrieval of Kant), we see how Gadamer's "hermeneutic turn" presupposes a deeper appreciation of the origin of language as the wellspring for the engenderment of new idioms, the birth of "meaning" itself (*Sinn*). A trajectory of meaning, in which the speaker can stand out within the larger expanse of what his/her possibilities are, is thereby born. Hidden in the background of Kant's transcendental methodology – even in its most esoteric variation in the guise of aesthetics – is a turn to language, which places that *method on a concrete footing*. The creation of an entry point into language through the *sensus communis*[456] suggests a further stage in Kant's Copernican revolution: meaning is not restricted to what is objectively definable, but instead extends to how our finitude can be revealed through examples set by our response to art.

---

**454** Gadamer, *Heidegger's Ways*, p. 100.
**455** See Risser, *Hermeneutics and the Voice of the Other*, pp. 144–157.
**456** For a further discussion of this point, see Laumakis, "The *Sensus Communis* Reconsidered", pp. 429–444.

Though references to the communicability of aesthetic experience run throughout the third *Critique*, the passage that Heidegger finds most intriguing, beginning with a footnote in the Kant-book,[457] occurs in section 59 dealing with symbol, analogy, and imagination. The fact that the experience of beauty can also awaken our moral sensibilities and art can become, as Kant suggests, a "symbol of morality,"[458] suggests how the axis of understanding extends beyond concepts to include the lived dimension of our being-in-the-world or *Verstehen*. For Kant, a symbol is a double way of referring, to an object that is given, and, by extension, to one which is not, in order that what cannot be conceptualized directly (in the schema of a concept) can be pointed to indirectly.[459] Thus, for example, the sky can symbolize the heights of moral sublimity. Kant's account of the role that imagination plays in this indirect form of communication is one of the rare instances in which he broaches the topic of language. "These forms which do not constitute the presentation of a given concept itself but only, as approximate representations of the imagination, express the consequences bound up with it and its relationship to other concepts, are called (aesthetical) *attributes* of an object ... Thus Jupiter's eagle with the lightning in its claws is an attribute of the mighty king of heaven, as the peacock is of his magnificent queen."[460] In this way, Kant defines as an "art of speech," an "art of conducting a free play of the imagination as if it were a serious business of the understanding."[461] Even *music implies a language* whose sensuous quality is communicable through the harmony it provokes in the listener:

> This tone indicates more or less an affection of the speaker and produces it also in the hearer, which affection excites in its turn in the hearer the idea that is expressed in speech by the tone in question. Thus as modulation is, as it were, a universal language of sensations intelligible to every man, the art of tone is by itself alone in its full force, viz. as a language of the affections ...[462]

Kant's account of the role that imagination plays in this indirect form of communication is one of the rare instances in which he broaches the topic of language. In its free play, imagination seeks a determinancy which can never be fulfilled by a concept, and *yet welcomes a complementary form of articulation — incomplete at*

---

457 GA 3, p. 160n; tr. 112n.
458 AA 5, KU, pp. 351–353; tr. 197–199.
459 See Watson, *Traditions*, pp. 232–234.
460 AA 5, KU, p. 314; tr. 158. For a discussion of this metaphor, see Pillow, "Jupiter's Eagle and the Despot's Hand Mill: Two Views of Metaphor in Kant", pp. 193–209.
461 AA 5, KU, pp. 320–321; tr. 165.
462 AA 5, KU, pp. 328–329; tr. 173.

*it is — through figurative vehicles of symbol and metaphor.*[463] When we juxtapose this tangential discussion of the role of language in the third *Critique* with Heidegger's overall effort to retrieve the power of imagination, *imagination re-emerges as that (temporal) dynamic which propels the human capacity to understand into the clearing.* Through art and imagination human beings do not just indulge in games of fantasy, but instead are endowed with the ability to participate in the clearing from which the impetus to philosophize arises. Though Heidegger was not particularly keen about evolutionary theory proclaiming the birth of "man,"[464] he might say, with Kant, that humanity's "second birth" occurs when human beings first engage in philosophy and experience its liberating spirit. "Let us ... establish philosophy [as a] work of human freedom."[465]

When we cast the third *Critique* in this light, it is more than just ceremonial, more than just a loose thread to tie up. For in following Heidegger's path of thinking, the thinkers who appear along that journey are not those whom we merely study in historical hindsight, but themselves spearhead the future of philosophy itself by *pioneering new methodologies*. In the *Prolegomena*, Kant remarks that "There are scholars for whom the history of philosophy (both ancient and modern) is philosophy itself."[466] The statement betrays a curious ambiguity, revealing on the one hand a kind of lack of appreciation for the inherently historical character of philosophical questions, but, on the other hand, suggesting that it is only by practicing thinking that we actually become philosophers ourselves. Heidegger straddles this ambiguity when he raises the question "what calls thinking forth?" For we cannot describe what thinking is, or arrive at a definition, merely by assuming the position of a spectator. Rather, only when we actually think do we arrive at what thinking is, such that, to put matter simply, we learn only by doing.

Perhaps Heidegger most eloquently most eloquently puts a more contemporary stamp on this issue in a passage from *Mindfulness*, which he makes, ironically, by alluding to the task of interpreting Kant's thought:

> For example, Kant's philosophy (what does it consist of) *can* be held to be *wrong* (and what does this mean?). Out of proving the wrongness of Kant's philosophy, one can make a career and a life's work. Except that is not philosophizing, not an inquiry into the sway of being.[467]

---

463 GA 3, p. 160n; tr. 122n. Heidegger asks whether Kant's allusion to symbolism is another instance of "schrinking back" (das *Zurückweichen!*), adding "but in what sense" (aber in welchem Sinn).

464 GA 29/30, pp. 402–403; tr. 277–278. See Schalow, "Essence and Ape: Heidegger and the Question of Evolutionary Theory", pp. 445–462.

465 GA 24, p. 17; tr. 12.

466 Kant, Prol., AA 4, p. 255. *Prolegomena to Any Future Metaphysics*, p. 3.

467 GA 66, p. 76; tr. 62.

In this passage, Heidegger echoes Kant's statement in his lectures on *Logic*: "No one can call himself a philosopher who cannot philosophize. Philosophizing, however, can be learned only through practice and the use of one's own reason ..."[468] Thus, for Heidegger, the question as to what calls thinking forth changes, by virtue of inviting us to think, into a concern for the topic (being) which, in turn, invites us to serve as respondents, in short, to heed the twofold and cultivating an abode for its self-gathering (*logos*) and appearance in speech. "Needful is the saying: beings to be."[469]

Just as the question about thinking reverts into its practice, so the exchange between thinkers proceeds through an increasingly fluidity of its language. For the basic philosophical terms are themselves open to transmutation, and the preservation of their force hinges upon that very possibility. A foremost example of the fluidity of philosophical terms occurs with Heidegger's ingenious, albeit controversial, development of etymologies. In his innovative development of etymologies, Heidegger recovers the root of the grounding words of philosophy (*Grundworte*), in order to allow a deeper meaning to resonate that is otherwise lost in the conventional usage of the term. Heidegger's approach proves to be controversial, because he resists any "semantic equivalency" between the term and the dictionary declension of its origin.[470] For Heidegger, however, the dictionary version assumes a strictly ideational content, which ignores the dynamic whereby language speaks through our co-respondence to it. By ignoring this dynamic, the stance of semantic equivalency remains oblivious to the pitch of attunement, the tonality of hearing, by which words evoke the meaning(s) they do. For what all etymological exercises assume, and the presupposition which Heidegger clarifies, is the contribution which history makes in providing the repository for the meaning of the key philosophical terms. The meaning of these terms is not simply a pure given, because they depend upon the enactment of being-historical thinking. As a result, only through a reciprocal movement of enowning, of the appropriation of tradition, can etymologies allow the grounding words of philosophy to speak from their historical depth.[471] In this way, being-historical thinking recalls the deeper meanings of words as they echo across the corridors of history.[472] The *echo* reverberates both with the

---

468 Kant, AA 9, p. 27; *Logic*, p. 29.
469 Heidegger, *What Is Called Thinking?*, p. 183.
470 Emad, *On the Way to Heidegger's Contributions to Philosophy*, pp. 11–12.
471 See Schalow, "Language and the Etymological Turn of Thought", pp. 187–203.
472 See De Gennaro, "Heidegger on Translation — Translating Heidegger", pp. 3–22.

distress of be-ing's refusal in remaining unspoken, and with the promise of its "gift" by intimating its "meaning" to mortals.[473]

If etymologies presuppose history in order to transmit their meaning, then their transmission depends upon a reciprocal appropriation of tradition in which language is embedded. Put simply, etymologies serve thinking, but it is only through a corollary exercise of thought that we can recall the ancestry of words. In this regard, etymologies exhibit a craftsmanship and style the hallmark of which is recollective thought. A primary instance of this occurs in Part IV of the Kant-book when Heidegger returns to the Greek ancestry of the word for being/ *Sein*, circumventing the truncation of the term in its Latinized cognate, or "substance," in favor of recollecting its hidden root as *ousia* or "permanent presence." Here is an example where thinking prevails over simple linguistics. What calls thinking forth, as the re-enactment of projecting being upon time, points back to the temporal derivation of the root of the term, permanence in presence. Thus, through his etymology of the Greek term, Heidegger accents the temporal connotation of the word, its affiliation with permanence and presence; he thereby draws upon the entire background of the philosophical tradition to recover the word from its deepest roots. Heidegger's deployment of etymologies, then, becomes a signpost along the path of thinking.

We cannot overlook, however, the way in which etymologies illustrates the creative tension or dynamic that animates thinking. Specifically, they embody the interplay between improvisation and law, freedom and governance, innovation and tradition. Do Heidegger's etymologies lack rigor; are they too loose in their formulation? Perhaps the best answer lies in the fact that they are champions, not of literalness, but, on the contrary, of imagination. Imagination invites the emergence of new possibilities, the weaving together of novel patterns of meanings, in which the saying of novelty reconnects us with, rather than severs us from, the roots of tradition. In the form of etymologies, imagination stretches the elasticity of language, in order to invite a multiplicity of responses, a multiviocality that allows the tradition to speak through the inflection of many different voices. By speaking through these various inflections, thought proceeds by disposing itself toward the deeper etymology of words. Herein lies the finite plea which delivers each thinker over to an exchange with his/her predecessors. Only by sustaining this otherness can language provide an abode for thought in which we can dwell with the deepest modesty and forbearance. Such forbearance is necessary, given that the promise offered by language's capacity for unconcealment is always

---

473 GA 65, pp. 45–46, 108; tr. 32, 75–76. For a further discussion of the significance of this "echoing," see Emad, *On the Way to Heidegger's Contributions to Philosophy*, pp. 60–65.

counter balanced by the refusal inherent in its tendency toward concealment. We experience the doubling of this tension, for example, when our attempt to translate basic philosophical words meets with the resistance of encountering the "materiality" and "particularity" endemic to language.[474]

In his "Letter on 'Humanism,'" Heidegger describes the special humility which is required for the vocation of thought: "Thinking is on the descent to the poverty of its provisional ownmost. Thinking gathers language into simple saying ... With its laying, thinking lays inconspicuous furrows in language. They are still more inconspicuous than the furrows that the farmer, slow of step, draws through the field."[475] Only by cultivating this poverty can we reap the rewards of thinking. In his "Notes to the Kant-book," Heidegger comments: "[the Kant-book:] an attempt to question what has not been said, instead of writing in a fixed way about Kant. What has been said is insufficient, what has not been said is filled with riches."[476] Conversely, the more proficient we become in the craft of thinking, the more we are disposed to re-examine the unspoken truth of Kant's transcendental philosophy.

## 2 Unwinding the Kantian Premise

At this juncture we no longer stand on either side of these great thinkers, but instead are transported, as it were, into the "midpoint" which turns the dialogue in different directions in order that new light can be cast as much on the thinking of the one as the other. This is particularly the case when we reconsider a text whose importance, if not largely discounted in Heidegger's exchange with Kant, is at least under emphasized and underplayed: the *Critique of Judgment*. When we move within the orbit of Heidegger's being-historical thinking, we are able to discover how apparently disparate motifs of Kant's philosophy can converge to form a new tapestry to interweave themes that would otherwise remain inaccessible. But might these new themes be, perhaps either art or nature, or even the power of creativity pervading both? The answer that we seek is not so straightforward, but can only be given by "unwinding" the premise of Heidegger's exchange with Kant precisely at the juncture where the former's interest in the latter seems to recede. If the problem of temporality had initially provided the focus of that interest, *then the gradual waning of Heidegger's emphasis on Kant turns the*

---

474 Schmidt, *Lyrical and Ethical Subjects*, p. 44.
475 GA 9, p. 369; tr. 276 (translation modified).
476 GA 3, p. 249; tr. 175.

*dialogue around to the counterpart of that problematic, that is, spatiality.* Obviously, spatiality no longer refers to "space" in the narrow sense of a numerical measure of length and width, as Kant initially construed it, but instead entails the specificity of a "location" in which expanse and depth interplay in their tension with each other.

If the beauty of art and the sublimity of nature are (among) the central themes of the third *Critique*, it is because through interfacing the problematic of spatiality shines forth. Put in simple terms, if we can fathom an avenue by which Heidegger revisits Kant's transcendental philosophy, then it is within the orbit of being-historical thinking where temporality and spatiality converge. As we have seen, in *Contributions to Philosophy* Heidegger describes this convergence as the free play of time-space. Conversely, the radicality of thinking time-space transposes Kant's discussions of art and nature into a wider compass of exploring our capacity for dwelling on and inhabiting the earth. Even in language itself, which in the previous chapter we have sought to bring to prominence as a nascent concern of the third *Critique*, comprises a domicile or an abode that each of us as Da-sein can also inhabit in offering a place for being to manifest itself.

Given these observations, perhaps we should not be surprised that scattered throughout two of his most complex and pivotal texts to be published posthumously — *Contributions to Philosophy* and *Mindfulness* — Heidegger offers some of his most intriguing comments about the importance of his destructive-retrieval of Kant's transcendental philosophy. For example, in the "Appendix" to *Mindfulness*, Heidegger alludes to the lecture course from the 1936/37 which, as we mentioned at the outset of this chapter, contains one his rare discussions of Kant's aesthetics (projected volume 84 of the *Gesamtausgabe*).[477] But, in light of the being-historical thinking which Heidegger first enacts in *Contributions to Philosophy*, his allusion (in this "Appendix") to art and aesthetics suggests not only the opening of a new landscape of inquiry, but also identifies the obstacles (within modern philosophy) which blocked Kant's access to it. Not only does the tension of this ambiguity emerge as Heidegger advances his critique of the entire history of philosophy, but it is also specifically interwoven into his *Auseinandersetzung* with Kant during the later half of the 1930s.

What then is being-historical thinking, such that its enactment opens up another chapter in Heidegger's exchange with Kant? Being-historical thinking not only criticizes metaphysics, but develops that criticism as part of a larger problem which casts a shadow over the Western tradition from its inception. That larger problem is the way in which metaphysics, born from the forgottenness of being,

---

477 GA 66, p. 419; tr. 371.

culminates in the historical phase of modernity. This epoch licenses the exploitation of all beings — including humanity and nature — in terms of its potential for production and consumption, i. e., technology. In *Contributions to Philosophy*, Heidegger first identifies this paradigm shift in Western history, which he later equates with modern technology, as the drive toward "machination."[478] Metaphysics then comes under criticism, albeit not only in contrast to Heidegger's own fundamental ontology. For metaphysics has an even more "problematic" origin, insofar as it is historically intertwined with the way in which the occurrence of neglecting the question of being has its specific repercussion the "abandonment of being." The sense of "abandonment" comes to light through the weight of the double genitive, such that not only is being excluded from questioning and thereby "forgotten"; but, correlatively, beings themselves emerge only "one-dimensionally," in effect "abandoned," insofar as they appear to be exclusively available for "instrumental" and "technocratic" purposes.

In his initial plan to "destroy the history of ontology," of which in its initial proposal the Kant-book would constitute its initial step as Division I, Part II of *Being and Time*, Heidegger considers only the first side of the double-genitive, the forgetting of being. In *Contributions*, he comes full circle to consider the other side whereby *Seinsvergessenheit* entails *Seinsverlassenheit*. As a result, the concern for machination arises for the first time, spearheading his later effort to pose "the question concerning technology." Within this larger landscape of questioning, Heidegger's exchange with Kant shoulders the ambiguity whereby the latter appears not only as the precursor to fundamental ontology, but also as entangled in the basic confusions of metaphysics. The term "metaphysics," as it first appears in the title of the Kant-book, becomes increasingly ambiguous as well, because it now carried the additional connotation of its historical unfolding into the problem posed by modern science and technology. As Heidegger points out in a parenthetical remark, "the title of the [Kant-book] is imprecise," such that the subsequent interpretation makes explicit that the term "metaphysics" has become increasingly questionable.[479] Two years later in *Contributions to Philosophy*, in justifying his initial attempt to "use force against Kant" in order "to work out the *transcendental power of imagination*," Heidegger reiterates his earlier points by stating: "And so the Kant-book is necessarily ambiguous ... because Kant continues to be the only one since the Greeks who brings the interpretation of beingness into a central relation to 'time' ..."[480]

---

**478** GA 65, pp. 128–135; tr. 90–94.
**479** GA 41, pp. 124–125.
**480** GA 65, pp. 252–253; tr. 178–179.

When viewed within the wider compass of the history of being, Kant's philosophy receives its importance *anew*, not only for what it positively offers as an inroad to the problematic of temporality/ finitude, but also for what it affords on the "negative" side by way of a contrast with the originality of being-historical thinking. Thus, in the aforementioned passage, Heidegger emphasizes the need to "overcome" Kant's transcendental beginning by way of developing a more radical point of departure through Da-sein, that is, in its relation to being. In the Kant-book, Heidegger had primarily emphasized the "positive" side of the problematic in drawing a parallel between his own inquiry into human finitude and Kant's. The need to heed the above "counter tension," however, requires accentuating the "negative" side as well: that finitude can no longer be thought exclusively in terms of "subjectivity," but, on the contrary, the "temporality" constitutive of it (which Kant first brought to the forefront through his schematism) must be re-examined in its reciprocity with being. But to consider time in this light is to address it as that dynamic which determines the possibility of being's disclosure and specifically *the allocation of a place* for that occurrence to unfold. Where Heidegger initially follows Kant's lead in emphasizing the priority of time, the counter movement of questioning must equally accommodate the importance of space in the search to locate a place for truth as unconcealment.

Rather than approaching Kant's thought as simply an ally, Heidegger now seeks in the former a *"counter point" from which to make explicit the presuppositions of his project and thereby facilitate its further radicalization.* As we will discover, the need to address temporality as equiprimordial with spatiality becomes central to this transformation, to unraveling the initial presupposition that springs from transcendental philosophy. Yet understood as the "turning around" of the question from "being and time" to "time and being," one permutation of *die Kehre* involves unwinding the aforementioned (Kantian) premise. In this manner, Heidegger rediscover his own hermeneutics as an historical possibility, as unfolding through the tension of inquiry in which he participates and *from whose transformation his thinking re-emerges.* By cleaving to this counter tension, the opposing movement of the *Auseinandersetzung*, allows for the interplay of *two distinct voices*, which plays itself out historically as a *dialogue* between Heidegger and Kant. As a result, we can appreciate for the first time not only the similarities which allow Heidegger to forge an alliance with his predecessor, but also the disparities which challenge the former to re-examine the place that his own thinking occupies within the wider landscape of the philosophical tradition.

Heidegger's brief revisiting of imagination in *Contributions to Philosophy* illustrates the importance of this historical development and transformation. Given the parallel between human finitude, as Kant construes it, and Dasein, as Heidegger initially addresses it through fundamental ontology, the topic of imagination marks the "crossing" that leads from the problem of subjectivity to a questioning which addresses the "place," the "Da" of be-ing's unconcealment. Rather than Kant's thinking coming under scrutiny, there is a double reflexivity, such that its appropriation yields a historical perspective which can illuminate the point of departure of Heidegger's own project. By participating in the larger historical drama of being's unconcealment, philosophy no longer considers man as "subject," but rather addresses him as belonging to history and as commissioned by what achieves unconcealment thereby, the dynamic of the "turning relation" of being to man. To quote another key passage from *Contributions to Philosophy*: "Kant's *Critique of Pure Reason*, in which after the Greeks another essential step is taken, has to presuppose this context without being able to grasp it as such and to ground it fully (the turning relation of Dasein and being)."[481]

Inherent in Heidegger's *Auseinandersetzung* with Kant is the creative tension whereby the questioning of one thinker aims at uncovering an omission in anther, and reciprocally, this act of disclosure accentuates further possibilities of inquiry (as far as questioning being goes). To be sure, Heidegger may be accused to exaggerating certain aspect of Kant's thinking at the expense of others. But this criticism ignores that fact it is through his open engagement with Kant's thought that Heidegger allows the former's insight to aid in transforming his own thinking, to provide a springboard from which to "leap" in order to radicalize his own project of *Being and Time*. Far from being merely "one-sided," we discover the "dia-logical" character of Heidegger's interpretation in these three ways. First, there are the parallels Heidegger draws between his own thinking and Kant's, as far their relevance for formulating the question being, e. g., finitude, temporality. Secondly, there is the attempt to discern the omissions and drawbacks in Kant's thinking; their discernment can thereby become a signpost, which points in the opposite direction to the keys in Heidegger's hermeneutic strategy for re-asking the question of being, e. g., addressing Dasein rather than "man," the practical orientation of everydayness rather than theoretical cognition. And, finally, there is the historical importance of allowing Kant's thinking to emerge as the backdrop against which Heidegger's can "project" his own task and, by way of contrast, establish its place of "originality" within the larger compass of the tradition. Although Heidegger may not explicitly identify these three points, each of them is at least implied in the concluding sections of Part IV of *Kant and the Problem of Metaphysics*.

And to the extent these points initially remain implicit, a deeper questioning, which is implemented through "being-historical thinking," first cast the spot-

---

**481** GA 65, p. 315; tr. 221.

light upon them. But in order for a "place" can be historically allocated for the hermeneutic project Heidegger undertakes, a further link must be made between, on the one side, the singularity of its expression through language, and, on the other, its access to the matter of thinking, to the self-showing of being or truth (ἀλήθεια). Beginning in *Contributions in Philosophy* and then in *Mindfulness*, Heidegger shows that inherent in the negativity of truth as untruth, as conceal-ment, is a dynamic that equally reserves a place for, and shelters, precisely the opposite. We see this dynamic in play in the fact that concealment (*Verbergung*), also implies the creation of a shelter (*Bergung*). In this sense, what is concealed is held in reserve and protected, even allowed a period of incubation (*Incubation-zeit*), as in mystery (*Geheimnis*) which is both preserved and protected in the advent of its re-emergence. Being thereby harbors its own mystery, insofar as its propensity for withdrawal yields a shelter to reserve its counter possibility of manifestness. That sheltering, however, requires its own factical element to grant access to participation by thought, in order that the mystery can provide a fountain for experience, even inspiration, rather than degenerate into something occult. And that locale which gives an avenue to thinking, because in its self-gathering it allows for the being's manifestation, can only be language. Lan-guage, however, can allow being to become manifest, however only by accommo-dating the opposite possibility of housing its own propensity for concealment. In the struggle with both the vagueness and imprecision of "finding the right word," for example, we experience both the limitations of language and the inevitability of our thrownness in it. As the crossroads where thinking and being meet, language necessarily gives way as much to the latter's negative tendency toward concealment as to its positive capability for unconcealment. That is, the power of sheltering and keeping in reserve can nowhere be more pronounced as in the (silent) depths of language. The fact that the word cannot resound without the counter resonance of silence, however, is tantamount to saying that language, in its capacity for sheltering, allows for the "unsaid" to arise. By resisting the prospect of total transparency, language necessarily gives reign to the sheltering as a specific haven granted to the "unsaid." In this regard, the unsaid (*Ungesagte*) is not merely a lack or privation, but instead embodies the inescapable abode to sustain a mystery — in its safekeeping and unfolding. By appealing to what remains "unspoken" in Kant, Heidegger assumes both that language can include this dimension of reservedness and that what pertains to being can shelter itself accordingly in order to prepare for its sudden breakthrough in questioning. When Heidegger then makes his dramatic allusion to the necessary "violence" of his interpretation, he presupposes the dynamic in surmounting the resistance of language, which the "setting into opposition" of the *Auseinandersetzung* presup-poses. Being-historical thinking makes explicit, what otherwise remains only implied, is how language opens up this crucible of conflict in which the tension between unconcealment and concealment play itself out. In this regard, the "Kant-interpretation" embodies a hermeneutic strategy whose presupposition can only be unraveled through a wider circle, which language yields to us as the precondition for our relating to what is most questioning worthy (i. e., mysterious) or being.

We arrive at the point where Heidegger's *Auseinandersetzung* with Kant, or its enactment, provides an example of the unique dynamic of language, namely, that hearing takes priority over speaking. If language is inherently disclosive, and dialogue is a way of participating in that process, then, to state perhaps the obvious, the exchange between thinkers receives its impetus from the tension that language plays out between unconcealment and concealment. The converse, however, is not so obvious, and thereby provides the foremost lesson of Heidegger's exchange with Kant. Specifically, history provides the ultimate stage for thinking, in such that a way that every philosophical advance is always predicated upon a return to one's predecessors, to a revival of what remains "unsaid" and unthought in their thinking. Because the question of being is inherently historical, whatever can be "said" about being must be developed historically through the diversity of idioms which the tradition itself spawns. These idioms are not abstractions, but instead define the basic words, indeed, the vocabulary by which thinkers carry out their "discussion" of the most perennial concern of all, being itself. In this regard, "*Überlieferung,*" or the handing down of tradition, is a "delivering into the freedom of discussion (*Freiheit des Gespräches*) with what has been."[482]

Thus freedom is what gives, and simultaneously refuses, the ground for thinking. As a result, the attempt to think, as least as far as addressing the meaning of being goes, necessarily leads to the precipice of the *Ab-grund*, as the "staying away" and "hesitating refusal of ground." As the overriding thrust of his Kant-interpretation, Heidegger shows that the attempt to "lay the foundation of metaphysics" arrives at imagination which, paradoxically speaking, usurps the authority of reason as the ultimate ground. In his famous declaration, he accept his unsettling insight into the imagination, overwhelmed by a vertigo which stems from the tendency to "shrink back" from the threshold of re-asking the question of being. In light of our preceding observations, we see, however, that is not simply due to a subjective unwillingness to abandon rationalism that Kant recoiled. Rather, he pulled back due to the appearance of a strange affinity between the temporal basis of imagination and its potential to engender new,

---

482 Heidegger, *What Is Philosophy?*, pp. 33, 35.

idioms which rely as much on a counter valence of "absence" as "presence." Because of this *imaginative* interplay of presence/absence, the linear kind of thinking which Kant initially equates with a rationality, must suddenly reverse course and move along a circular path.

In the final chapter of *Mindfulness*, "The Be-ing Historical Concept of Metaphysics," Heidegger states parenthetically: "The Kant-book is meant to show *in a certain* way that Kant is thrust into the sphere of the truth of be-ing, but shrinks back from it and does not show the question that belongs to the truth of be-ing and cannot know that question within the basic stance of metaphysics itself."[483] In the passage quote earlier from *Contributions*, Heidegger emphasizes that we can no longer consider imagination "transcendentally." What is "imaginative" is no longer the unity of a temporal synthesis, but instead the gestures and idioms that designate being through the counter valence of absence as well as presence. In this way, the power of imagination re-emerges through its essential unity with freedom, which Heidegger describes as the free-play of time-space of Dasein.[484] While to a certain extent Heidegger, following Kant, had privileged time over space, the thrust of begin-historical thinking is to address the conjunction of the time, time-space (*Zeit-Raum*). For space is the counterpoint to time, in offering the enclave of a shelter in which the withdrawal of being can reside. and hence in reserving the possibility of its unconcealment to the contingencies of a specific historical place (*Ort*).

Could time-space become the new name for imagination? The message of the three passages which we have examined, when taken together, would seem to point in this direction. In this respect, the path that Heidegger follows in his exchange with Kant leads to radicalizing the question of being, not simply as an either-other proposal of abandoning the Kantian legacy, but rather as reaping its full benefits. Precisely because, and not merely in spite of Heidegger's *Auseinandersetzung* with Kant, thinking arrives at the historical crossroads where time conjoins with space, in order to lend depth as well as breath to the openness of being's manifestation. The interplay of time-space establishes a locale through which a specific form of dwelling takes precedent over all others, namely, the haven of language in which we already reside. We occupy language as an ecstatic openness that provides a shelter for being to appear and ultimately a "house" in which its truth can flourish.

To be sure, a critic might suggest that we are in engaging in a creative license with metaphors in defining space through such dimensions as "sheltering,"

---

**483** GA 66, p. 377; tr. 335.
**484** GA 66, p. 101; tr. 85.

"housing," "abiding," "dwelling," and then suggesting that they are endemic to an "openness" which language can alone can foster in order for being to appear. Yet the creativity at play is not merely arbitrary, but instead distinguishes a unique polyvalency into which imagination evolves. If this is the case, then we arrive the crossing where imagination both enacts and undergoes the transformation, in order that being can become accessible or yield to thought, (i. e., *"es gibt"*) in a more original way. The upshot of marking this crossing, however, lies in formulating a crucial, if not unexpected insight. Specifically, the concern for imagination, and its emergence through Heidegger's exchange with and Kant, do not fall by the wayside, but instead "come in their own" as distinguishing the "back and forth" movement between the "hermeneutic/transcendental" perspective of *Being and Time* and the perspective of "being-historical thinking." Because thinking is in need of some experience, there is always going to be a "phenomenological dimension" to its activity.

At this historical crossing, the direction of questioning "turns around" from addressing beings to be-ing itself, according to an *imaginative play* of a variations: "the gifting-refusing," in which "revelation [*Offenbarkeit*]" belongs to the "basic thrust of self-sheltering-concealing."[485] The gathering together of these dimensions into their simplest economy occurs through the "last god," which provides an image for the "crossing" to the "other beginning." The importance of such an image recalls for thinking the need of always having to acknowledge the withdrawal that precedes what still can be thought. In view of these observations, the most telling statement Heidegger makes after the close of his Kantian decade, "imagination as 'occurrence'" of the clearing itself," takes on an even richer meaning. In what becomes a "postscript" to Heidegger's exchange with Kant, (the play of) imagination re-emerges to "light up" the clearing itself.

Through this play, space contributes to the dynamic, speared by time, which unfolds the clearing as the open expanse for the manifestation of what is. Space re-emerges into the forefront, not as a geometrical measure, but as a distributive process of reassigning limits, of expanding and contracting. In this way, the limits revolve around a locale, not as a constriction, but, on the contrary, as spawning the widest birth of openness, and, correlatively, circumscribe an expanse that reverts into the differentiation of specific sites, of "making room." The conjunction of time and space embodies the momentum which "projects-open" the clearing in its widest possible radius, the "highest actuality in the domain of imagination."[486] The "free-play of time-space" thereby facilitates our participa-

---

485 GA 65, p. 405; tr. 285.
486 GA 65, p. 312; tr. 219.

tion in the occurrence of being's openness and manifestation.[487] If the work of art provides an occasion for this free-play, and thereby "inaugurates a clearing of being," it is only due to the fact that space contributes equally with time to project-open this clearing.[488]

The polyvalent, polymorphic character of space fulfills a double occupancy, both in allowing for the enactment of care ownmost to human beings, or "dwelling," and in allocating a place reserved for being's manifestations, or its residence within language. Given the determination of space as "place," language emerges as a domicile, a "house," where (the truth of) being resides,[489] and conversely, our "dwelling" constitutes a form of stewardship in which we cultivate a "site" for being to manifest itself. As a result of this spatial modality, human beings can exemplify "care of the word" (*Sorge des Wortes*) that is, safeguard language as a "habitat" — rather than use it as an "instrument" in the sense of machination — by engaging in the reciprocal activities of thinking and poetry.[490] The double play of space thereby means that thought is closely conjoined with the activities whereby human beings inhabit the world, most notably, art, and conversely, the stewardship over one's existence is also connected with the philosophical mission of allowing being to become manifest in language.

*By unwinding his initial "Kantian" premise*, Heidegger allows the *differences* as well as the similarities to shape his exchange with his predecessor, thereby transposing his hermeneutic inquiry into a wider historical orbit. Accordingly, Heidegger's awakening to his own place within the tradition marks the inception of being-historical thinking, the unfolding of its dimension of "mindfulness" (*Besinnung*), the "*inceptual* self-mindfulness of philosophy."[491] Even at its most exalted heights, being-historical thinking remains rooted in the experiential dimension of our "being-in-the-world," in the enactment of our dwelling. In this regard, the lasting legacy of Heidegger's exchange with Kant lies in directing us to the historical place where being can manifest itself and assume "residence" in the most primordial idioms of all. Because language determines our ability to think, we participate in this "clearing" only as our idioms respond more precisely to the unique occurrence of manifestation and bear the tension of the "*Ab-grund*" in which the creativity of the word resides. Within the depths of this silence resides the "unsaid," which resounds when thinking heeds the claim of being and is enowned by the ringing stillness of language. By acclimating itself to this

---

487 GA 65, p. 240; tr. 169.
488 GA 66, p. 31; tr. 23.
489 GA 9, p. 332.
490 GA 54, p. 18.
491 GA 66, p. 24; tr. 18.

stillness, and to the tonality of the word, thinking undertakes the *task of transcribing the grounding words*, or their intralingual translation. The possibility of such an intralingual translation, however, provides the *hermeneutic foothold for one thinker, in this case, Heidegger, to engage his predecessor, in this case, Kant, thereby sparking a conversation between them and allowing the former to undertake a translation of the latter's major work*, The Critique of Pure Reason.

By tracing the historical curvature of the hermeneutic circle, we mark the axis along which Heidegger's exchange with Kant turns. Insofar as the movement of history predicates every philosophical advance on a reciprocal return, Heidegger's project is continually *undergoing a journey of coming in its own* by reclaiming and deepening the hermeneutic, phenomenological roots of its origin through an *Auseinandersetzung* with his precedessors. As he states: "We must then ourselves, through our thinking, go to meet philosophy on the path it is traveling."[492] Does not the rebirth of imagination as the "play of time-space" signal the first step along this journey, the imminent "self-mindfulness of philosophy"?

## 3 The Mystery of Nature and the Idiom of the Word

Having then brought the play of time-space into the forefront of Heidegger's exchange with Kant, what can we distinguish as still remaining unthought in one of the most enigmatic of all the latter's texts, the third *Critique*? Whether Heidegger considers the possibility of knowledge as it pertains to theoretical reason, or action as its pertains to practical reason, in one way or another the concern for world orients these discussions. But when Kant addresses the sensation of pleasure corresponding to the experience of beauty, or the sublimity awakened by encountering the awesome power of nature, the focus shifts to the "materiality" of our existence. These are the dimensions which cannot easily be thematized within the framework of Kant's construction of universal principles, either for theoretical or practical reason. Hence the task falls on the shoulders of a (reflective) judgment to address the niches and crevices within experience that withdraw from intelligibility and re-emerge only through the examples of the materiality of art and nature. Insofar as the sublimity of nature can exhibit the dual faces of terror and awe, the sublime can provide an occasion to "thinking matter" as much as a cosmic principle of creativity as indeterminate stuff.[493] In Heideg-

---

492 Heidegger, *What Is Philosophy?*, p. 69.
493 Grant, "Kant after Geophilosophy", p. 53.

gerian terms, these examples point back to what most epitomizes the withdrawal into concealment, or the earth.

Ironically, Kant begins his Critical enterprise by developing an analogy between his own philosophical approach and a new cosmology in which the earth would revolve around the sun. The rotation of the earth then provides new focal point from which to envision the dynamic of knowledge in relation to its object. The third *Critique* allows us to see how the concern for the earth can re-emerge as a key motif in Heidegger's exchange with Kant. For Heidegger, the earth carries a unique dynamic, as indicated, for instance in his reference to our "sojourn" upon it.[494] The earth thereby exhibits the dual indices of homecoming and exile, of arrival and departure. The earth points both to our emergence into the domesticity of inhabitation and the crossing of those boundaries with the wildness of nature. Even in the most civilized of surroundings, nature can still erupt in all its terror and majesty. Living in New Orleans, who can forget the devastation wrought by Hurricane Katrina? Indeed, there is a certain randomness to the forces of nature, and to its violence — as witnessed in hurricanes — that escapes human mastery and even technological control. The earth thereby serves as a reminder of our incarnality, our affinity with nature, that makes explicit the material element in our occupation of a world.

In the "Critique of Teleological Judgment," Kant acknowledges this materiality when he rejects Spinoza's attempt to "reduce our concepts of the purposive in nature to our own consciousness of existing in all-embracing (though simple) Being."[495] In today's world, however, the concept of the purposiveness of nature, implying a divine architect, has been replaced by the calculus of artificial intelligence, that is, the paradigm of machination or technology When transposed into this new context, the flip side of Kant's insight is that the awesome, if not destructive power of nature, erupts precisely in the glitches and gaps of the monolithic plan machination. When unpredictable mutations of viruses outstrip the ability of the newest vaccines to combat them, the power of nature propels us toward that eventuality which is "not to be outstripped," in spite of the benefits of the latest medical advances. In our technological age, what Kant proposes as the purposiveness of nature may assume the form, instead, of a "counter" purposiveness, insofar as the materiality of the earth resists our anthropocentric designs

---

**494** GA 7, p. 63. For a translation, not based on the *Gesamtausgabe edition*, see Heidegger, *The Question concerning Technology and Other Essays*, p. 180.
**495** AA 5, KU, p. 393; tr. 241. See Heidegger's brief reference to section 76 of the *Critique of Judgment* and the question of its "teleological" exercise, GA 86, p. 200. For an interesting comparison with Goethe, on the question of teleology versus mechanism, see Tantillo, *The Will to Create: Goethe's Philosophy of Nature*, pp. 101–102.

and restores a balance at the expense of the willful, self-serving ends of technological progress.

As Gadamer remarks: "The earth, in truth, is not stuff, but that out of which everything comes forth and into which everything disappears."[496] Given that being-in-the-world is grafted upon the roots of our earthly sojourn, the boundaries of the human community may extend to include sentient beings. But does our materiality, as it were, tell us about what we have in common with animals? And how we address that root of commonality in phenomenological terms? Part of our incarnality is such that, as "factically dispersed," we are instantiated in a body.[497] So instantiated, we are also differentiated in regard to sex or gender. As Heidegger states in his 1928 lectures on logic, "As such, Dasein harbors the intrinsic possibility for being factically dispersed into bodiliness and thus into sexuality. ... As factical, Dasein is, among other things, in each case dispersed in a body and concomitantly, among other things, in each case disunited [*Zwiespältig*] in a particular sexuality."[498] Given the materiality of our embodiment, the differentiation between the sexes occurs. Obviously, neither Heidegger nor Kant gives specific voice to the topic of sexual difference, although Kant makes an indirect reference in a rare example from the "Analytic of the Sublime."

> "Nature is no longer judged inasmuch as it appears like art, but in so far as it *is* actual (although superhuman) art; and the teleological judgment serves as the basis and condition of the aesthetical, as a condition to which the latter must have respect. In such a case, e. g., if it is said 'That is a beautiful woman,' we think nothing else than this: nature represents in her figure the purposes in view in the shape of a woman's figure."[499]

Moreover, in his ethics Kant subordinates the sexual impulse to the claims of rationality and the moral principle of respect for persons.[500] Kant, however, diverges from natural law theory because he does not make reproduction the primary moral requirement for sexual relations. For while he accepts marriage as a precondition of sexual intimacy, he argues that it is the authority of reason (i. e., respect), rather the authority of God, which grounds that requirement. Because sexual desire is inherently exploitative due to the impulse to use the other as an object of gratification, marriage, as a way of reaffirming the rational dimension of our humanity, proves to be the only way of avoiding such objectification.[501] By

---

**496** Gadamer, *Heidegger's Ways*, p. 104.
**497** GA 26, p. 172; tr. 136.
**498** GA 26, p. 173; tr. 137. See Schalow, "Heidegger, Martin (1889–1976)", pp. 435–439.
**499** AA 5, KU, pp. 311–312; tr. 154.
**500** Kant, *Vorlesungen*, AA 27, pp. 155–160. *Lectures in Ethics*, pp. 162–169.
**501** See Brake, "Kant, Immanuel (1724–1804)", pp. 544–545.

the embodied dimension of selfhood, contemporary ethicists like Sara Ruddick argue that respect, when transposed into a sexual context, constitutes an ecstatic form of mutual gratification. Her emphasis on reciprocal caring, to employ a Heideggerian term, *retrieves* the dimension of respect within the *tactile space of emotional and physical intimacy.*[502] But just as Kant reserves the third *Critique* to address such tangential issues as the experience of beauty, pleasure, and nature, so Heidegger enters the domain of metontology in order to question the self's embodiment. In either case, materiality is a concern that occupies the periphery of their thinking, even though it would be a mistake to claim that Heidegger and Kant completely neglect this problematic. Perhaps Heidegger most aptly summarizes the difference between his own understanding of the importance of the body from that of Kant, in this passage from *Zollikon Seminars* (occurring in proximity to Heidegger's final essay on Kant, "Kant's Thesis about Being" (1962): "Being-in-the-world as such is a bodying forth, but not *only* a bodying forth. There is no sensory affection [sensory intuition] which must be supplemented by a concept of the understanding [*Verstand*] as Kant believed."[503]

In a letter from *Zollikon Seminars* (1963), Heidegger reaffirms, however, the importance of studying Kant's philosophy: "It does not do any harm for physicians to have something about Kant in their libraries too."[504] In these seminars with the Swiss psychiatrist, Medard Boss, Heidegger provides perhaps his fullest treatment of the issues of embodiment, love, and sexuality. Heidegger suggests that Kant's groundbreaking insight into human finitude brings forth preconceptions about human existence that underlie the medical field's regional inquiries into our relative health or sickness. For example, one's sexuality pertains to the state of one's overall welfare; for how the self takes over its sexual desires exacts a concern about its identity, posing a question about who it is. Indeed, the fact of being dispersed into a body puts back to Dasein about the pursuit of its desires (*eros*), its companionship with others, its capacity for intimacy (e. g., a "significant other"), and the institutionalizing of those interrelationships through co-habitation, marriage, child-rearing, and family. We are confronted with the irrepressibility of erotic feelings, not merely as psycho-physical sensations, but as indicative of thrownness into and ex-posure to beings. The question about my friend's health and welfare "can be meant as an inquiry into the very factical [*faktish*] situation of the other. However, such a condition is to be distinguished from what is interpreted as ontological disposition [*Befindlichkeit*] in *Being and*

---

502 Ruddick, "Better Sex", pp. 218–225. Also see O'Neill, "Kantian Ethics", pp. 175–185.
503 Heidegger, *Zollikon Seminars*, p. 199.
504 Heidegger, *Zollikon Seminars*, p. 267.

*Time*. It is the attunement determining Da-sein in its particular relationship to the world, to the Dasein-with [*Mitdasein*] other humans, and of itself. Ontological dispositions found the particular feelings of ... discontent yet is itself founded again in the human being's being exposed [*Ausgesetzheit*] toward beings in a whole [*das Seiende im Ganzen*]."[505]

Through the dynamic of our "bodying forth," *eros* is not just a reactionary impulse, but is also the striving after, going over and beyond, which seeks to reclaim one's ownedness. *Eros* is, as it were, the fundamental, attuned response to the self's vulnerability to its own ex-posed openness to beings. The experience of eros, then, transposes Dasein into the openness, and, to employ Heidegger's expression in the Kant-book, is "self-affective" in that sense. Because it operates without necessarily requiring the object of its desire to be present, *eros* bears an affinity to the free-play of imagination. For example, the imaginative play of fantasies exults in possibility, in such a way as to allow the absence of what is sought to prevail over its presence. "... pure turning-one's attention to ... pure affecting ...; means: becoming affected in the absence of experience, i.e., self-affecting."[506] In this way, the appeal to *eros* and embodiment, to sexuality and desire, brings us back to the double-play of open-exposure, the retrieval of the sensible as sensible, to which imagination reserves a place. As John Sallis emphasizes, Heidegger's retrieval of imagination has as its unspoken corollary, which reverberates throughout the labyrinth of the third *Critique*, namely, the recovery of the sensible, not in subordination to and in opposition to the intelligible, but, instead, as set free, liberated, and returned into its own element.[507]

When released into its own element, the sensible can acquire meaning in its own right apart from its metaphysical opposition to the intelligible. The sense, as in sensory, can thereby acquire "sense" (*Sinn*), on a par even with the *sensus communis* of the third *Critique*. As Sallis describes this transformation in his *Force of Imagination*:

> Beginning with sense requires both turning to it and letting it go. It requires turning to the expanse open to sense while releasing the sensible from the imperative of being only the appearance of another, remote truth. It requires also that in turning to the sensible one let go of sense in another sense, in the sense heretofore determined as that other, remote truth: Its retreat is not to be granted, endured, as one ventures to engender sense. As in remembrance.[508]

---

505 Heidegger, *Zollikon Seminars*, p. 139 (translation modified).
506 GA 3, p. 190; tr. 133.
507 Sallis, *Echoes: After Heidegger*, pp. 87–92.
508 Sallis, *Force of Imagination*, p. 77.

What can be designed by the "sensual," however, can have a plurality of senses. The sensual is not just what corresponds to sensation in the Humean guise or empirical intuition in the language of the first *Critique*. Nor is the sensual restricted even to the arousal of a pleasure response when the individual experiences the beauty of the formal purposiveness of art. Rather, the sensual includes the entire panorama of responses to our sexuality, to nature, and the chain of signifiers that direct us back to our rootedness in the earth. Thus, the simple act of petting a cat may be soothing both to the animal and the individual, releasing endorphins in the one and lowering the blood pressure of the other. But there is also a sense of the bond which arises from the commonality of our belonging to nature.

Within the play of imagination, the sensual aligns with concealing power of the earth, which provides that counter-reference, as it were, out of which the limits of all intelligibility emerge. In this context, we might be mindful of the Pre-Socratic thinker, Anaximander who addresses the emergence of beings as circumscribing the limited from out of the unlimited. Heidegger considers Anaximander as a thinker at the historical cusp of addressing the twofold, the differentiation between being and beings, precisely insofar as the difference *as* difference withdraws within the history of metaphysics. But the "as" incubates the pregnancy of the possible throughout this history, in unlikely forms like the retrieval of the sensible as sensible. Through this retrieval, the dynamic of differentiation to which Anaximander alludes re-emerges across the chasm of the forgottenness of being. Where do we then stand in this upheaval of the ground of metaphysics, indeed, even in the laying of the ground of metaphysics which Heidegger first brings into question through his exchange with Kant? Where can we stand, if we can do so at all? Indeed, we can only stand where we already are, as shaky as the footing may be, with the spin that it has, like a top, moving on its orbit across the dark night of the universe?

In his 1939 lectures on Herder and the origin of language, Heidegger quotes a line from Stefan George poetry: "Listen to what the somber earth speaks."[509] From its entrails, the earth speaks to us about the mystery of our origins, posing questions about the quality of its habitat (space), of our inheritance and protection of it for future generations (time). The more we rely upon the various benefits that modern technology offers, the more the earth provides the counter-resonance to the self-evidence of technological progress. As Heidegger states toward the close of his essay, "Overcoming Metaphysics," "It is one thing to use the earth, another to receive the blessing of the earth and to become at home in the law of

---

**509** GA 85, p. 67; tr. 58.

this reception in order to shepherd the mystery of being and watch over the inviolability of the possible."[510]

As we try to bring the third *Critique* into context, including where it stands within the wider landscape of Heidegger's retrieval of Kant, we cannot help but raise the third of Kant's three questions of philosophy that correspond to each of the three parts of the Critical philosophy: "What can I hope?". Insofar as the 1st and 2nd *Critique* address "what can I know?" and "what should I do?", respectively, the third *Critique* ponders the furthest vistas of my personal concern for fulfillment. The question of my own search for fulfillment springs from the profoundest depths of human need. As Heidegger remarks in Part IV of the Kantbook: "All expecting [of hope], however, requires a privation. If this neediness arises in the innermost interest of human finitude, then it attests to that reason as one which is essentially finite."[511] While hope may point to the heights of transcendence, as an index of our finitude, hope speaks to the contingency of our circumstances, to the materiality of our factical natures. Drawing upon Heidegger's early hermeneutics of facticity, including his 1921 lectures on St. Paul, Joanna Hodge defines hope in this way: "Hope anticipates glory and the life to come, which brings into the dirempted time of human finitude a fulfillment of meaning and a redemption of time."[512] Precisely due to our finitude, and our awakening to our earthly origins, we become capable of the most ethereal spiritual aspirations. In Kant's terms, hope is humanity's birth into the sensible that points over and beyond to our supersensible destination," to the "supersensible in us."[513] The possibility of the self's spiritual rebirth becomes, in Kant's language, a "boundary concept" that points ahead to the forefront of the world's disclosure and back to the life-situation within which the self discovers its individuality, its commitment toward others, and its affinity with nature.

In emphasizing the materiality of our emergence within, rather than our divorce from nature, the third *Critique* provides a forgotten locus to address the dynamics of our experience of the divine. Undoubtably, Kant provides the best clue to this possibility when he discusses our experience of the sublimity of nature. The *sublime* constitutes our response to the simultaneity of the awe and terror of nature, allowing the majesty of its destructive power to evoke in us an even more exalted sense of our capacity for resilience and courage.

---

510 See GA 7, pp. 139–140. For an earlier translation, not based on the *Gesamtausgabe* edition, see Heidegger, *The End of Philosophy*, p. 109.
511 GA 3, p. 216; tr. 152.
512 Hodge, "Phenomenologies of Faith and Hope", p. 50.
513 AA 5, KU, pp. 340–341; tr. 186.

Bold, overhanging, and as it were threatening rocks; clouds piled up in the sky, moving with lighting flashed and thunder peals; volcanoes in all their violence of destruction; hurricanes with their track of devastation; the boundless ocean in a state of tumult; the lofty waterfall of a mighty river, and such like — these exhibit our faculty of resistance as insignificantly small in comparison with their might. But the sight of them is the more attractive, the more fearful it is provided only that we are in security; and we willingly call these objects sublime, because they raise the energies of the soul above their accustomed height and discover in us a faculty of resistance of a quite different kind, which gives us courage to measure ourselves against the apparent almightiness of nature.

Now, in the immensity of nature and in the insufficiency of our faculties to take in a standard proportionate to the aesthetical estimation of the magnitude of its *realm*, we find our own limitation, although at the same time in our rational faculty we find a different, nonsensuous standard, which has that infinity itself under it as a unity, in comparison with which everything in nature is small, and thus in our mind we find a superiority to nature, even in its immensity.[514]

The experience of the sublime thereby offers an example of how which human beings transcend toward what offers the possibility of their fulfillment. For Kant, imagination is the primeval power which enables the self to traverse this arc, allowing the limits that our finitude imposes upon us — in our temporal-spatial incarnation — to provide the impetus for overcoming these limits. For him, imagination not only grants us the wings of aspiration. But in doing so, imagination allows the sensible to direct us across the chasm separating us from the opposite, and, conversely, allows the light of spirituality to shine forth in the beauty *and* sublimity of nature. In a manner that Schelling later explored, nature emerges as a phenomenon in its own right, the embodiment of the *logos* that "speaks to us" through "symbolic language," conveying a more graphic depiction of the heights and depths of the human soul.[515]

To be sure, the need to address the confluence of nature and spirit — the religious dimension of Kant's thought — takes a backseat in Heidegger's retrieval thereof. By the same token, the third *Critique* marks the point of crossing where imagination brings us into proximity with the sacred, to an experience of the divine that does not rest on the rigid preconceptions of onto-theo-logy. The god(s) of aesthetic imagination is less the deity of orthodox Christianity, and more the *promise* of a divinity that arrives with the passing of the "last god." "[Gods] not from within 'religion'; not as something extant, nor as an expedient of man; rather, they come from out of be-ing, as its decision; they are futural in the

---

**514** AA 5, KU, pp. 261–262; tr. 100–101.
**515** For an illumination discussion of Schelling's treatment of nature, in relation to the *logos*, see Watson, *Tradition(s)*, pp. 146–148, 162–164.

uniqueness of the *last one*."[516] When we reach this zenith of the holy, Heidegger's retrieval of Kant ceases to be merely an ontological thesis "about being," and instead becomes a mosaic about the multidimensional appearance of be-ing as it crisscrosses the realms of art and nature, truth and beauty, thought and faith. Insofar as we can experience this mosaic in all its facets, it is because we are endowed with the power of imagination and the beneficiaries of its *freedom*.

When seen in this light, the "third" of the three *Critiques* takes on new significance. That is, the numeric characterization of this text, i. e., as "three" becomes an icon for the a path of inter-mediation leading back and forth between Heidegger and Kant, marking a "crossroads" bridging their philosophies. For Kant, the crossing is configured through the power of imagination, for Heidegger, through the figure of Hermes and its ontological enactment in the task of translating the grounding words of philosophy. By marking the dual vectors of this "crossing," we illuminate the key insight of our thesis: namely, that language is the catalytic element in the unfolding, development, and, appropriation of the *Critique of Judgment*, the final step in retrieving Kant's critical project from its *unspoken* premise.

---

516 GA 65, p. 508; tr. 357.

# Postscript
# The "Echo" of Kant and the Path of Thinking

If it is the case that Kant shrank back from the centrality of imagination, it is also the case that this occurrence points to the sheltering of a mystery which still remains worthy of questioning. The need to supply a ground for thinking, or even the effort to "lay the foundation of metaphysics," reverts into a destabilizing distress, the rising up of the *Ab-grund*. In contrast to the stability of the first beginning of the Greeks, the vertigo of confronting the *Ab-grund* propels us to "leap" toward the opening of the "there" as the "other beginning" of philosophy. The imagination ceases to be merely one among other cognitive powers, but rather re-emerges as the clearing within the possibility to understand. In this trans-position, the self becomes a participant in the clearing, and man becomes he/she who sustains and "suffers" the tension of its open expanse. Where Kant emphasized imagination's role in engaging the "free play" of our cognitive faculties, the freedom on which they are predicated disengages them as distinctly human powers and instead resurrects them as emissaries of imagination. The powers in question are then liberated from the shackles of their search for a ground as a rational foundation. This search in turn yields to the gathering which first prepares a place for the clearing, or language. Imagination is thereby the *detour* in the history of metaphysics which leads back to the convergence of these concurrent events: the temporality and breakthrough of the "there," the emergence of the word from the entrails of nature, the (re-)birth of "man" from the soil of philosophy. "As the work of the freedom of human Dasein, the possibilities and destinies of philosophy are bound up with humanity's existence, and thus with temporality and with historicality."[517] Through this rebirth we stand at the *threshold of freedom*.

Insofar as the power of imagination resurfaces in the third *Critique*, it can no longer "recur in express relationship to laying the ground for metaphysics." For it is this recoil from a ground which draws us back into another, more alien abode: namely, the dependence of thought upon its partnership with what is radically other, the creativity of the word in its birth from the depths of silence. It is precisely at this momentous point, where thought renounces its sovereignty in favor of the humility of its dependence on language, that Heidegger can find in Kantian imagination a detour around German Idealism as the end and completion of Western metaphysics. By following the curves of this detour, the path of thinking (*Denkweg*) rises up before us.

---

**517** GA 24, p. 28; tr. 19–20.

As we re-examine Heidegger's relation to Kant, the third *Critique* assumes greater and greater importance. For this work *echoes the voice of a counter reply*, a "counter resonance," which directs us back to our residence within language, to the silent stirring of *logos*. In this regard, Kant's nascent concern for language provides an example of how silence simultaneously serves as both a shelter and as an emissary of the word. As Heidegger states at the conclusion to *Contributions to Philosophy*, in which reverberates the profoundest echoes of what remains "unthought" and "unsaid" throughout the history of philosophy: "Language is grounded in silence. It holds the measure, in that it first sets up measures ... And insofar as language [is] the ground of Da-sein, the measuring lies in this [Da-sein] and indeed as the ground of the strife of world and earth."[518] Accordingly, the more we seek sustenance from what remains "unsaid," the more we can *experience the gift of its riches*. The echo reverberates both with the distress of be-ing's refusal in remaining unspoken, and with the promise of its "gift" by intimating its "meaning" to mortals. Indeed, of all of Kant's writings, the third *Critique* most directly touches the soil of the *unsaid* from which language originates, the silent breath of the word that first gives voice to thought and its enactment of the turning relation of be-ing, the turning in enowning (*die Kehre im Ereignis*). "The riches of the turning relation of be-ing to Da-sein, which is en-owned by be-ing, are immeasurable. The fullness of the enowning is incalculable."[519] By heeding "unsaid" that is both sheltered in and intimated by Kant's third *Critique*, we experience the hallmark of "*die Kehre*" as the dynamic of Da-sein's thrownness into the clearing of be-ing, as dwelling within it and projecting it open through language (λόγος).

While the emphasis on the pivotal issues may change, the challenge remains of allowing the exchange between Heidegger and Kant to strike the chord to speak what still remains worthy of questioning today concerning our own *venture with freedom* in the midst of today's social and environmental crises. This venture transports us into the orbit of being-historical thinking, releasing us toward "the immeasurable possibilities for our history."[520] As we safeguard this freedom, assuming responsibility for its administration in both thought and language, in activism and dissent, we arrive at the "crossroads" which joins Heidegger's philosophy with Kant's. This arrival is not merely a destination, but a departure that points the way to a more promising future.

---

**518** GA 65, p. 510; tr. 359.
**519** GA 65, p. 7; tr. 8. For a discussion of this sense of "richness," see Emad, *On the Way to Heidegger's Contributions to Philosophy*, p. 64.
**520** GA 65, p. 412; tr. 289.

# Bibliography

## General Bibliography

Allison, Henry. *Kant's Transcendental Idealism*. New Haven: Yale University Press, 1983.

Arendt, Hannah. *The Human Condition*. Chicago: The University of Chicago Press, 1958.

Arendt, Hannah. *Lectures on Kant's Political Philosophy*. Chicago: The University of Chicago Press, 1982.

Arendt, Hannah. *The Life of the Mind*, Vol. II. New York: Harcourt, Brace, Jovanovich, 1978.

Ballard, Edward G. "Heidegger on Bringing Kant to Stand", in: *The Southern Journal of Philosophy*, 7/1, 1969: 91–103.

Ballard, Edward G. *Philosophy at the Crossroads*. Baton Rouge: Louisiana State University Press, 1971.

Bambach, Charles. *Heidegger, Dilthey, and the Crisis of Historicism*. Ithaca: Cornell University Press, 1995.

de Beistegui, Miguel. *Heidegger and the Political*. London: Routledge Press, 1998.

Bell, Martin. "Relations and Reversals: Deleuze, Hume, and Kant", in: A. Rehberg, R. Jones (ed.). *The Matter of Critique: Readings in Kant's Philosophy*. Manchester Clinamen Press, 2000: 183–201.

Blattner, William. *Heidegger's Temporal Idealism*. Cambridge: Cambridge University Press, 1999.

Birmingham, Peg. "Ever Respectfully Mine: Heidegger on Agency and Responsibility", in: A. Dallary, C. Scott, and H. Roberts (ed.). *Ethics and Danger*. Albany, NY: SUNY Press, 1992: 109–124.

Birmingham, Peg. "*Logos* and the Place of the Other", in: *Research in Phenomenology*, 20, 1990: 34–54.

Bowie, Andrew. *Introduction to German Philosophy from Kant to Habermas*. Cambridge: Cambridge University Press, 2003.

Brake, Elizabeth. "Kant, Immanuel (1724–1804)", in: A. Soble (ed.). *Sex from Plato to Paglia*. Westport, Conn.: Greenwood Press, 2006: 544–545.

Brogan, Walter. *Heidegger and Aristotle*. Albany, NY: SUNY Press, 2005.

Buren, John van. *The Young Heidegger*. Bloomington: Indiana University Press, 1994.

Caputo, John D. *The Mystical Elements in Heidegger's Thought*. Bronx: Fordham University Press, 1978.

Cassirer, Ernst. "Kant und das Problem der Metaphysik: Bemerkungen zu Martin Heideggers Kant-Interpretation", in: *Kant-Studien*, 36, 1931: 1–26.

Cassirer, Ernst. "Remarks on Martin Heidegger's Interpretation of Kant", in: M.S. Gram. *Kant: Disputed Questions*, Chicago: Quadrangle Books, Inc., 1967: 131–157.

Churchill, James (tr.), Martin Heidegger: *Kant and the Problem of Metaphysics*, Bloomington: Indiana University Press, 1962.

Cristaudo, Wayne. "Heidegger and Cassirer: Being, Knowing, and Politics", in: *Kant–Studien*, 82/4, 1991: 473–483.

Crowe, Benjamin. "Philosophy, World-View, and the Possibility of Ethics in *The Basic Problems of Phenomenology*", in: *Journal of the British Society for Phenomenology*, 34/2, 2003: 184–202.

Crowell, Steven. "Subjectivity: Locating the First Person in *Heidegger's Being and Time*", in: R. Polt (ed.). *Heidegger's Being and Time: Critical Essays*. Lanham, MD: Rowman and Littlefield, 2005: 307–331.

Dahlstrom, Daniel O. "Heidegger's Kant Courses at Marburg", in: T. Kisiel, J. van Buren (ed.). *Reading Heidegger from the Start*. Albany, NY: SUNY Press, 1994: 293–323.

Dahlstrom, Daniel O. "Heidegger's Kantian Turn: Notes on His Commentary to the *Kritik der reinen Vernunft*", in: *Review of Metaphysics*, XLVII, Dec. 1991: 329–361.

Dahlstrom, Daniel O. "Heidegger's Transcendentalism", in: *Research in Phenomenology*, 35, 2005: 29–54.

Dahlstrom, Daniel O. *Philosophical Legacies: Essays on the Thought of Kant, Hegel, and Their Contemporaries*. Washington D.C.: Catholic University Press of American, 2008.

David, Pascal. "From Fundamental Ontology to Being-historical Thinking", in: *Heidegger Studies*, 17, 2001: 191–204.

David, Pascal. "A Philosophical Confrontation with the Political", in: *Heidegger Studies*, 11, 1995: 191–204.

De Gennaro, Ivo. "Heidegger on Translation — Translating Heidegger", in: *Phänomenologische Forschungen*, 5, 2000: 3–22.

De Gennaro, Ivo. *Logos — Heidegger liest Heralkit*. Berlin: Dunker & Humbolt, 2001.

Derrida, Jacques. *Of Spirit*. Translated by Geoff Bennington and Rachel Bowlby. Chicago: The University of Chicago Press, 1988.

Derrida, Jacques. *The Truth in Painting*. Translated by Garrett Barden. London: Shed & Ward, 1975.

Descartes, René. *Discourse on Method*, Translated by John Veitch, in: *The Rationalists*. New York: Anchor Books, 1974.

Emad, Parvis. "Boredom as Limit and Disposition", in: *Heidegger Studies*, 1, 1985: 63–78.

Emad, Parvis. "A Conversation with Friedrich-Wilhelm von Herrmann on *Beiträge zur Philosophie*", in: B. Hopkins (ed.). *Phenomenology: Japanese and American Perspectives*. Dordrecht: Kluwer Academic Publishers, 1999: 145–166.

Emad, Parvis. "A Conversation with Friedrich-Wilhelm von Herrmann on *Mindfulness*", in: *The New Yearbook for Phenomenology and Phenomenological Philosophy* VI, 2006: 1–20.

Emad, Parvis. "The Echo of Being in *Beiträge zur Philosophie*", in: *Heidegger Studies*, 7, 1991: 15–35.

Emad, Parvis. "Heidegger's Originary Reading of Heraclitus–Fragment 16", in: K. Maly, P. Emad (ed.). *Heidegger on Heraclitus — A New Reading*. Lewiston, NY: The Edwin Mellen Press, 1986: 103–120.

Emad, Parvis. *On the Way to Heidegger's Contributions to Philosophy*. Wisconsin: The University of Wisconsin Press, 2007.

Emad, Parvis. "Thinking More Deeply into the Question of Translation", in: J. Sallis (ed.). *Reading Heidegger: Commemorations*. Bloomington: Indiana University Press, 1993: 323–340.

Emad, Parvis. *Translation and Interpretation: Learning from Beiträge*, Edited by F. Schalow. Bucharest: Zeta Books, 2012.

Esposito, Costantino. "Kausalität als Freiheit: Heidegger liest Kant", in: *Heidegger Studies*, 20, 2004: 101–125.

Gosetti-Ferencei, Jennifer Anna. *Heidegger, Hölderlin, and the Subject of Poetic Language*. Bronx, NY: Fordham University Press, 2004.

Ferrarin, Alfredo. "Kant's Productive Imagination and its Alleged Antecedents", in: *Graduate Faculty Philosophy Journal*, 18/1, 1995: 65–92.

Freydberg, Bernard. *Imagination in Kant's Critique of Practical Reason*. Bloomington: Indiana University Press, 2005.

Franklin, Julian H. *Animal Rights and Moral Philosophy*. Columbia: Columbia University Press, 2005.

Gadamer, Hans-Georg. *Heidegger's Ways*. Translated by John Stanley. Introduction by Dennis J. Schmidt. Albany, NY: SUNY Press, 1994.

Gadamer, Hans-Georg. *Philosophical Apprenticeships*. Translated by Robert Sullivan. Boston: The MIT Press, 1985.

Gadamer, Hans-Georg. *Philosophical Hermeneutics*. Translated by David E. Linge. Berkeley: The University of California Press, 1976.

Gordon, Haim. *The Heidegger-Buber Controversy: The Status of the I-Thou*. Westport, CT: Greenwood Press, 2003.

Gordon, Peter E. *Continental Divide: Heidegger, Cassirer, Davos*. Cambridge, Mass.: Harvard University Press, 2010.

Haar, Michel. *Heidegger and the Essence of Man*. Translated by William McNeill. Albany, NY: SUNY Press, 1995.

Grant, Iain Hamilton. "Kant after Geophilosophy", in: A. Rehberg, R. Jones (ed.). *The Matter of Critique: Readings in Kant's Philosophy*. Manchester: Clinamen Press, 2000: 37–60.

Habermas, Jürgen. *The Theory of Communicative Action: Reason and Rationalization of Society*. Translated by Thomas McCarthy. Boston: Beacon Press, 1984.

Hanna, Robert. "The Trouble with Truth in Kant's Theory of Meaning", in: *History of Philosophy Quarterly*, 10/1, 1993: 1–20.

Hatab, Lawrence. *Ethics and Finitude*. Lanham, MD: Roman & Littlefield Publishers, Inc., 2000.

Hegel, G.W.F. *Logic*. Translated by William Wallace. Oxford: Oxford University Press, 1975.

Herrmann, Friedrich-Wilhelm von. "'*Gelassenheit*' bei Heidegger und Meister Eckhart", in: B. Babich (ed.). *From Phenomenology to Thought, Errancy, and Desire: Essays in Honor of William J. Richardson, S. J*. Dordrecht: Kluwer Academic Publishers, 1995: 115–127.

Herrmann, Friedrich-Wilhelm von. *Subjekt und Dasein*. Frankfurt am Main: Vittorio Klostermann, 1985.

Herrmann, Friedrich-Wilhelm von. *Wege ins Ereignis: Zu Heideggers "Beiträge zur Philosophie"*. Frankfurt am Main: Vittorio Klostermann, 1994.

Hiltscher, Richard; Klingner, Stefan. (eds.). *Die Vollendung der Transzendentalphilosophie in Kants "Kritik der Urteilskraft"*. Berlin: Duncker & Humblot, 2006.

Hodge, Joanna. "Disjunctive Reading: Kant, Heidegger, Irigarary", in: A. Rehberg, R. Jones (ed.). *The Matter of Critique: Readings in Kant's Philosophy*. Manchester: Clinamen Press, 2000: 163–181.

Hodge, Joanna. "Phenomenologies of Faith and Hope", in: *Journal of the British Society for Phenomenology*, 37/1, Jan. 2006: 37–52.

Hyde, Michael J. "A Matter of the Heart: Epideictic Rhetoric and Heidegger's Call of Conscience", in: D. Gros, A. Kemmann (ed.). *Heidegger and Rhetoric*. NY: SUNY Press, 2005: 81–104.

Janicaud, Dominique; Mattéi, Jean-Francois (eds.). *Heidegger from Metaphysics to Thought*. Translated by Michael Gendre. Albany, NY: SUNY Press, 1995.

Japaridze, Tamar. *The Kantian Subject*. Albany, NY: SUNY Press, 2000.

Kalary, Thomas. "Hermeneutic Phenomenology and Related Questions: The Emotional, the Political, and the Godly", in: *Heidegger Studies*, 21, 2005: 135–158.

Kalary, Thomas. "Hermeneutic Pre-conditions for Interpreting Heidegger: A Look at Recent Literature (Part One). German Introduction to Heidegger's Thought and Its Place in Western Philosophy", in: *Heidegger Studies*, 18, 2002: 159–180.

Kalary, Thomas. "Hermeneutic Pre-conditions for Interpreting Heidegger: A Look at Recent Literature (Part Two). Focusing on Thinking after *Beiträge*", in: *Heidegger Studies*, 19, 2003: 129–157.

Kalary, Thomas. "New Access to *Being and Time*: Focusing on Friedrich-Wilhelm von Herrmann's Commentary on *Sein und Zeit*", in: *Heidegger Studies*, 24, 2008: 183–195.

Kant, Immanuel. *Akademie Ausgabe. Kants Gesammelte Schriften*. Berlin: de Gruyter, 1902.

Kant, Immanuel. *Akademie Ausgabe. Kants Gesammelte Schriften. Band 9, Logik*. Berlin: de Gruyter, 1902.

Kisiel, Theodore. *The Genesis of Heidegger's Being and Time*. Berkeley, CA: The University of California Press, 1993.

Klein, Ted. "Being as Ontological Predicate: Heidegger's Interpretation of 'Kant's Thesis about Being'", in: *Southwestern Journal of Philosophy*, 4/3, 1973: 35–51, 88–100.

Körner, Stephan. *Kant*. Baltimore, MD: Penguin Books, 1974.

Kovacs, George. "Heidegger's *Contributions to Philosophy* and the Failure of 'A Grassroots Archival Perspective'", in: *Studia Phaenomenologica*, VI, 2006: 319–345.

Kovacs, George. "Heidegger in Dialogue with Herder: Crossing the Language of Metaphysics toward Be-ing-historical Language", in: *Heidegger Studies*, 17, 2001: 45–63.

Kovacs, George. "Philosophy as Primordial Science", in: T. Kisiel, J. van Buren (eds.). *Reading Heidegger from the Start*. Albany, NY: SUNY Press, 1994: 91–107.

Kovacs, George. "The Unthought at the Limit of Heidegger's Thought", in. *Existentia*, 17/5–6, 2007: 337–355.

La Rocca, Claudio. "Schematismus und Anwendung", in: *Kant-Studien*, 80/2, 1989: 129–154.

Laumakis, Stephen J. "The *Sensus Communis* Reconsidered", in: *American Catholic Philosophical Quarterly*, 82/3, 2008: 429–444.

Levinas, Emmanuel. *Collected Philosophical Papers*. Translated by Alphonso Lingis. The Hague: Martinus Nijhoff, 1987.

Lewis, Michael. *Heidegger and the Place of Ethics*. London: Continuum Press, 2005.

Llewelyn, John. "Prolegomena to Any Future Phenomenological Ecology", in: C. Brown, T. Toadvine (eds.). *Eco- Phenomenology*. Albany, NY: SUNY Press, 2003: 51–72.

Lynch, Dennis A. "Ernst Cassirer and Martin Heidegger: The Davos Debate", in: *Kant-Studien* 81/3, 1990: 360–370.

Lyotard, François. *Heidegger and the "jews"*. Translated by Andreas Michel and Mark Roberts. Minneapolis: The University of Minnesota Press, 1990.

Lyotard, François. "Reflection in Kant's Aesthetics", Translated by Charles T. Wolf. In: *Graduate Faculty Philosophy Journal*, 16. 2, 1993: 375–411.

Makkreel, Rudolf A. *Imagination and Interpretation in Kant: The Hermeneutic Import of the Third Critique*. Chicago: The University of Chicago Press, 1990.

Maly, Kenneth. *Heidegger's Possibilities*. Toronto: The University of Toronto Press, 2008.

Maly, Kenneth. "Translating Heidegger's Works into English: The History and the Possibility", in: *Heidegger Studies*, 16, 2000: 115–138.

Mattéi, Jean-Francois. "The Heideggerian Chiasmus", Translated by Michael Gendre. In: D. Janicaud, J.-F. Mattéi (eds.). *Heidegger from Metaphysics to Thought*. Albany, NY: SUNY Press, 1995.

McCumber, John. *The Company of Words*. Evanston: Northwestern University Press, 1993.

McNeill, William. *The Glance of the Eye*. Albany, NY: SUNY Press, 1997.

McNeill, William. *The Time of Life*. Albany, NY: SUNY Press, 2006.

Morrison, Ronald P. "Kant, Husserl, and Heidegger on Time and the Unity of Consciousness", in: *Philosophy and Phenomenological Research*, 39, 1978: 182–198.

Munzel, Felicitas. *Kant's Conception of Moral Character: The "Critical" Link of Morality, Anthropology, and Reflective Judgement*. Chicago, IL: University of Chicago Press, 1998.

Nelson, Eric Sean. "Begründbarkeit und Unergründlichkeit bei Wilhelm Dilthey". In: *Existensia*, XII/1–2, 2002: 7–9.

Nelson, Eric Sean. "Die Formale Anzeige der Fakitizität als Frage zer Logik", in: A. Denker, H. Zoborowski (eds.). *Heidegger und die Logik*. Amsterdam and Atlanta: Editions Rodopi, 2006: 31–48.

Nelson, Eric Sean. "Heidegger and Ethics of Facticity", in: E.S. Nelson, F. Raffoul (eds.). *Rethinking Facticity*. Albany, NY: SUNY Press, 2008: 129–147.

Nelson, Eric Sean. "Questioning Practice: Heidegger, Historicity and the Hermeneutics of Facticity", in: *Philosophy Today*, 44, 2001: 150–159.

Nietzsche, Friedrich. *Thus Spoke Zarathustra*. *The Portable Nietzsche*. Edited and Translated by Walter Kaufmann. New York: Viking Press, 1954.

Nuyen, A. T. "On Interpreting Kant's Architectonic in Terms of the Hermeneutical Model", in: *Kant-Studien*, 84/2, 1993: 154–166.

O'Neill, Onora. "Kantian Ethics", in: P. Singer (ed.). *A Companion to Ethics*. Oxford: Blackwell Publishers, 1991: 175–185.

Orth, Ernst W. "Martin Heidegger und der NeuKantianismus", in: *Man and World*, 25/3–4, 1992: 421–444.

Paton, Herbert J. *Kant's Metaphysics of Experience*, Vol. I. New York: Macmillan, 1936.

Petzet, Heinrich Wiegand. *Encounters & Dialogues with Martin Heidegger (1929–1976)*. Translated by Parvis Emad and Kenneth Maly. Chicago: The University of Chicago Press, 1993.

Pillow, Kirk. "Jupiter's Eagle and the Despot's Hand Mill: Two Views of Metaphor in Kant", in: *Journal of Aesthetics and Art Criticism*, 59, 2001: 193–209.

Pöggeler, Otto. *Martin Heidegger's Path of Thinking*. Translated by Daniel Magurshak and Sigmund Barber. Atlantic Highlands, NJ: Humanities Press International, Inc., 1989.

Polt, Richard (ed.). *Heidegger's Being and Time: Critical Essays*. Lanham, MD: Rowman and Littlefield, 2005.

Radloff, Bernhard. *Heidegger and the Question of National Socialism: Disclosure and Gestalt*. Toronto: The University of Toronto Press, 2007.

Radloff, Bernhard. "Machination and the Political in Heidegger's Mindfulness", in: *Heidegger Studies*, 24, 2008: 167–181.

Raffoul, François. *The Origins of Responsibility*. Bloomington: Indiana University Press, 2010.

Richardson, William J., S. J. *Heidegger: Through Phenomenology to Thought,* 4th ed. Bronx, NY: Fordham University Press, 2003.

Ricoeur, Paul. *Fallible Man*. Chicago: Henry Regnery Company, 1965.

Ricoeur, Paul. *On Translation*. Translated by Eileen Brennan, "Introduction" by Richard Kearney. London: Routledge, 2006.

Rilke, Rainer Maria. *On Love and Other Difficulties*. Translated by J. L. Mood. New York: W. W. Norton & Company, 1975.

Risser, James. *Hermeneutics and the Voice of the Other*. Albany: SUNY Press, 1997.

Roth, Klas; Surprenant, Chris (eds.). *Kant on Education: Interpretations and Commentary*. London: Routledge, 2011.

Ruddick, Sara. "Better Sex", in: M. D. Bayles, K. Henley (eds.). *Right Conduct*. New York: Random House, Inc., 1983: 218–225.

Sallis, John. *Double Truth*. Albany, NY: SUNY Press, 1995.

Sallis, John. *Echoes: After Heidegger*. Bloomington: Indiana University Press, 1990.

Sallis, John. *Force of Imagination*. Bloomington: Indiana University Press, 2000.

Sallis, John. "Free Thinking", in: F. Raffoul, D. Pettigrew (eds.). *Heidegger and Practical Philosophy*. Albany, NY: State University of New York Press, 2002: 3–12.

Sallis, John. *The Gathering of Reason*. Athens, Ohio: Ohio University Press, 1980.

Schalow, Frank. "Beyond Decisionism and Anarchy: The Task of Re-thinking Resolve", in: *Man and World*, 28/4, 1995: 359–376.

Schalow, Frank. "Essence and Ape: Heidegger and the Question of Evolutionary Theory", in: *American Catholic Philosophical Quarterly*, 82/3, 2008: 445–462.

Schalow, Frank. "At the Crossroads of Freedom: Ethics without Values", in: R. Polt and G. Fried (eds.). *The Companion to Introduction to Metaphysics*. New Haven: Yale University Press, 2001: 250–262.

Schalow, Frank. "Freedom, Finitude, and the Practical Self: The Other Side of Heidegger's Appropriation of Kant", in: F. Raffoul and D. Pettigrew (eds.). *Heidegger and Practical Philosophy*. Albany, NY: SUNY Press, 2002: 29–41.

Schalow, Frank. "Freedom, Truth, and Responsibility in the Recent Translations of the *Gesamtausgabe*", in: *Heidegger Studies*, 23, 2007: 97–111.

Schalow, Frank. "The Gesamtausgabe Nietzsche: An Exercise in Translation and Thought", in: *Heidegger Studies*, 9, 1993: 139–152.

Schalow, Frank. "Heidegger, Martin (1889–1976)", in: A. Soble (ed.). *Sex from Plato to Paglia: A Philosophical Encyclopedia*. Westport, CT: Greenwood Publishing Group, 2006: 435–439.

Schalow, Frank. "Heidegger and the Hidden Task of Kant's Schematism", in: *Existentia*, 16/5–6, 2006: 425–436.

Schalow, Frank. "Heidegger and Kant in Conversation: The Search for a Hermeneutic Guideline," in: *Existentia*, 22/3–4, 2012: 338–348.

Schalow, Frank. *Heidegger and the Quest for the Sacred: From Thought to the Sanctuary of Faith*. Dordrecht: Kluwer Academic Publishers, 2001.

Schalow, Frank. "Attunement and Translation", in: F. Schalow (ed). *Heidegger, Translation, and the Task of Thinking: Essays in Honor of Parvis Emad*. Dordrecht: Springer Publishers, 2011: 291–312.

Schalow, Frank. "How Viable Is Dreyfus's Interpretation of Heidegger? Anthropoligism, Pragmatism and Misunderstanding of Texts", in: *Heidegger Studies*, 20, 2004: 17–33.

Schalow, Frank. "Imagination and Embodiment: The Task of Reincarnating the Self from a Heideggerian Perspective", in: *International Studies in Philosophy*, Vol. 4, 2004: 201–215.

Schalow, Frank. *Imagination and Existence: Heidegger's Retrieval of the Kantian Ethic*. Lanham, MD: University of America Press, 1986.

Schalow, Frank. *The Incarnality of Being: The Earth, Animals, and the Body in Heidegger's Thought*. Albany, NY: SUNY Press, 2006.

Schalow, Frank. "Kant, Heidegger, and the Performative Character of Language in the First Critique", in: *Epoché*, Vol. 8, No. 1, 2003: 91–106.

Schalow, Frank. "Kant and the Question of Values", in: I. De Gennaro (ed.). *Value. Sources and Readings in a Globalized World*. Leiden: Brill Publishers, 2012: 131–147.

Schalow, Frank. "The Kantian Schema of Heidegger's Late Marburg Period", in: T. Kisiel and J. van Buren (eds.). *Reading Heidegger from the Start*. New York: SUNY Press, 1994: 309–323.

Schalow, Frank. *Language and Deed*. Amsterdam and Atlanta: Editions Rodopi, 1998.

Schalow, Frank. "Language and the Etymological Turn of Thought", in: *Graduate Faculty Philosophy Journal*, 18/1, 1995: 187–203.

Schalow, Frank. "Language and Temporality in Heidegger and Kant", in: *Southwest Philosophy Review*, 11/2, 1995: 131–144.

Schalow, Frank. "Methodological Elements in Heidegger's Employment of Imagination", in: *Journal of Philosophical Research*, 23, 1998: 117–132.

Schalow, Frank. "Position, Place, and Language: Revisiting Heidegger's Final Essay on Kant", in: *Southwest Philosophy Review*, 15/2, 1999: 57–69.

Schalow, Frank. "Questioning the Search for Genesis: A Look at Heidegger's Early Freiburg and Marburg Lectures", in: *Heidegger Studies*, 21, 2000: 167–186.

Schalow, Frank. "Reinscribing the *Logos* in Transcendental Logic: Revisiting Kant's Highest Principle of Synthetic Judgments Revisited", in: *Existentia*, 19/3–4, 2009: 195–205.

Schalow, Frank. *The Renewal of the Heidegger-Kant Dialogue: Action, Thought, and Responsibility*. Albany, NY: SUNY Press, 1992.

Schalow, Frank. "Textuality and Imagination: The Refracted Image of Hegelian Dialectic", in: *Research in Phenomenology*, 26, 1996: 155–170.

Schalow, Frank. "Thinking at Cross Purposes with Kant — Reason, Finitude, and Truth in the Cassirer-Heidegger Debate", in: Kant-Studien, 87, 1996: 198–217.

Schalow, Frank. "The Third Critique and a New Nomenclature of Difference", in: Epoché, 4/1, 1996: 71–95.

Schalow, Frank. "Thought and Spatiality: The Later Heidegger's Quandary", in: Southwest Philosophy Review, 12/2, 1996: 157–170.

Schalow, Frank. "The Topography of Heidegger's Concept of Conscience", in: J. D. Caputo (ed.). Heidegger. American Catholic Philosophical Quarterly, 69, 1995: 255–273.

Schalow, Frank. "Toward a Concrete Ontology of Practical Reason in Light of Heidegger's Lectures on Human Freedom", in: Journal of the British Society for Phenomenology, 29/3, 1986: 361–376.

Schalow, Frank. "The Twofold Image of Space: Heidegger's Unwinding of the Kantian Premise", in: Existentia, 17/ 5–6, 2007: 357–371.

Schalow, Frank. "The Unique Role of Logic in the Development of Heidegger's Dialogue with Kant", in: Journal of the History of Philosophy, 32/1, 1994: 103–125.

Schalow, Frank. "The Unity of Vorträge und Aufsätze and its Loss in the English Translations", in: Heidegger Studies, 18, 2002: 45–58.

Schalow, Frank; Alfred Denker. Historical Dictionary of Heidegger's Philosophy, 2nd edition. Lanham, MD: Scarecrow Press, 2010.

Scheler, Max. On the Eternal in Man. Translated by Berhard Noble. London: SCM Press, 1969.

Schelling, F. W. J. Of Human Freedom. Translated by James Gutman. Chicago: Open Court Publishers, 1936.

Schmidt, Dennis J. "Changing the Subject: Heidegger, 'the' National and Epochal", in: Graduate Faculty Philosophy Journal, 14.2/ 15.1, 1991: 441–462.

Schmidt, Dennis J. Lyrical and Ethical Subjects. Albany, NY: SUNY Press, 2005.

Schmidt, Dennis J. The Ubiquity of the Finite. Cambridge, Mass.: The MIT Press, 1988.

Schrag, Calvin O. Communicative Praxis and the Space of Subjectivity. Bloomington: Indiana University Press, 1989.

Schrag, Calvin O. "Heidegger and Cassirer on Kant", in: Kant–Studien, 58/1, 1967: 87–100.

Scott, Charles E. "The De-struction of being and time in Being and Time", in: Man and World, 21/1, 1988: 91–106.

Scott, Charles E. "The Horizon of Time and the Ontological Difference", in: J. Kockelmans (ed.). Hermeneutic Phenomenology. Lanham, MD: University Press of America, 1988: 72–80.

Scott, Charles E. The Question of Ethics. Bloomington: Indiana University Press, 1991.

Sheehan, Thomas (ed.). Heidegger: The Man and the Thinker. Chicago: Precedent Press, 1981.

Sherover, Charles M. Are We in Time? Evanston, IL: Northwestern University Press, 2003.

Sherover, Charles M. Heidegger, Kant, and Time. Bloomington: Indiana University Press, 1971.

Sherover, Charles M. From Kant and Royce to Heidegger. Washington, D.C.: Catholic University Press, 2002.

Sherover, Charles M. "Heidegger and the Reconstruction of the Kantian Ethic", in: Akten des XIV. Internationalen Kongresses für Philosophie (1968). Vienna: Herder, 1970: 527–534.

Sherover, Charles M. "Time and Ethics. How Is Morality Possible?", in: The Study of Time, Vol. 2. New York: Springer-Verlag, 1975: 216–230.

Sherover, Charles M. Time, Freedom, and the Common Good. Albany, NY: SUNY Press, 1984.

Sherover, Charles M. "Two Kinds of Transcendental Objectivity: Their Differentiation", in: Philosophical Topics, 12/2, 1981: 251–278.

Silber, John. "The Copernican Revolution in Ethics: The Good Re-Examined", in: R. P. Wolff (ed.). Kant: A Collection of Critical Essays. New York: Doubleday Anchor Books, Inc., 1967: 266–290.

Sluga, Hans. Heidegger's Crisis. Cambridge, MA.: Harvard University Press, 1993.

Smith, Joseph T. "Heidegger's Kant-Interpretation", in: Philosophy Today, 11, 1967: 254–264.

Stenstad, Gail. Transformations: Thinking after Heidegger. Madison, WI: The University of Wisconsin Press, 2005.

Sullivan, Roger J. An Introduction to Kant's Ethics. Cambridge: Cambridge University Press, 1994.

Surber, Jere Paul. Language and German Idealism. Atlantic Highlands, NJ: Humanities Press, 1996.

Taminiaux, Jacques. Poetics and Speculation. Albany: SUNY Press, 1993.

Tantillo, Astrida. The Will to Create: Goethe's Philosophy of Nature. Pittsburgh: The University of Pittsburgh Press, 2002.

Tillich, Paul. "Heidegger and Jaspers", in: A. M. Olson (ed.). Heidegger and Jaspers. Philadelphia: Temple University Press, 1993.

Thomä, Dieter. "Being and Time in Retrospect: Heidegger's Self-Critique", Translated by D. Dwyer. In: R. Polt (ed.). Heidegger's Being and Time: Critical Essays. Lanham, MD: Rowman and Littlefield, 2005: 215–234.

Vallega-Neu, Daniela. The Bodily Dimension in Thinking. Albany, NY: SUNY Press, 2005.

Vallega-Neu, Daniela. Heidegger's Contributions to Philosophy: An Introduction. Bloomington: Indiana University Press, 2003.

Vallega-Neu, Daniela. "Poietic Saying", in: C. E. Scott (ed.). A Companion to Heidegger's Contributions to Philosophy. Bloomington: Indiana University Press, 2001: 67–80.

Velkley, Richard. Being after Rousseau: Philosophy and Culture in Question. Chicago: The University of Chicago Press, 2002.

Velkley, Richard. Freedom and the End of Reason: On the Moral Foundation of Kant's Critical Philosophy. Chicago: The University of Chicago Press, 1989.

Velkley, Richard. *Heidegger, Strauss, and the Presuppositions of Philosophy.* Chicago: The University of Chicago Press, 2011.

Volpi, Franco. *"Being and Time*: A 'Translation' of *Nichomachean Ethics*?", Translated by John Protevi. In: T. Kisiel and J. van Buren (ed.). *Reading Heidegger from the Start.* Albany: SUNY Press, 1994: 195–211.

Watson, Stephen. "Heidegger, Rationality, and the Critique of Judgment", in: *Review of Metaphysics*, 41, 1988: 461–499.

Watson, Stephen. *Traditions.* Bloomington: Indiana University Press, 1997.

Weatherston, Martin. *Heidegger's Interpretation of Kant: Categories, Imagination, and Temporality.* New York: Palgrave Macmillan, 2002.

Wolin, Richard. *The Politics of Being.* Columbia, NY: Columbia University Press, 1990.

Zammito, John. *The Genesis of Kant's Critique of Judgment.* Chicago: The University of Chicago Press, 1992.

Zimmerman, Michael E. *Contesting Earth's Future.* Berkeley, CA: The University of California Press, 1993.

Zimmerman, Michael E. *The Eclipse of the Self.* Athens, OH: University of Ohio Press, 1981.

Zimmerman, Michael E. "Heidegger's 'Completion' of *Sein und Zeit*", in: *Philosophy and Phenomenological Research*, 34, 1979: 537–560.

Zimmerman, Michael E. *Heidegger's Confrontation with Modernity.* Bloomington: Indiana University Press, 1990.

Zimmerman, Michael E. "Heidegger's Phenomenology and Contemporary Environmentalism", in: T. Toadvine (ed.). *Eco-Phenomenology: Back to the Earth Itself.* Albany, NY: SUNY Press, 2002: 73–101.

# Heidegger's Works Cited

Heidegger, Martin. "Die Armut", in: *Heidegger Studies*, 10, 1994: 5–11.

Heidegger, Martin. *Der Feldweg.* Frankfurt am Main: Vittorio Klostermann, 1962.

Heidegger, Martin. *Gesamtausgabe.* Vol. 2, *Sein und Zeit.* Frankfurt am Main: Vittorio Klostermann, 1977.

Heidegger, Martin. *Gesamtausgabe.* Vol. 3, *Kant und das Problem der Metaphysik.* Frankfurt am Main: Vittorio Klostermann, 1991.

Heidegger, Martin. *Gesamtausgabe.* Vol. 4, *Erläuterungen zu Hölderlins Dichtung.* Frankfurt am Main: Vittorio Klostermann, 1981.

Heidegger, Martin. *Gesamtausgabe.* Vol. 5, *Holzwege.* Frankfurt am Main: Vittorio Klostermann, 1978.

Heidegger, Martin. *Gesamtausgabe.* Vol. 7, *Vorträge und Aufsätze.* Frankfurt am Main: Vittorio Klostermann, 2000.

Heidegger, Martin. *Gesamtausgabe.* Vol. 9, *Wegmarken.* Frankfurt am Main: Vittorio Klostermann, 1976.

Heidegger, Martin. *Gesamtausgabe.* Vol. 10, *Der Satz vom Grund.* Frankfurt am Main: Vittorio Klostermann, 1997.

Heidegger, Martin. *Gesamtausgabe.* Vol. 11, *Identität und Differenz.* Frankfurt am Main: Vittorio Klostermann, 2006.

Heidegger, Martin. *Gesamtausgabe*. Vol. 12, *Unterwegs zur Sprache*. Frankfurt am Main: Vittorio Klostermann, 1985.

Heidegger, Martin. *Gesamtausgabe*. Vol. 13, *Aus der Erfahrung des Denkens*. Frankfurt am Main: Vittorio Klostermann, 1983.

Heidegger, Martin. *Gesamtausgabe*. Vol. 17, *Einführung in die phänomenologische Forschung*. Frankfurt am Main: Vittorio Klostermann, 1994.

Heidegger, Martin. *Gesamtausgabe*, Vol. 19, *Platon: Sophistes*. Frankfurt am Main: Vittorio Klostermann, 1992.

Heidegger, Martin. *Gesamtausgabe*, Vol. 20, *Prolegomena zur Geschichte des Zeitbegriffs*. Frankfurt am Main: Vittorio Klostermann, 1979.

Heidegger, Martin. *Gesamtausgabe*, Vol. 21, *Logik. Die Frage nach der Wahrheit*. Frankfurt am Main: Vittorio Klostermann, 1976.

Heidegger, Martin. *Gesamtausgabe*, Vol. 22, *Grundbegriffe der antiken Philosophie*. Frankfurt am Main: Vittorio Klostermann, 1993.

Heidegger, Martin. *Gesamtausgabe*. Vol 24, *Die Grundprobleme der Phänomenologie*. Frankfurt am Main: Vittorio Klosterman, 1975.

Heidegger, Martin. *Gesamtausgabe*. Vol. 25, *Phänomenologische Interpretation von Kants Kritik der reinen Vernunft*. Frankfurt am Main: Vittorio Klostermann, 1977.

Heidegger, Martin. *Gesamtausgabe*. Vol. 26, *Metaphysische Anfangsgründe im Ausgang von Leibniz*. Frankfurt am Main: Vittorio Klostermann, 1978.

Heidegger, Martin. *Gesamtausgabe*. Vol. 27, *Einleitung in die Philosophie*. Frankfurt am Main: Vittorio Klostermann, 1996.

Heidegger, Martin. *Gesamtausgabe*. Vol. 28, *Der deutsche Idealismus (Fichte, Schelling, Hegel) und die philosophische Problemlage der Gegenwart*. Frankfurt am Main: Vittorio Klostermann, 1997.

Heidegger, Martin. *Gesamtausgabe*. Vol. 29/30, *Die Grundbegriffe der Metaphysik*. Frankfurt am Main: Vittorio Klostermann, 1983.

Heidegger, Martin. *Gesamtausgabe*. Vol. 31, *Vom Wesen der menschlichen Freiheit. Einleitung in die Philosophie*. Frankfurt am Main: Vittorio Klostermann, 1982.

Heidegger, Martin. *Gesamtausgabe*. Vol. 32, *Hegels Phänomenologie des Geistes*. Frankfurt am Main: Vittorio Klostermann, 1980.

Heidegger, Martin. *Gesamtausgabe*, Vol. 33, *Aristoteles: Metaphysik Θ 1–3: Vom Wesen und Wirklichkeit der Kraft*. Frankfurt am Main: Vittorio Klostermann, 1981.

Heidegger, Martin. *Gesamtausgabe*, Vol. 34, *Vom Wesen der Wahrheit. Zu Platons Höhlengleichnis und Theätet*. Frankfurt am Main: Vittorio Klostermann, 1988.

Heidegger, Martin. *Gesamtausgabe*, Vol. 40, *Einführung in die Metaphysik*. Frankfurt am Main: Vittorio Klostermann, 1983.

Heidegger, Martin. *Gesamtausgabe*. Vol. 41, *Die Frage nach dem Ding. Zu Kants Lehre von den transzendentalen Grundsätzen*. Frankfurt am Main: Vittorio Klostermann, 1984.

Heidegger, Martin. *Gesamtausgabe*. Vol. 42, *Schelling: Vom Wesen der menschlichen Freiheit*. Frankfurt am Main: Vittorio Klostermann, 1988.

Heidegger, Martin. *Gesamtausgabe*. Vol. 43, *Nietzsche: Der Wille zur Macht als Kunst*. Frankfurt am Main: Vittorio Klostermann, 1985.

Heidegger, Martin. *Gesamtausgabe*. Vol. 48, *Nietzsche: Der europäische Nihilismus*. Frankfurt am Main: Vittorio Klostermann, 1986.

Heidegger, Martin. *Gesamtausgabe*. Vol. 49, *Die Metaphysik des deutschen Idealismus. Zur erneuten Auslegung von Schelling: Philosophische Untersuchungen über das Wesen der menschlichen Freiheit und die damit zusammenhängenden Gegenstände (1809)*. Frankfurt am Main: Vittorio Klostermann, 1991.

Heidegger, Martin. *Gesamtausgabe*. Vol. 51, *Grundbegriffe*. Frankfurt am Main: Vittorio Klostermann, 1981.

Heidegger, Martin. *Gesamtausgabe*. Vol. 53, *Hölderlins Hymne "Der Ister"*. Frankfurt am Main: Vittorio Klostermann, 1984.

Heidegger, Martin. *Gesamtausgabe*. Vol. 54, *Parmenides*. Frankfurt am Main: Vittorio Klostermann, 1982.

Heidegger, Martin. *Gesamtausgabe*. Vol. 55, *Heraklit*. Frankfurt am Main: Vittorio Klostermann, 1979.

Heidegger, Martin. *Gesamtausgabe*. Vol. 56/57, *Bestimmung zur Philosopohie*. Frankfurt am Main: Vittorio Klostermann, 1987.

Heidegger, Martin. *Gesamtausgabe*. Vol. 59, *Phänomenologie der Anschauung und des Ausdrucks. Theorie der philosophischen Begriffsbildung*. Frankfurt am Main: Vittorio Klostermann, 1993.

Heidegger, Martin. *Gesamtausgabe*. Vol. 60, *Phänomenologie des religiösen Lebens*. Frankfurt am Main: Vittorio Klostermann, 1995.

Heidegger, Martin. *Gesamtausgabe*. Vol. 61. *Phänomenologische Interpretationen zu Aristoteles*. Frankfurt am Main: Vittorio Klostermann, 1994.

Heidegger, Martin. *Gesamtausgabe*. Vol. 63, *Ontologie: Hermeneutik der Faktizität*. Frankfurt am Main: Vittorio Klostermann, 1988.

Heidegger, Martin. *Gesamtausgabe*. Vol. 64, *Der Begriff der Zeit*. Frankfurt am Main: Vittorio Klostermann, 2004.

Heidegger, Martin. *Gesamtausgabe*. Vol. 65, *Beiträge zur Philosophie (Vom Ereignis)*. Frankfurt am Main: Vittorio Klostermann, 1989.

Heidegger, Martin. *Gesamtausgabe*. Vol. 66, *Besinnung*. Frankfurt am Main: Vittorio Klostermann, 1997.

Heidegger, Martin. *Gesamtausgabe*. Vol. 67, *Metaphysik und Nihilismus*. Frankfurt am Main: Vittorio Klostermann, 1999.

Heidegger, Martin. *Gesamtausgabe*. Vol. 69, *Die Geschichtes des Seyns*. Frankfurt am Main: Vittorio Klostermann, 1998.

Heidegger, Martin. *Gesamtausgabe*. Vol. 85, *Vom Wesen der Sprache. Die Metaphysik der Sprache und die Wesung des Wortes. Zu Herders Abhandlung "Über den Ursprung der Sprache"*. Frankfurt am Main: Vittorio Klostermann, 1999.

Heidegger, Martin. *Gesamtausgabe*. Vol. 86, *Seminare. Hegel–Schelling*. Frankfurt am Main: Vittorio Klostermann, 2011.

Heidegger, Martin. *Nietzsche, Zweiter Band*. Pfullingen: Günther Neske, 1961.

Heidegger, Martin. "Seinsvergessenheit", in: *Heidegger Studies*, 20, 2004: 9–16.

Heidegger, Martin. "Über das Prinzip 'Zu den Sachen selbt'", *Heidegger Studies*, 11, 1995: 5–8.

# Translations of Heidegger's Works Cited

Heidegger, Martin. *Aristotle's Metaphysics Θ 1–3: On the Essence and Actuality of Force*. Translated by Walter Brogan and Peter Warnek. Bloomington: Indiana University Press, 1995.

Heidegger, Martin. *Basic Concepts*. Translated by Gary E. Aylesworth. Bloomington: Indiana University Press, 1993.

Heidegger, Martin. *Basic Concepts of Ancient Philosophy*. Translated by Richard Rojcewicz. Bloomington: Indiana University Press, 2008.

Heidegger, Martin. *The Basic Problems of Phenomenology*. Translated by Albert Hofstadter. Bloomington: Indiana University Press, 1982.

Heidegger, Martin. *Off the Beaten Track*. Translated by Julian Young and Kenneth Haynes. Cambridge: Cambridge University Press, 2003.

Heidegger, Martin. *Being and Time*. Translated by John Macquarrie and Edward Robinson. New York: Harper & Row, Publishers, Inc., 1962.

Heidegger, Martin. *The Concept of Time*. Translated by William McNeill. Oxford: Blackwell, 1992.

Heidegger, Martin. *Contributions to Philosophy (From Enowning)*. Translated by Parvis Emad and Kenneth Maly. Bloomington: Indiana University Press, 1999.

Heidegger, Martin. *Towards the Definition of Philosophy*. Translated by Ted Sadler. London: Continuum Press, 2000.

Heidegger, Martin. *Discourse on Thinking*. Translated by John Anderson and E. Hans Freund. New York: Harper & Row, Publishers, Inc., 1966.

Heidegger, Martin. *Early Greek Thinking*. Translated by Frank Capuzzi and David Farrell Krell. New York: Harper & Row, Publishers, Inc., 1975.

Heidegger, Martin. *Elucidations of Hölderlin's Poetry*. Translated by Keith Hoeller. Amherst, NY: Humanity Books, 2000.

Heidegger, Martin. *The End of Philosophy*. Translated by Joan Stambaugh. New York: Harper & Row, Publishers, Inc., 1973.

Heidegger, Martin. *On the Essence of Language. The Metaphysics of Language and the Essencing of the Word. Concerning Herder's Treatise "On the Origin of Language"*. Translated by Wanda Torres Gregory and Yvonne Unna. Albany, NY: SUNY Press, 2004.

Heidegger, Martin. *Existence and Being*. Edited by Werner Brock. Chicago: Henry Regenry Company, 1949.

Heidegger, Martin. *Four Seminars*. Translated by François Raffoul and Andrew Mitchell. Bloomington: Indiana University Press, 2003.

Heidegger, Martin. *The Fundamental Concepts of Metaphysics*. Translated by William McNeill and Nicholas Walker. Bloomington: Indiana University Press, 1995.

Heidegger, Martin. *Hegel's Phenomenology of Spirit*. Translated by Parvis Emad and Kenneth Maly. Bloomington: Indiana University Press, 1988.

Heidegger, Martin. *History of the Concept of Time*. Translated by Theodore Kisiel. Bloomington: Indiana University Press, 1985.

Heidegger, Martin. *Hölderlin's Hymn "The Ister"*. Translated by William McNeill and Julia Davis. Bloomington: Indiana University Press, 1996.

Heidegger, Martin. *Identity and Difference*. Translated by Joan Stambaugh. New York: Harper & Row, Publishers, Inc., 1969.

Heidegger, Martin. *Introduction to Metaphysics*. Translated by Gregory Fried and Richard Polt. New Haven: Yale University Press, 2000.

Heidegger, Martin. *Introduction to Phenomenological Research*. Translated by Daniel Dahlstrom. Bloomington: Indiana University Press, 2007.

Heidegger, Martin. *Kant and the Problem of Metaphysics* (4th ed.). Translated by Richard Taft. Bloomington: Indiana University Press, 1997.

Heidegger, Martin. *The Metaphysical Foundations of Logic*. Translated by Michael Heim. Bloomington: Indiana University Press, 1984.

Heidegger, Martin. "My Way to Phenomenology". In: *On Time and Being*. Translated by Joan Stambaugh. New York: Harper & Row, Publishers, Inc., 1972.

Heidegger, Martin. *Nietzsche, Vol. I. The Will to Power as Art*. Edited and translated by David Farrell Krell. New York: Harper & Row, Publishers, Inc., 1979.

Heidegger, Martin. *Nietzsche, Vol IV. Nihilism*. Edited by David Farrell Krell. Translated by Frank A. Capuzzi. New York: Harper & Row, Publishers, Inc., 1982.

Heidegger, Martin. *Ontology — The Hermeneutics of Facticity*. Translated by John van Buren. Bloomington: Indiana University Press, 1988.

Heidegger, Martin. *Parmenides*. Translated by André Schuwer and Richard Rojcewicz. Bloomington: Indiana University Press, 1992.

Heidegger, Martin. *Pathmarks*. Edited by William McNeill. Cambridge: Cambridge University Press, 1998.

Heidegger, Martin. "The Pathway". Translated by Thomas F. O'Meara. In: T. Sheehan (ed.). *Heidegger: The Man and the Thinker*. Chicago: Precedent Press, 1981: 69–94.

Heidegger, Martin. *Phenomenological Interpretation of Kant's Critique of Pure Reason*. Translated by Parvis Emad and Kenneth Maly. Bloomington: Indiana University Press, 1995.

Heidegger, Martin. *The Piety of Thinking*. Edited and Translated by James G. Hart and John C. Maraldo. Bloomington: Indiana University Press, 1976.

Heidegger, Martin. *Plato's Sophist*. Translated by R. Rojcewicz and A. Schuwer. Bloomington: Indiana University Press, 1997.

Heidegger, Martin. *Poetry, Language, Thought*. Translated by Albert Hofstadter. New York: Harper & Row, Publishers, Inc., 1971.

Heidegger, Martin. "Poverty". Translated by Thomas Kalary and Frank Schalow. In: F. Schalow (ed.). *Heidegger, Translation, and the Task of Thinking: Essays in Honor of Parvis Emad*. Dordrecht: Springer Publishers, 2011: 5–11.

Heidegger, Martin. *The Principle of Reason*. Translated by Reginald Lilly. Bloomington: Indiana University Press, 1991.

Heidegger, Martin. *The Question of Being*. Translated by Jean T. Wilde and William Kluback. New Haven: Twayne Publishers, 1958.

Heidegger, Martin. *The Question Concerning Technology and Other Essays*. Translated by William Lovitt. New York: Harper & Row, Publishers, Inc., 1977.

Heidegger, Martin. *Schelling's Treatise on the Essence of Human Freedom*. Translated by Joan Stambaugh. Athens: Ohio University Press, 1985.

Heidegger, Martin. *Sojourns*. Translated by John P. Manoussakis. Albany, NY: SUNY Press, 2004.

Heidegger, Martin. "Der Spiegel Interview — 'Only a God Can Save Us'". Translated by Maria Alter and John D. Caputo. In: G. Neske, E. Kettering (ed.). *Martin Heidegger and National Socialism*. New York: Paragon House, 1990.

Heidegger, Martin. *On Time and Being*. Translated by Joan Stambaugh. New York: Harper & Row, Publishers, Inc., 1972.

Heidegger, Martin. *On the Way to Language*. Translated by Joan Stambaugh. New York: Harper & Row, Publishers, Inc., 1971.

Heidegger, Martin. *What Is Called Thinking?* Translated by J. Glenn Gray and Fred Wieck. New York: Harper & Row, Publishers, Inc., 1968.

Heidegger, Martin. *What Is Philosophy?* Translated by Jean T. Wilde and William Kluback. New Haven: Twayne Publishers, 1959.

Heidegger, Martin. *What Is a Thing?* Translated by W. B. Barton and Vera Deutsch. Chicago: Henry Regnery Company, 1967.

Heidegger, Martin. *Zollikon Seminars.* Translated by F. Mayr. Evanston, IL: Northwestern University Press, 2001.


## Translations of Kant's Works Cited

Kant, Immanuel. *Anthropology, History, and Education.* Edited by G. Zoeller and R. Louden. Cambridge: Cambridge University Press, 2007

Kant, Immanuel. *Cambridge Edition of the Works of Immanuel Kant.* Edited by Paul Guyer and Allen Wood. Cambridge: Cambridge University Press, 1999.

Kant, Immanuel. *Critique of Judgment.* Translated by J. H. Bernhard. New York: Macmillan Publishers, 1951.

Kant, Immanuel. *Critique of Judgment.* Translated by James Creed Meredith. Oxford: Oxford University Press, 1952.

Kant, Immanuel. *Critique of Practical Reason.* Translated by Lewis White Beck. Indianapolis: The Bobbs-Merrill Company, Inc., 1959.

Kant, Immanuel. *Critique of Pure Reason.* Translated by Norman Kemp Smith. New York: St. Martin's Press, 1965.

Kant, Immanuel. *The Doctrine of Virtue.* Translated by Mary J. Gregor. New York: Harper & Row, Publishers, Inc., 1964.

Kant, Immanuel. *Dreams of a Spirit Seer Illustrated by Dreams of Metaphysics.* Translated by E. F. Goerwitz. New York: MacMillan Co., 1900.

Kant, Immanuel. *Foundations for the Metaphysicy of Morals.* Translated by Lewis White Beck. Indianapolis: The Bobbs-Merrill Company, 1954.

Kant, Immanuel. *Grounding for the Metaphysicy of Morals.* Translated by J. Ellington. Indianapolis: Hackett, 1981

Kant, Immanuel. *First Introduction to the Critique of Judgment.* Translated by James Haden. Indianapolis: The Bobbs-Merrill Company, Inc., 1965.

Kant, Immanuel. *Lectures in Ethics.* Translated by Louis Infield. London: Metheun & Company, 1963.

Kant, Immanuel. *Logic.* Translated by Robert Hartman and Wolfgang Schwarz. Indianapolis: The Bobbs-Merrill Company, Inc., 1974.

Kant, Immanuel. "Perpetual Peace: A Philosophical Sketch", in: *Political Writings.* Translated by H. B. Nisbet. Cambridge: Cambridge University Press, 1991: 93–130.

Kant, Immanuel. *Philosophical Correspondence 1759–99.* Chicago: University of Chicago Press, 1967.

Kant, Immanuel. *Prolegomena to any Future Metaphysics.* Translated by Lewis White Beck. Indianapolis: The Bobbs-Merrill Company, 1950.

Kant, Immanuel. *Religion within the Limits of Reason Alone.* Translated by Theodore M. Greene and Hoyt H. Hudson. New York: Harper & Row, Publishers, Inc., 1960.

# Index

10680437R00150

Printed in Great Britain
by Amazon